Socio-Economic
Review 2011

Socio-Economic Review 2011

A NEW AND FAIRER IRELAND

Securing
Economic Development,
Social Equity and
Sustainability

Seán Healy, Brigid Reynolds and Micheál Collins

Social Justice Ireland

Social Justice Ireland
Working to build a just society

ISBN No. 978-1-907501-04-3

First Published May 2011

Published by
Social Justice Ireland
Arena House
Arena Road
Sandyford
Dublin 18

www.socialjustice.ie

Tel: 01- 2130724

e-mail: secretary@socialjustice.ie

This Socio-Economic Review has been produced as follows:

Analysis and Policy: Brigid Reynolds and Seán Healy, Directors, *Social Justice Ireland*.

Data and Content: Micheál Collins, Department of Economics, Trinity College Dublin.

TABLE OF CONTENTS

1.	**INTRODUCTION**	1
2.	**IRELAND IN 2011: The Context**	3
	2.1 How Ireland got here: the background to the crises	4
	2.2 Ireland in 2011: the context	11
	2.3 The Need for Vision: where is Irish society going?	26
	2.4 Priorities for a New Ireland	29
	2.5 Focusing on Specific Issues	39
3.	**A NEW AND FAIRER IRELAND**	41
	Objectives, Analysis and Policy Proposals	
	3.1 Income	41
	(a) Poverty	41
	(b) Income Distribution	67
	(c) Maintaining an Adequate Level of Social Welfare	76
	(d) Basic Income	81
	3.2 Taxation	86
	3.3 Work	124
	3.4 Public Services	136
	3.5 Housing and Accommodation	144
	3.6 Healthcare	159
	3.7 Education and Education Disadvantage	176
	3.8 Intercultural & Migration Issues	188
	3.9 Participation	194
	3.10 Sustainability	200
	(a) Promoting Sustainable Development	200
	(b) Environmental Issues	204
	3.11 Rural Development	216
	3.12 The Developing World	226
4.	**VALUES**	235
5.	**CONCLUSION**	239
	REFERENCES	240
	APPENDIX	254

INTRODUCTION

Ireland and Irish society have changed dramatically over the past few years. As the economy rapidly declined the phenomena of unemployment and emigration returned. Government signed a bailout agreement with the IMF/ECB/EC in late-2010 and poor people were forced to bear an inordinate proportion of the burden of rescuing failed banks and bondholders even though they had no hand, act or part in the reckless gambling and questionable activity engaged in by these bodies. Today, we are faced with substantial challenges and choices as we respond to the current crisis, acknowledge the national policy failures of recent years and plan for the years to come. The future that emerges will result from the decisions taken now. These decisions involve making difficult choices all of which need to combine to build a logical and coherent agenda for *A New and Fairer Ireland*.

In chapter 2 we present an analysis of how Ireland came to be where it is today and identify a series of false assumptions and conclusions that underpinned Ireland's policy-making in recent decades. We look at Ireland today and identify key features of the economic, political, social and cultural context and reflect on how individualism, anxiety and greed, among other things, played a major role in Ireland's poor decision-making. We set out a vision of an Ireland based on the values of human dignity, sustainability, equality and the common good and then identify a series of policy priorities that are required to move in that direction.

In chapter 3 we outline in greater detail what *A New and Fairer Ireland* would entail and how, through making better choices, Ireland can recover to become a fairer society. The specific issues we address are: income, taxation, work, public services, housing and accommodation, healthcare, education and educational disadvantage, intercultural and migration issues, participation, sustainability and the environment, rural development and the developing world. On each of these issues, we propose a core policy objective. We also provide an analysis of the present situation, review relevant initiatives and outline key policy priorities aimed at constructing a better future. In doing this, we clearly indicate the choices *Social Justice Ireland* believes should be made in the years immediately ahead.

In chapter 4 we set out the values that underpin our analysis.

In presenting our analysis and proposals we pay special attention to how Ireland is experienced today by those who are disadvantaged. All our proposals are presented within responsible fiscal policy parameters. *Social Justice Ireland* does not claim to have all the answers. However, we make our proposals as a contribution to the public debate on what the key priorities in the socio-economic arena should be now and in the years ahead. All responses are most welcome.

2. IRELAND IN 2011

In this chapter we set the scene for this *Socio-Economic Review*. To do so, we present a narrative outlining what happened over recent decades to bring Ireland to where it is today, where exactly Ireland finds itself now, where Ireland should go into the future and what it needs to do to get there. The remainder of this *Review* will address key policy areas, present a detailed analysis and highlight the key policy initiatives that are required if a New Ireland is to emerge from the current series of crises.

Given the limits of space available to us it is not possible to address all issues that need to be addressed or to present extensive detail on particular policy areas. Our focus in this chapter is on the broad socio-economic reality that has emerged. We do not accept many of the assumptions and so-called analysis that are guiding much of the commentary in public and policy-making arenas in recent times. The analysis of the past that seems to have underpinned decision-making is flawed and inaccurate. While some of the policy decisions that have been adopted did move in the right direction:

- Many initiatives since the current crises emerged have been deeply flawed and are likely to lead to growing inequality.
- They are built on a vision of the future that is unsustainable.
- They fail to put human dignity and the common good at the core of the policy-making process.
- In particular, they seem to be guided by a questionable vision of Ireland's future.

The scale and severity of the crises Ireland is currently facing raise obvious questions regarding how they occurred. We provide a commentary on the background to these events. We also address questions about how Ireland can recover from these crises and more importantly how we can shape a future Ireland that cares for the well-being of all its people and protects the environment.

The chapter is structured in four parts:
    2.1 How Ireland got here: the background to the crises
    2.2 Ireland in 2011: the context
    2.3 The Need for Vision: where is Irish society going?
    2.4 Priorities for a New Ireland

2.1 How Ireland got here: the background to the crises

There are both international and national roots to the current crises. From the perspective of Irish society, few would dispute that the latter is of major significance and the dominant factor. In this section we consider both these backgrounds.

2.1.1 The International Background

The origin of the international financial crisis can be traced back to the decisions taken by Ronald Reagan and Margaret Thatcher when they led their respective governments in the early 1980s. In the preceding decades there had been rapid economic growth driven by the reconstruction of Europe and East Asia that had been devastated by war. In that period the world's economies were regulated through strong state controls over market activity and strong state intervention to minimise inflation and recession (through control of monetary policy for example). These were accompanied by relatively high wages which were seen as essential to stimulate and maintain demand for what was being produced. It was the era of the Keynesian state.

However, as the reconstruction of Germany and Japan reached completion and the capacity of other economies began to grow also (e.g. Brazil, Taiwan and South Korea) a new problem emerged. The world's capacity for economic growth was increasing dramatically. A major problem of over-production was emerging. As production capacity exceeded demand two kinds of responses were encouraged – the first was to create huge competition between the various producers and the second was to increase the demand people had for products and services. The former led to a process of driving down costs which in turn led to reduction in many people's wages. This had the effect of increasing inequality both within countries and between countries. It had the added effect of driving down demand as people could not afford the products being produced which, in turn, led to the erosion of profitability among companies. The huge increases in the price of oil in 1973 and 1979 also impacted on this situation in a negative way.

Since the late 1970s capitalism has tried three approaches to solving the problem of overproduction i.e. neoliberal restructuring, globalisation and financialisation. The first of these was the route chosen by Reagan and Thatcher. This has been followed by globalisation which in turn was followed by financialisation. The problems produced by financialisation are the immediate cause of what happened to the financial system in recent years.

Neo-Liberal Restructuring: Reagan and Thatcher agreed that the way to save capitalism was to promote capital accumulation and they did this by:

- Removing state constraints on the growth, use and flow of capital and wealth; and
- Redistributing income from the poor and middle classes to the rich on the understanding that the rich would then be motivated to invest their new profits and reignite economic growth.

This theory proved false in that it saw global growth averaging 1.4 per cent in the 1980s and 1.1 per cent a year in the 1990s. This compared with an average of 3.5 per cent in the 1960s and 2.4 per cent in the 1970s when state interventionist policies were the accepted norm. This neo-liberal approach redistributed income to the rich and seriously damaged the incomes of the poor and the middle classes. It did not increase the demand for products on the scale required since those whose incomes were being damaged didn't have the resources to spend and the rich did not invest a great deal of their new gains as expected.

Globalisation: The second approach used to try to save capitalism was globalisation. Great effort has gone into the creation of a global market. Countries that had been outside the market or had been non-capitalist were integrated into the global market. This was accompanied by trade liberalisation, the removal of barriers to the mobility of global capital and the abolition of barriers to foreign investment. This was seen as the solution to overproduction. China was the largest non-capitalist country to move into this system. This process, however, worsened the problem of overproduction. While the world's consumption grew this was surpassed by growing production capacity. The profits of major corporations were not growing as fast as had been the case in preceding decades. In the 1960s the annual profit margin of the Fortune 500 companies was 7.15 per cent. This went down to 5.3 per cent in the 1980s and 2.29 per cent in the 1990s. Profit margins continued to fall in the early years of this century.

Financialisation: In order to increase profitability the capitalist world turned to 'financialisation'. In the past the financial sector made the funds of savers available to entrepreneurs to finance their production capacity. With the continued reality of overproduction the financial world began to invest surplus funds in the financial world itself and in property. A whole range of new financial 'products' were created that could be bought and sold. Interest rates were lowered to facilitate this process. The increasing resources available for purchasing property led to huge increases in the price of property. Mortgage companies became more aggressive in marketing their products introducing innovations such as 100 per cent mortgages, 'interest only' mortgages and 40-year mortgages. House prices soared. Lending standards were lowered. Many of these mortgages were held by people who could not afford to repay on the agreed terms i.e. these were 'subprime' mortgages. A further problem was created as these mortgages, were included with other assets in new derivative products called 'collateralised debt obligations' (CDOs). These products were sold to banks and financial institutions that were not aware of what these products really contained. As interest rates rose it became apparent that many of these products were not worth their face value. The total value of these products is not known but is estimated to run into trillions of dollars. Companies such as Lehman Brothers, Merrill Lynch, Fannie Mae, Freddie Mac and Bear Stearns in the USA and others across the world were simply overwhelmed by these products as their reserves could not meet the losses being faced. Some collapsed. Others were bought out. The major international insurance company AIG (American International Group) was brought down by its huge exposure in the area of 'credit default swaps' which are derivatives that make it possible for investors to bet on the possibility that companies will default on repaying loans. George Soros the well known investor estimated that €45 trillion are invested in a market on these swaps – a market that is totally unregulated. The seriousness of this situation was further exacerbated by the broad adoption of a policy of light-touch regulation for financial markets.

What we have been witnessing over the past few years is the collapse of financialisation - the third strategy to rescue capitalism from its core problem of overproduction.

Taken together these experiences imply a number of questions including the following:

- What is needed to ensure effective and efficient regulation at both national and international level of the world's financial systems?
- Does the world need to recognise that there is a fundamental flaw in capitalism that needs to be addressed?
- What needs to be done to ensure that economic development and social development are given equal priority in countries across the world?

2.1.2 The Irish Background

Given that Ireland is a small open economy, any form of international recession is bound to have implications for economic growth, jobs and trade. Consequently, the severity of the recent international recession would by itself have had serious implications for Ireland and would have guaranteed that this country experienced some form of recession. However, the recession experienced over the past three years has been a lot more severe due to an array of national policies and decisions over recent decades. Indeed, Ireland has been unlucky that both an international and national recession struck at the same time. However, Ireland was heading for a substantial slowdown independent of international developments.

Looking back, by the mid-1970s Ireland was well placed to have a period of strong economic growth. We had: just joined the European Union; were pursuing well-focused industrial policies; had low corporate tax rates; had an emerging legacy from the strong investment in education made since the mid-1960s; had a favourable geographic location for European markets; and our workforce spoke English. However, poor fiscal and monetary policy from 1977-1986 failed to provide the stability required to deliver this potential economic growth. Eventually, Government was forced to pursue appropriate policies and from 1987 onwards Social Partnership provided the framework to secure the stability required.

Since the late 1980s Ireland's population changed its relationship to employment; a change which provided a stimulus to economic growth in three ways.[1] First, the proportion of Ireland's population that was employed converged with the levels experienced elsewhere in Europe and the OECD. In 1989 only 31 per cent of Ireland's population was employed and this climbed to over 45 per cent by the end of the following decade. Second, the proportion of the labour force that was employed grew dramatically in the decade and a half from the early 1990s and the proportion unemployed fell dramatically after a period of jobless growth in the early 1990s. Thirdly, the labour force itself grew dramatically, increasing by over 900,000 during the 1990s. The key change in all of this was the increase in female participation in the labour force. Between 1990 and 2000 the number of females in the Irish labour force increased by almost 250,000 and the female labour force participation rate rose from 44 per cent to 56 per cent (OECD Labour Force Database, 2010).

---

[1] We explore these trends in more detail in section 3.3 of this review.

Complementing this labour force driven growth, was a very strong growth in productivity (average output) during the 1990s. Productivity growth helped Ireland become richer. However, as Ireland grew richer its productivity drew closer to the productivity levels of world-leading countries and its productivity growth slowed down. Subsequently, in the later years of the 'Celtic Tiger' it was population growth and not productivity or an increased employment ratio that was driving growth. This population growth, and the consequent increase in labour supply and economic activity, was being supported by a huge increase in immigration and was not likely to be sustainable over a long period. Put simply, by 2000/2001 Ireland had lost focus on productivity growth as the key to improving living standards and focussed simply on economic growth.

In effect, Ireland had reached a false conclusion on the issue of growth. Government policy became fixated on economic growth. It became convinced that economic growth was good in itself and the higher the rate of economic growth the better it would be for Ireland. Whatever supported economic growth was to be facilitated. Whatever controlled or limited economic growth was to be resisted. Consequently, Ireland followed a very questionable pathway as it put its faith (and huge incentives) in construction to continue the high growth levels that had been seen in previous years.

From 2000/2001 onwards, growth in housing construction masked Ireland's deteriorating 'fundamentals' for several years.[2] As Ireland's per-capita income grew the demand for housing grew. As we detail in section 3.5 of this review, Ireland's housing construction rose from 19,000 completions in 1990 to a peak of over 93,000 completions in 2006. While there were 48,413 households on local authority waiting lists for social housing in 2002, this level of housing construction was unsustainable by any standards. Most of the new construction was for private housing. Of the 57,695 houses completed in 2002, 51,932 were private housing. Of the 93,419 completed in 2006, 88,211 were private housing. Overall, the number of houses in Ireland rose from 1.2 million homes in 1991 to 1.4 million in 2000 and then exploded to 1.9 million in 2008. By 2007, construction accounted for 13.3 per cent of all employment, the highest share in the OECD (OECD, 2010).

This level of construction was encouraged and supported by a combination of factors of which three were:

---

[2] We examine Housing and Accommodation issues in more detail in section 3.5 of this review.

- Very low interest rates. These were dictated by the large EU economies which unlike Ireland were experiencing very low growth levels. Interest rates were reduced to very low levels to encourage investment in those countries. The same rates applied in Ireland, however, which was at the opposite end of the economic cycle.
- Large tax incentives for construction provided by the Irish Government.
- Unsustainable house price inflation and profiteering.

The results of this housing boom were catastrophic where Ireland was concerned

During this period Ireland had reached another false conclusion, this time on taxation.[3] It had come to believe: that low taxation was good in itself; that reducing tax rates would lead inevitably to an increase in tax-take; and that "giving people back their own money", through reducing taxes, was far better than investing that money in developing and improving infrastructure and services. The result of these beliefs was that by the end of the Celtic Tiger years Ireland had one of the lowest total tax-takes in the EU. At the same time, while there were improvements in areas such as housing, public transport and social welfare during those years, there was no doubt that Ireland's infrastructure and social services were far below an EU-average level. Despite very strong efforts from some policy analysts to convince Government and others otherwise, the strong assumption was maintained that infrastructure and social services at an EU-average level could be delivered with one of the lowest total tax-takes in the EU.

By 2007 Ireland had 'run out of road'. There was no further room for substantial improvement in the population/labour force/employment context. The labour market was over-heated and relying on inward migration to sustain labour supply. Productivity was weakening and the economy, and the total tax-take, were over-reliant on a housing construction sector that had already over-expanded. While a serious slowdown was inevitable the General Election of 2007 was fought on the generally accepted assumption that growth would average 4.5 per cent per year over the 2007-2012 period. All political parties except one drew up their manifestos on this basis. Many of those who challenged this assumption were rejected with derision.

Overall, Ireland's policy-making during this period was under-pinned by a series of false assumptions and conclusions that included the following:

---

[3] We review these issues in greater detail in section 3.2 of this review.

- Economic growth was good in itself and the higher the rate of economic growth the better it would be for Ireland. Whatever supported economic growth was to be facilitated. Whatever controlled or limited economic growth was to be resisted. So the promotion of growth as an end in itself became the focus of policy.
- The benefits of economic growth would trickle down automatically. Everyone would benefit.
- Infrastructure and social services at an EU-average level could be delivered with one of the lowest total tax-takes in the EU.
- The growing inequality and the widening gaps between the better-off and the poor that followed from this approach to policy-development were not important as everyone was gaining something.
- Low taxation was good.
- Reducing tax rates would lead inevitably to an increase in tax-take.
- "Giving people back their own money", through reducing taxes, was far better than investing that money in developing and improving infrastructure and services. The sum of Irish people's individual decisions would produce far better results for Ireland than allowing Government to decide how best to use the money.
- Ireland had a great deal to teach the rest of the world particularly about how it could reach full employment, generate huge economic growth and provide for all the society's needs while having one of the lowest total tax-takes in the Western world.

Arising from this series of false policy assumptions, there were many resulting policy failures. Among the failures were the following:

- Failure to take action to broaden the tax base by, for example:
  - introducing a property tax;
  - removing outstanding tax exemptions where there is not a demonstrated benefit-cost advantage;
  - introducing user service charges.
- Failure to promote tax equity by for example, introducing Refundable Tax Credits.
- Failure to overcome infrastructure deficiencies, such as broadband, public transport, primary health care, water, energy and waste.
- Failure to adequately address high energy costs.
- Failure to address high local authority charges on business.

- Failure to promote competition in sheltered sectors of the economy, such as professions.
- Failure to appropriately regulate the banking and financial services sector.
- Failure to manage the growth of personnel numbers in the public service.

2.2 Ireland in 2011: the context

In this section we analyse where Ireland stands today. We assess various dimensions of the current crisis and subsequently explore the present context in economic, social, political and cultural terms.

2.2.1 Ireland's Five-Part Crisis

Today, Ireland continues to be in crisis. At the outset of this period the National Economic and Social Council (NESC, 2009) summarised the nature of this crisis as one possessing five closely related dimensions. We briefly review and summarise each of these.

A Banking Crisis in which the taxpayer is taking responsibility for rescuing all the major banks and financial institutions from the consequences of the dishonesty and incompetence of individuals and institutions who were in charge of running and regulating our financial system. As NESC has pointed out (2009: x), the policy response to the banking crisis must also address:

- The need to ensure that recent policy measures provide protection to the increasing number of households with mortgage arrears;
- The need to ensure that recent government action prompts a renewed flow of credit to businesses in Ireland;
- The need to convince Irish society as a whole, and particularly groups making visible sacrifices, that those who led Irish financial institutions into their current reliance on the state, and who were major beneficiaries of the boom, are being held accountable and are bearing their share of the adjustment burden;
- The need to persuade our EU partners, other international institutions and the global financial market actors that a new regulatory regime and governance culture is being created in Ireland.

A Public Finance Crisis because we are borrowing far more than we are collecting in taxes. To bring Ireland back into line with our EU/IMF commitments, major budgetary adjustments have been required and will be required over the next few years. We discuss the nature of these changes later in this chapter. However, as NESC has noted, these fiscal adjustments need to be considered and implemented not just with regard to how they address the gap between taxes and spending but also with regard to how these adjustments impact on the other dimensions of Ireland's challenge: the economic crisis, the social crisis and the country's reputation (2009: *x*).

An Economic Crisis because we have lost many jobs and, throughout much of the last decade, fundamentally undermined our competitiveness. The speed, depth and nature of Ireland's economic decline necessitates a policy response which collectively addresses what NESC describes as "a difficult set of overlapping and competing objectives and factors" (NESC: *xi*). These include:

- The employment situation - particularly the threat of further unemployment and in particular large levels of long-term unemployment;
- Ireland's loss of competitiveness over the past decade;
- The pressures on certain enterprises created by the devaluation of sterling;
- The evolution of prices, including policy instruments that influence input costs to business, professional fees and rents;
- The level of domestic demand;
- The state of the public finances, which are directly affected by public sector pay developments and indirectly influenced by wider unemployment, economic and income developments;
- The burden of mortgage debt, particularly on those who become unemployed;
- Social solidarity, encompassing the whole of Irish society, not just those whose incomes are determined in collective bargaining.

We outline the nature of this economic crisis in greater detail later in this section.

A Social Crisis because our social services and social infrastructure are being eroded, unemployment is increasing, incomes are falling, debt levels are rising and the prospect of a sustained period of high long-term unemployment levels now seems likely. While the economic crisis, and in particular the collapse of private construction, provides some opportunities to address the social housing deficit (see section 3.5 of this review), policy makers need to be keenly aware that their responses to the other crises should not further undermine the vulnerable in Irish society and the social services and infrastructure on which they depend. We outline the nature of this social crisis in greater detail later in this chapter.

A Reputational Crisis because our reputation around the world has been damaged for several reasons (NESC, 2009: *xii*):

- The perception that Ireland has, along with a number of other countries, had a lax and ineffective system of regulation of the financial sector;
- The perception that Ireland's response to the banking crisis may not include sufficient change in governance and personnel
- The uncertainty about Ireland's willingness to participate in major developments in the EU;

These are added to by the perception that Ireland's public finances are vulnerable to default because of a combination of low growth, contingent liabilities to the banking system and the increasing ratio of debt to GDP;

2.2.2 The Economic Context

The dramatic and sudden turn-around in Ireland's economic experiences since 2007 needs to be considered in the context of our economic growth and expansion throughout the last decade. Clearly, as indicated earlier, there have been a number of major policy failures behind some of this growth (e.g. excessive fuelling of the construction industry and an unregulated banking sector). However, as table 2.1 shows, Ireland's Gross Domestic Product (GDP) and Gross National Income (GNI) have increased significantly since 1997.[4] The final column of the table tracks the per-capita value of GNI over the last decade. During that time it increased in real-terms (after taking account of price changes) by over 30 per cent.[5] The current economic slowdown has brought per capita income levels back to the levels experienced in the early years of this century.

---

[4] GDP is calculated as the value of all economic activity that occurs in Ireland. GNI is calculated as GDP minus the net outflow of income from Ireland (mainly involving foreign multinational repatriating profits), minus EU taxes and plus EU subsidies (for further information see CSO, 2008:76).

[5] We examine the distribution of this income, which was far from even, in section 3.1.

Table 2.1:	Ireland's National Income, 1997-2009		
Year	GDP (€b)	GNI (€b)	GNI per capita*
1997	68.1	60.8	n/a
1998	78.7	69.8	n/a
1999	90.4	77.8	n/a
2000	105.0	90.5	€30,700
2001	117.1	99.0	€31,400
2002	130.5	108.3	€31,900
2003	140.0	119.7	€33,100
2004	149.3	127.9	€33,900
2005	162.3	139.9	€35,200
2006	177.3	155.4	€36,600
2007	189.4	164.1	€37,200
2008	180.0	156.0	€35,300
2009**	159.6	132.6	€31,300

Source: CSO, 2010:17
Note: * Gross National Income per capita at constant 2008 prices;
** Preliminary Figures

Chart 2.1: Ireland's GDP Growth, 1995-2014 (%)

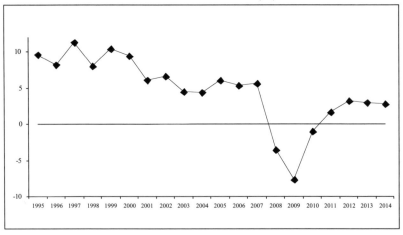

Source: OECD Factbook 2008, CSO (2011) and Department of Finance (2010).

The speed and severity of Ireland's economic decline is also visible in chart 2.1. It shows the strength of economic growth since 1995 (most developed world countries experience 2-3 per cent growth per annum) and the rapid decrease between 2007-09. While the nature, timing and pace of the recovery remain unclear, all agree that there is likely to be a return to small positive annual GDP growth rates from 2011.

Among the components driving the decline in GDP growth rates has been the rapid decrease in house building. A housing bubble, where both prices and the number of units completed soared, saw Ireland move from building just 30,000 units in 1995 to a peak of 93,419 in 2006; in 2009 approximately 23,000 units were completed falling to approximately 14,000 units in 2010 (Department of Environment, Heritage and Local Government, 2009; AIB, 2011). It also produced over-priced housing, paid for by irrational borrowing, foolish lending and unrealistic profit expectations. The legacy of this policy disaster has been empty housing units (many of them in inappropriate locations), negative equity and high numbers of unemployed construction workers.

Similarly, the scale of the international recession has had an impact on the level of exports. These fell by almost 3 per cent in 2009 but recovered to grow by 6 per cent in 2010. During that period as production declined, both the number of workers and hours worked per worker were reduced.

For the public finances, the combined effects of these changes have been dramatic. Over the last decade the state had become dependent on construction related revenues which provided increased stamp duty, building related VAT and income taxes. Table 2.2 shows that as the economy turned these revenues rapidly declined. Overall, total tax receipts have fallen from in excess of €47 billion in 2007 to €32.5 billion in 2009; and fell further to €31.5 billion in 2010.

The state continues to invest in infrastructure and other capital projects and, as in previous years, has borrowed money to make these investments. However, given the aforementioned collapse in taxation revenues, the state has, since 2008, been borrowing to pay its day-to-day (current account) costs. This is a serious and unsustainable development. In 2009 the government borrowed over €12 billion to meet its day-to-day costs and a further €13 billion for capital investment (including contributions to fund the rescue of Anglo Irish Bank and to bail out the major banks via investment contributions from the national pensions reserve fund). By November 2010, the scale of the exchequer deficit and the ongoing, and escalating,

A New and Fairer Ireland

bank bailout costs forced the state to turn to outside agencies for economic support. An agreement was reached with the IMF and EU for €85 billion in funding over the period 2010-2013. The bailout funds comprise €50 billion to facilitate state borrowing and refinancing over the period and up to €35 billion to rescue the banking system. In return for securing the right to borrow this money, the Irish Government signed a *Memorandum of Understanding* which set out a severe austerity programme over the period to 2014.[6] Budget 2011 commenced this programme with tax increases and spending cuts combining to a total of €6 billion in 2011. It also projected that in 2011 the government will need to borrow over €11.5 billion to meet its day-to-day costs and €8.8 billion for capital purposes; this money is being drawn down from the bailout funds.

Table 2.2: The changing nature of Ireland's current tax revenues				
	Estimated Outturn 2007 €m	Estimated Outturn 2008 €m	Estimated Outturn 2009 €m	Estimated Outturn 2010 €m
Customs	285	255	209	230
Excise Duties	5,815	5,581	4,575	4,620
Capital Gains Tax	3,145	1,710	385	400
Capital Acquisitions Tax	383	320	260	240
Stamp Duties	3,195	1,780	900	975
Income Tax ★	13,605	13,200	11,810	11,125
Corporation Tax	6,349	6,000	3,790	3,775
Value Added Tax	14,545	13,525	10,640	10,165
Other Levies	3	1	1	0
Total Tax Receipts★★	**47,325**	**42,372**	**32,570**	**31,530**

Source: Department of Finance, Budget Documents 2007-2011
Notes: ★Including income levy in 2009 and 2010.
★★These figures do not incorporate other tax sources including revenues to the social insurance fund, the health levy and local government charges. These are incorporated into the totals reported in table 3.2.4 below.

---

[6] The memorandum has subsequently been revised by the Government elected in 2011.

Taken together, Ireland's General Government Balance (GGB) as a percentage of GDP (the key indictor used by the European Central Bank to judge fiscal policy control) will be 9.4 per cent, down from 11.6 per cent in 2010. These figures are well in excess of the 3 per cent limit set in the EU *Stability and Growth Pact*. Consequently, the objective of Government economic (fiscal) policy, as agreed with the EU and IMF, for the next few years is to reduce the GGB deficit indicator to 3 per cent by 2014. Table 2.3 outlines the pathway signalled by the outgoing Government to achieve this; a pathway that has been endorsed by the EU and IMF.

Table 2.3: Plan to reduce the General Government Balance, 2010-2014					
	2010	2011	2012	2013	2014
GGB €m	-18,175	-15,150	-12,270	-10,170	-5,140
GGB as % GDP	11.6	9.4	7.3	5.8	2.8

Source: Calculated from Department of Finance, Budget 2011: D27.

While the international and national economic recovery are likely to somewhat assist in achieving this objective, it is clear that further tax increases and expenditure reductions must form a part of that transition. This guarantees a number of challenging Budgets in the years ahead. It is also assumed that the ongoing banking crisis does not require the exchequer to further invest in the banks and that the excessive budgetary cuts in Budget 2011 do not damage the economy so badly that it spirals further into recession, a risk we highlighted in our *Analysis and Critique of Budget 2011* (Social Justice Ireland, 2010). Were either of these to occur, they would undermine the sustainability of the EU/IMF deal in its current format and require additional years for Ireland to reach the 3 per cent of GDP threshold – indeed the IMF and EU have already signalled that this is likely.

Table 2.4 presents a summary of the projections for Ireland over the years 2011-2012. Most of this data is derived from the Department of Finance's Budget 2011 documentation and we highlight where necessary where these Government projections are unreliable given the economic and banking events that have occurred since December 2010 when the Budget was presented.

Table 2.4: Ireland's Economic Position, 2011-2012

National Income
GDP in 2011 (€m)#	€161,200
GNP in 2011 (€m) #	€127,900
GDP growth in 2011#	1.75%
GNP growth in 2011#	1.00%
GDP growth 2011-2014 (average) #	2.7% per annum

Exchequer Budgetary Position
Current Budget Balance, 2011 (€m)##	-€11,530
Net Capital Investment, 2011 (€m)	€8,800
Capital Investment paid from current resources, 2011 (€m)	Zero
Capital Investment paid from borrowing, 2011 (€m)	All
Exchequer Borrowing, 2011 (€m)	€18,400
General Government Balance (%GDP)	-9.10%
Current Budget Balance 2012 (€m)	-€8,795
Current Budget Balance 2013 (€m)	-€5,280
Net Capital Investment 2011-2014 (€m)	€8,700 (average)
Exchequer Borrowing 2011-2014 (€m)	€14,100 (average)
National Debt 2011 % GDP★	107%
National Debt plus NAMA 2011 % GDP★★	125%

Inflation and the Labour Market
HICP inflation in 2011	0.70%
HICP inflation 2011-2014 (average)	1.3% per annum
Unemployment rate in 2011##	13.25%
Employment growth in 2011	-0.25%
Unemployment rate 2011-2014 (average)##	11.50%
Employment growth 2011-2014 (average)	1.06%

Source: Department of Finance, Budget 2011 (various tables) and separate calculations where indicated.

Notes: ★ Adjusted upwards to account for subsequent CSO revisions to GDP and borrowing to fund capital injections into the banks.
★★ Including a figure of €29 million to account for NAMA borrowings (NAMA, 2011:3). # This is a Department of Finance Budget 2011 estimate and the actual number is likely to be smaller. ## This is a Department of Finance Budget 2011 estimate and the actual number is likely to be larger.

Ireland in 2011: the context

Table 2.5: EU-27 Rankings (highest to lowest) on Three National Policy Indicators

Taxation as a % of GDP	Total Government Expenditure as a % of GDP	Total Social Protection Expenditure as a % of GDP
Denmark	Sweden	France
Sweden	France	Sweden
Belgium	Denmark	Belgium
France	Hungary	Netherlands
Finland	Austria	Denmark
Italy	Belgium	Germany
Austria	Italy	Austria
Netherlands	Finland	Italy
Germany	Portugal	United Kingdom
Slovenia	Netherlands	Finland
United Kingdom	Germany	Portugal
Hungary	Greece	Greece
EU-27 AVERAGE	United Kingdom	**EU-27 AVERAGE**
Cyprus	**EU-27 AVERAGE**	Slovenia
Spain	Cyprus	Hungary
Czech Rep	Czech Republic	Spain
Portugal	Malta	Luxembourg
Luxembourg	Slovenia	Poland
Bulgaria	Poland	Czech Republic
Malta	Bulgaria	Cyprus
Poland	Spain	**IRELAND**
IRELAND	Luxembourg	Malta
Greece	Romania	Slovakia
Estonia	Latvia	Bulgaria
Latvia	**IRELAND**	Romania
Lithuania	Estonia	Lithuania
Slovakia	Lithuania	Estonia
Romania	Slovakia	Latvia

Source: Eurostat online database (2009)
Note: A more extensive assessment of each of these indicators can be found in corresponding tables throughout this review. They are: table 3.2.1, table A1 and table 2.8.

A further insight into Ireland's economic standing is presented in table 2.5. Using figures highlighted throughout this review it outlines where Ireland stands relative to our fellow EU members on three key indicators – total taxation, total

Government expenditure and total social protection expenditure. In all cases, Ireland is near the bottom of the rankings. The rankings are based on Eurostat data compiled before the current economic collapse - the abnormal nature of fiscal policies since 2007 across all EU countries suggests that it would be inappropriate to make structural comparisons using this data.[7]

The obvious question arising from this table is: against whom do we benchmark ourselves as a society? Is it Latvia, Lithuania, Estonia, Slovakia and Romania? Are these the countries we wish to emulate in terms of public services, pensions, social welfare payments and wage rates (private and public)?

2.2.3 The Social Context

Throughout much of this review Ireland's social context is considered; this section provides a brief overview.

The ramifications for Ireland's people of the recent economic turmoil have been severe. Most notably, in the space of a few months, one of the great achievements of recent years has been reversed with unemployment returning as a widespread phenomenon.[8] In late 2006, 90,300 people were recorded as unemployed by the CSO's quarterly national household survey (QNHS), a figure which represented 4.2 per cent of the labour force. Four years later, the number of people unemployed tripled to reach almost 300,000 (approximately 14.1 per cent of the labour force). Suddenly, Ireland has returned to unemployment levels equivalent to those experienced in the mid-1980s. Behind each of these figures are people and families - the society-wide impact of these increases cannot be over-estimated.

The scale of this unemployment crisis, and the simultaneous collapse in employment opportunities, has resulted in many becoming stranded in unemployment. Consequently long-term unemployment, defined as those unemployed for more than one year, has rapidly increased. By late 2010 the long-term unemployment rate had reached 7.3 per cent of the labour force (almost 154,000 people) and this figure looks set to climb towards 200,000 during 2011. It is of some concern that a large proportion of the newly long-term unemployed possess skills for which there is likely to be limited demand over the next few years. In particular, large numbers of males who formerly worked in the construction

---

[7] See the Appendix of this review for more details.
[8] The data cited in this section comes from the CSO's QNHS, the official measure of employment and unemployment. We analyse the live register figures in section 3.3.

sector have joined this group and they will require significant assistance and retraining before many of them can return to employment.[9]

Another of the social ghosts of the 1980s and 1990s has also returned – emigration. While there are no official figures, estimates by the ESRI in their December 2010 *Quarterly Economic Commentary* have suggested that there was a net outflow of almost 34,500 people in the year ending April 2010 and they have projected a further net 100,000 people will leave by April 2012 (60,000 to April 2011 and 40,000 in the subsequent 12 months). However, they warn that these are assumptions rather than forecasts as there is little official data available. As the international economy recovers, something that is likely to precede Ireland's recovery by 12-18 months, it is expected that emigration will remain at these high levels with a large outflow of young and skilled Irish-born people.

The aforementioned collapse in taxation revenues has forced the government into five challenging budgets and a series of spending cutbacks in 2008, 2009 (twice), 2010 and 2011. Throughout this review we highlight and critique many of the cuts in social spending including the unacceptable cut to most social welfare payments delivered in Budgets 2010 and 2011. In the area of both national and local social services and initiatives, it is particularly difficult that these cuts are being implemented just as the demands for these services are increasing. The impact of these cuts, and the threats of further similar cuts, continues to undermine the social structures within Irish society and their ability to cope in the present circumstances.

The collective implications of these actions were well summarised by Magdalena Sepulveda, the UN independent expert on Human Rights and Extreme Poverty, who visited Ireland following an invitation from Government in January 2011.[10] In her preliminary report, she stated that "the current economic and financial crisis poses a disproportionate threat to those who did not benefit much from the Irish economic boom and is a serious threat to the milestones achieved in social protection". This is further reflected in the experience of the Society of St Vincent de Paul who reported that throughout the last 18 months calls for assistance dramatically increased with many from 'first-timers' struggling to cope with the impact of the current crisis. Similarly, Central Bank data has indicated that in 2010 €113m was out on loan from registered moneylenders (up 25 per cent since 2008) and in Dublin City Council there have been growing rent arrears levels among local authority tenants (€20m in 2010 which is up 40 per cent since 2009).

---

[9] We analyse the issues of unemployment, employment and work in Section 3.3.
[10] *Social Justice Ireland* held a detailed meeting with the UN delegation in January 2011.

Aside from growing unemployment and long-term unemployment, emigration, service and funding cutbacks and the ongoing problems of inequality and poverty, we continue to live in a society with alarming numbers of people with literacy difficulties across all age groups, schools with leaking roofs and 'temporary' portacabins and a two-tier health system where the availability of services is related to income rather than need. Clearly, Ireland in 2011 has a social crisis.

2.2.4 The Political Context

At a Government level, the result of the 2011 General Election has produced a new government with a large majority and a mandate to address the broad economic and social problems we have been outlining. The new *Programme for Government* covers a wide range of issues at different levels and we have published a review of the document on our website (www.socialjustice.ie). The programme contains very welcome commitments on some issues while being very vague on how it proposes to address other issues. It contains very few numbers or target dates. Its implementation will be very dependent on the EU/IMF bailout agreement being renegotiated so as to reduce the burden and to enable sufficient economic activity to ensure a viable future. Overall, it is clear that difficult choice will need to be made in the years ahead and *Social Justice Ireland* urges the new Government to place the protection of the vulnerable at the core of these decisions.

Finally the issue of governance is of major importance for society at large. There is a substantial role for civil society in the huge task that Ireland currently faces. Social dialogue is a critically important component of any effective decision-making in a modern democracy. Recently the process of consultation and society-wide cooperation has been undermined with the process often demonised and its significant positive contributions ignored. The severity of Ireland's current situation is reminiscent of the situation in the late 1980s when social dialogue was seen as the key to economic and social recovery; the lessons learnt then should be remembered now.

We believe governance along these lines can be developed in Ireland. *Social Justice Ireland* seeks real, effective engagement with the new Government – an engagement that reflects the value of social dialogue and the need for good governance characterised by transparency, accountability and inclusion.

2.2.5 The Cultural Context (assumptions, values and attitudes)

At times of crisis it is often the case that strategic thinking and planning are set-aside. This approach has been very visible in Ireland since the inception of the current crises. Its most visible manifestation has been the acceptance into the conventional wisdom of a series of largely unchallenged assumptions that are not valid. These include:

- That the economy should have priority over all else.
- That preventing all the major banks from collapse is the major economic priority.
- That cuts in public expenditure are the key. (They are only part of the solution.)

These assumptions fail to grasp the fact that economic development and social development are two sides of the one coin. Economic development is required to provide resources for social development. On the other hand social development is essential if economic development is to be successful. There will be no lasting economic development of substance without the provision of social services and infrastructure. For example, it will not be possible to promote a smart, green, hi-tech economy without having an education system that ensures people are capable of taking up jobs in these areas. Likewise infrastructure in areas such as public transport and Information and Communication Technology (ICT) are essential for a successful economy in the twenty first century. Thinking we can have economic development first and then follow-up with social development is to ignore many of the major lessons that have been learned over the past two decades.

There are other assumptions which are only half true that are repeated like mantras in policy discussion and commentary. These include:

- That everybody should make a contribution to the adjustment required.
- That fairness is important but taxes should not be increased.

Yes, we agree everyone should make a contribution insofar as they can. But we do not accept that some people should be driven into poverty because of the contribution that is demanded of them. To do this would be to solve one problem by creating a deeper and more long-lasting one. We reject any attempt to solve Ireland's problems by increasing inequality or by forcing the most vulnerable members of the population into a situation where they do not have the resources to live life with dignity. It is profoundly wrong also that poor people carry a major burden while senior bond-holders, who carry a part of the responsibility for Ireland's implosion, make no contribution to sharing the burden. We also agree that fairness is critically important but we do not believe that Ireland's socio-economic situation can be rectified fairly while we persist in having one of the lowest total tax-takes in the EU.

There are other values that are regularly repeated that we do accept. These include:

- That there should be far better value got for public expenditure.
- That the reform of the public sector is a major priority.

The widely quoted assumptions listed in this section have been adopted with limited consideration of their meaning or implications. Consequently, those that are not valid generate ill-considered policies which are met with widespread opposition and anger. As a society we are lacking a coherent set of guiding values and assumptions to shape the policies and actions of the decade to come.

But that is not all. Developments over the past decade and more and the response to the multi-faceted crises Ireland has been encountering have produced a situation which is dominated by individualism, anxiety and greed.

Individualism in the sense of people being seen as isolated, self-sufficient, economic individuals grew dramatically in recent years. More and more the individual has come to be seen as the primary unit of social reality and community connectedness is down-played and resisted. In practice, policy has done much to undermine this community dimension. This kind of individualism is seen as a virtue. Such an individual is seen as autonomous, owing nothing to anybody, accountable to nobody, responsible for nothing and can rely on nobody only himself or herself. This kind of person is seen almost exclusively in economic terms. This is the kind of person who deserves to "get their own money back" through keeping taxation low according to much of the rhetoric of recent years. As we have highlighted already this was justified on the false assumption that such people were far better at investing that money in developing and improving infrastructure and services. According to this understanding the sum of Irish people's individual decisions would produce far better results for Ireland than allowing Government to decide how best to use the money. We have seen the falsehood of this assumption. However, there has been a further development for those individuals themselves and for society as a whole and that has been the consequent emergence of anxiety as a constant in Ireland's core.

Anxiety follows the growing realisation that individualism as described above is not an adequate basis for making long-term progress or securing people's well-being. Endless anxiety emerges for one never has enough or has done enough to be safe and satisfied. As a result, the autonomous individual that is championed in much current economic theory is caught in an endless rat race of achievement that produces bottomless anxiety – about the market, about performance, about self-worth.[11] This anxiety, in turn, leads many such people to experience growing insecurity, pressure and threat. This in turn feeds into the wider society and how it experiences itself. The individual person experiencing anxiety often responds by seeking to get more, to have more, so as to control the future. This often leads to greed.

Greed generates what Brueggemann calls "ravenous acquisitiveness" so that life becomes a passionate pursuit of every form of security and self-worth, especially through money. This in some ways explains why people who have the most usually think they do not have enough. Those with less imitate this ravenous greed. It is not difficult to see how this played a large part in a process where lenders were attracted to give out loans because of the easy income that would supposedly flow from interest payments and borrowers took the loans as they imagined a better future beyond their current deprivation or a more secure future that would counteract the anxiety they were experiencing. This situation was exacerbated by a 'bonus' culture which saw many lenders and others gaining huge bonuses.

This series of developments which saw the growth of individualism, anxiety and greed formed part of the core of why Ireland (and much of the Western world) got to be where it is today. A pathway out of this morass is needed. That pathway should be guided by a vision of Irish society, a New Ireland, towards which policy can be guided. We now move on to address the issue of what Ireland's guiding vision should be and what we need to do to move towards that vision.

---

[11] For further development of these points cf. Walter Brueggemann, *From Anxiety and Greed to Milk and Honey*, Sojourners, http://www.sojo.net/

2.3 The Need for Vision: where is Irish society going?

The scale of the ongoing crises facing Ireland today is dramatic. They imply a period of recovery, one that will take a number of years. The nature of that recovery has both international and national aspects. While the former is out of our control, decisions regarding our national policy responses to these crises will need to be considered and taken over the next few months and years. *Social Justice Ireland* believes that these national decisions should be framed in the context of one central question: Where does Ireland, and Irish society, want to be in 10 years time?

2.3.1 A Guiding Vision for a New Ireland

Overall, at this time there is a need for vision. A guiding vision that charts the future direction and shape of Irish society is needed; one that takes a long-term perspective and implements policy to achieve this. *Social Justice Ireland* believes that Ireland should be guided by the core values of:

- Human dignity
- Sustainability
- Equality and Human Rights
- The Common Good.

Being a little more specific, Ireland needs to see these values at the core of the vision of its future as a country where:

- Every man, woman and child has what is required to live life with dignity i.e.
  - Has sufficient income,
  - Has access to the necessary services and
  - Is actively included in a genuinely participatory society.
- Sustainability (economic, social and environmental) is a central motif in policy development. This would mean that:
  - Economic development, social development and environmental protection are seen as different sides of the same reality, all interdependent.
  - Balanced regional and global development would be at the heart of the vision of Ireland's future.
- Equality and a rights-based approach are at the core of public policy.
- International economic competitiveness is developed and sustained
- The common good is a constant goal of policy development.

2.3.2 The Developmental Welfare State – a useful model for social development

The formation of future policy should take account of the perspective that is offered by NESC in its report entitled *The Developmental Welfare State* (NESC, 2005). Chart 2.2 presents the core structure of the model NESC presented. It is developed on the understanding that every person in Ireland should have what is required to secure human dignity in three interrelated areas: (i) services, (ii) income supports and (iii) innovative measures that would secure active inclusion.

Chart 2.2: The Core Structure of the Developmental Welfare State

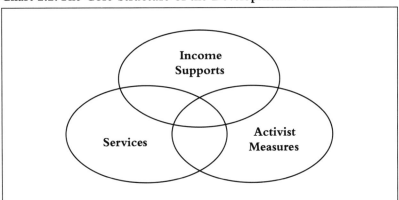

Services	Income Supports	Activist Measures
• Childcare	• Progressive child income support	• Social inclusion
• Education	• Working age income for participation	• Area-based strategies
• Health		• Particular community /group projects
• Eldercare	• Minimum pension guarantee	• Emerging new needs
• Housing		• Novel approaches
• Transport	• Capped tax expenditures	
• Employment services		
• Training		

Source: NESC (2005:144, 156)

Table 2.6: NESC Life-cycle approach to delivering the Developmental Welfare State

	Who?	What?	How?
0-17yrs	Integration of services, income support and activist measures	Governance and leadership	Standards and rights
18-29yrs			
30-64yrs			
65+ yrs			
People challenged in their personal autonomy			

Source: NESC (2005:147)

In building the developmental welfare state NESC argued that Irish society should take a 'life-cycle' approach to ensuring that all three dimensions were delivered. As table 2.6 shows, such an approach would focus on identifying the needs of children, young adults, people of working age, older people and people challenged in their personal autonomy such as those in care or having a disability. The council suggested that for each group, policy should focus on securing an effective combination of income supports, services and active inclusion measures.

Successfully implementing this approach would underscore each of these group's ability to play a real and sustained role in Irish society and thereby play an important part in tacking social exclusion. This approach provides each sector involved with key challenges if the best options are to be taken and if the approach is to be successfully developed as a template for policy. A major part of the *Towards 2016* national agreement uses this approach to social development. It identifies 23 high-level goals across these age groups and interlinked areas. *Social Justice Ireland* believes that the Developmental Welfare State model and the *Towards 2016* high level goals should play a central role in implementing the social aspects of the vision for Ireland we articulate here.

2.4 Policy Priorities for Moving Towards the Vision

Social Justice Ireland believes that moving towards the vision outlined above, would require among other things:

- Raising Ireland's total tax-take in a fair and equitable manner while keeping Ireland a low-tax economy (i.e. below 35% of GDP which is the cut-off level provided by Eurostat for a low-tax economy).
- Providing the necessary resources over time to raise Ireland's infrastructure and social services at least to the EU-average level.
- Focusing economic growth on increasing per-capita National Income.
- Reforming the Public Service to ensure it maximises its capacity and delivers appropriate outcomes.
- Ensuring Ireland's economy is internationally competitive.
- Addressing the reality of unemployment for both short-term and long-term unemployed people.
- Reducing poverty with a particular focus on reducing child poverty.
- Developing long-term planning and ensuring all actions taken are sustainable economically, environmentally and socially.
- Tackling inequality and developing a rights-based approach to policy development.
- Developing a 'shared responsibility' approach to policy development.
- Ensuring that getting value for money is the norm where public expenditure is concerned.
- Minimising the exposure of the tax-payer to the losses incurred by banks and the consequent expenditure of tax-payers money on rescuing these.
- A commitment to reach the 23 high-level goals for various stages of the life-cycle set out in *Towards 2016*.
- Prioritise balanced local and regional development.
- The role of the Community and Voluntary sector being respected and supported.
- Dialogue with social partners being a central part of policy development.
- Ensuring all policy development is evidence-based and outcome-focused.
- Avoiding upward redistribution in the process of supporting banks, bondholders and developers.

We explore a number of these issues in greater depth below. Others are examined elsewhere throughout this *Socio-Economic Review*.

Raising Ireland's total tax-take in a fair and equitable manner

Social Justice Ireland believes that Ireland should remain a low-tax economy. However, it should be one that collects sufficient taxes to meet the provision of an acceptable level of public services. In that regard we note Eurostat's selection of 35 per cent of GDP as the dividing line between high and low tax economies (2008:5). Ireland should bring its overall level of taxation to 34.9 per cent of GDP.

The achievement of this low-tax benchmark is particularly relevant given the recent collapse of taxation revenues (detailed earlier in this chapter) and the obvious and immediate need for Government to rebuild the Irish taxation base. According to the Department of Finance (2010), in 2011 Ireland's total tax-take is likely to fall to approximately 30.5 per cent of GDP. It is this decrease that has placed the exchequer in such a precarious position and put so much unnecessary pressure on public services.

Table 2.7 estimates the scale of tax revenues that should be collected using this low-tax benchmark (34.9 per cent of GDP) with the Department of Finance's projected tax take for the years 2011-2014. The total taxation figure represents not just those taxes collected centrally by the exchequer but also contributions to the social insurance fund and revenues collected by local authorities.[12] As we show, if we increase our tax take to the level proposed by Social Justice Ireland significant additional revenue would be raised. While we do not suggest this change should be immediate, we believe Government should outline a pathway to achieve this target.

Table 2.7: Potential Irish Total Tax Revenues, 2011-2014 (€m)

Year	GDP	Tax @ 34.9%	Tax @ DOF %	Difference
2011	161,200	56,259	49,166	7,093
2012	168,100	58,667	52,952	5,715
2013	175,400	61,215	56,654	4,560
2014	183,500	64,042	60,555	3,486

Source: Calculated from Department of Finance Budget 2011: D9 and D25.
Note: See also Table 3.2.4.

---

[12] There are also some EU related taxes but these are small in the overall context.

Policy Priorities for Moving Towards the Vision

In the longer term it is an obvious reality that Ireland can never hope to address its deficits in infrastructure and social provision if we continue to collect substantially less tax income than that required by other European countries. As we outline in some detail in section 3.2 of this review, *Social Justice Ireland* believes that these tax reforms should not be attained through increasing income tax rates, but rather via reforming and broadening the tax base so that Ireland's taxation system becomes fairer.

> **The recent bank bailouts and rescues have further added to the debt levels being carried by Ireland. Associated with this debt are large and increasing annual debt servicing costs which may consume between 15-20 per cent of the Department of Finance's annual projected taxation revenues. Later in 2011, once the process of bank bailouts, interest rate adjustments and debt restructuring has completed,** *Social Justice Ireland* **will revisit our proposed taxation benchmark and test its adequacy. Subsequently, we will publish an analysis and revise the benchmark upwards if appropriate.**

Adequately resource Ireland's infrastructure and social provision
When considering the adequacy of the resources allocated to infrastructure and social provision, an analysis of Ireland's spending on social protection against that of other EU countries is telling. Social protection expenditure is defined by Eurostat to include spending on: sickness/health care, disability, old age, survivors, family/children, unemployment, housing and social exclusion initiatives not elsewhere classified (2007: 125). Table 2.8 uses the most recent figures, published by Eurostat, to show the size of this expenditure as a percentage of GDP for 2008 (the latest year for which figures are available). A comparison is also made with Ireland's GNP.

In 2008, Ireland's spending on social expenditure was below the EU average (of 26.3 per cent of GDP). Although the Irish figure has been rising in recent years, and is likely to increase further due to the large growth in unemployment, it is by-and-large only poorer new member states that record lower proportions of social expenditure. Chart 2.3 develops this analysis further and examines the difference between the proportion of GDP allocated to social protection expenditure by each of the EU-27 countries and the EU average.

A New and Fairer Ireland

Table 2.8: National Social Protection Expenditure as a % of GDP, for the EU-27 in 2008

Country	% of GDP	Country	% of GDP
France	30.8	Hungary	22.7
Denmark	29.7	**IRELAND GDP**	**22.1**
Sweden	29.4	Slovenia	21.5
Netherlands	28.4	Luxembourg	20.1
Belgium	28.3	Malta	18.9
Austria	28.2	Czech Republic	18.7
Italy	27.8	Poland	18.6
Germany	27.8	Cyprus	18.4
Finland	26.3	Lithuania	16.2
Greece	26.0	Slovakia	16.0
IRELAND GNP	**25.7**	Bulgaria	15.5
Portugal	24.3	Estonia	15.1
United Kingdom	23.7	Romania	14.3
Spain	22.7	Latvia	12.6

Source: Eurostat online database (2011) and CSO (2011:4)
Note: EU-27 average in 2008 = 26.3% of GDP

Chart 2.3: Percentage Divergence in National Social Protection Expenditure levels from the EU average*

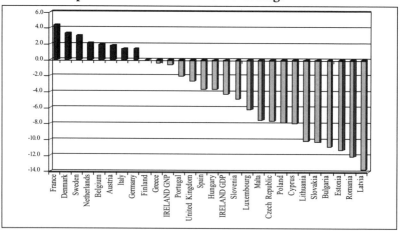

Source: Eurostat online database (2011) and CSO (2011:3)
Note: *EU-27 average in 2008 = 26.3% of GDP

Policy Priorities for Moving Towards the Vision

When social expenditure is assessed on a per capita basis Ireland's position marginally improves. However, when these figures are compared to other countries the Eurostat figures show that the German government spends 7 per cent more per person on social expenditure than Ireland does. Other comparisons against spending per Irish person include: Belgium 9 per cent more, France 11 per cent more, Austria 17 per cent more and Netherlands 28 per cent more.[13]

In the context of these figures, it is of no surprise that the reports mentioned earlier (and others detailed in section 3.1) highlight the high levels of poverty and exclusion in Ireland. *Social Justice Ireland* believes that it is important that Ireland, as a society, focuses on protecting our social provision in the years to come. It is of serious concern that to date, many of those dependent on services and supports in this area have experienced severe cutbacks as a result of various measures in recent Budgets. As we recover from the current crises, it is important that society continues to protect and assist its most vulnerable.

Focus policy to target growth of per-capita National Income
Social Justice Ireland believes that a series of new indicators is needed to measure the development of societies. The inadequacy of out current metrics was the theme of our 2009 Social Policy conference and the subsequent publication entitled *Beyond GDP: What is progress and how should it be measured?* (Reynolds and Healy, 2009). Later in this review we discuss the need to develop such alternative scorecards and in particular address the commitment to investigate the possibility of developing a set of shadow national accounts (see section 3.10).

In the years to come, as Ireland recovers, we believe that it is worthwhile for economic policy to focus on growing per capita national incomes rather than just their nominal levels. Per capita national income is calculated by dividing GNP (or GDP) by the population – establishing GNP per person. Moving to such an approach is particularly important in the context of projected population growth (see below). Reporting and monitoring increases in these indicators would enhance policy making and provide a more realistic yardstick to assess economic developments.

---

[13] All figures sourced from Eurostat online database (2011) and adjusted for purchasing power standards (PPS).

Ensure Ireland's economy is Internationally Competitive

Ireland lost competitiveness throughout almost all of the last decade. While National Income climbed so too did wages. Simultaneously, our infrastructure, both physical and technological, failed to keep pace with the rest of Europe while many of our public institutions performed badly.[14] Overall, we slipped backwards relative to our international competitors; a dangerous phenomenon for an export-orientated economy.

Without doubt, a key feature of Ireland's recovery is the need to rebuild this competitiveness. Already unit labour costs have fallen relative to our EU counterparts and this trend looks set to continue in 2011 (Irish wages are likely to be static at best while other EU countries will record small increases). However, as the World Economic Forum's *Global Competitiveness Reports* have pointed out, competitiveness is about more than just labour costs. Therefore, as Ireland recovers attention needs to be paid to the other key areas of competitiveness including infrastructure, technological connectivity, public sector efficiency, innovation and education/skills.

Address Unemployment and Target Long-term Unemployment

The past three years have seen Ireland return to the phenomenon of widespread unemployment. The transition from near full employment to high-unemployment has been a critically important characteristic of this recession. The implications for people, families, social cohesion and the exchequer's finances have been serious. Economic forecasts for the remainder of 2011 indicate that unemployment will increase further. There can be little doubt that we are entering a very challenging period where high levels of long-term unemployment once again become a characteristic of Irish society.

In Section 3.3 of this review we present a detailed outline of the approaches *Social Justice Ireland* believes the new Government should take to comprehensively addressing this crisis. The scale of these challenges is enormous. However, it is crucial that Government, commentators and society in general remember that each of these policy priorities affect people who are experiencing dramatic and, in many cases, unexpected turmoil in their and their families' lives. As Irish society comes to terms with the enormity of this issue, this perspective should remain central.

---

[14] See section 3.2 where we examine competitiveness in greater detail.

Reduce Poverty

The European wide social survey SILC (Survey on Income and Living Conditions) allows accurate comparisons to be made between the levels and rates of various socio-economic phenomena across the member states. The most recent poverty data indicate that throughout the EU-25 the average risk of poverty in 2008 (the latest year for which comparable statistics are available) was 16.5 per cent. In recent years Ireland's poverty levels have been falling, driven by the increases in social welfare payments delivered in the Budgets of 2005-2007. These increases compensated only partly for the distance social welfare rates had fallen behind other incomes in society over the preceding two decades. However, the recent cuts to these payments combined with reductions in wages and employment numbers is likely to see the poverty figure increase once again. There is a real danger that Irish society will let those on the lowest incomes, and in particular those dependent on social welfare, fall behind once again as it did in the late 1990s (see section 3.1(a)).

One of the most shocking current social statistics relates to child poverty. Of all the children (under 18 years) in Ireland, 18.6 per cent live in poverty - this amounts to approximately 205,000 children. The scale of this statistic is alarming and in recent years it has been increasing. Given that our children are our future, this situation is not acceptable. Furthermore, the fact that such a large proportion of our children is living below the poverty line has obvious implications for the education system, for the success of these children within it, for their job prospects in the future and for Ireland's economic potential in the long-run. Consequently, addressing child poverty must be a priority.

Despite recent policies, over the next few years *Social Justice Ireland* believes that it is possible to reduce Ireland's poverty rate further as most Irish people desire. This can be achieved through policies which continue to: benchmark social welfare payments; provide equity of social welfare rates across genders; provide adequate payments for children and deliver higher and universal state pensions and cost of disability payments. Throughout section 3.1 of this review we outline these policies.

As the economy recovers, a policy agenda focused on maintaining this position would equally be important and would reflect a clear willingness to include all of society in the fruits of the recovery. It would be a great mistake for Ireland, and Irish policy makers, to repeat the experience of the late 1990s, where economic growth benefited only those who were employed while others such as those dependent on pensions and other social welfare payments slipped further and further behind.[15]

---

[15] See section 3.1 and the paragraphs on 'Poverty and social welfare recipients' which provide details of the late 1990s experience.

Develop Long Term Planning

An essential element of any society is its ability to plan for the future. In that context an important insight into Ireland's future was provided in April 2008 as part of the Central Statistics Office (CSO) report on expected population trends. Entitled *Population and Labour Force Projections, 2011-2041* the report signalled a dramatic demographic transformation due to occur in Ireland over the next three decades.[16] Table 2.9 presents its main findings.

Table 2.9: Projected growth of the Irish population, 2002-2041		
Year	Population Growth	% increase from 2002
2002	3,917,000	–
2006	4,232,900	8.06
2011	4,421,900	12.89
2016	4,606,900	17.61
2021	4,763,700	21.62
2026	4,883,000	24.66
2031	4,976,300	27.04
2036	5,055,500	29.07
2041	5,122,000	30.76

Source: CSO (2004; 2008: 27, 33). Using the CSO's demographic assumptions M0F1 – zero migration and high fertility.

As table 2.9 shows the CSO forecast that Ireland's population will climb from approximately 4.2 million people today to over 4.7 million people by 2121 and on to exceed 5.1 million people by 2041. The figures in table 2.6.4 reflect the most conservative CSO assumptions for population growth. While it is likely that the current recession and associated emigration will have some impact on these figures, the differences are unlikely to be substantial.

There are major implications for many public policy areas as a result of this projected increase. Where will all these extra people live? How will they travel around? What additional education and health facilities are required to provide for such additional numbers? How can Ireland ensure that we build a fair, inclusive and sustainable society which can adequately cater for all these extra people?

---

[16] See also Punch (2006).

Social Justice Ireland believes that these figures necessitate the development of long term planning. Rather than cope with the implications of this population growth once it has happened, we believe it is important to begin to plan now for its arrival. To do this successfully, policies need to be framed within a time frame of at least 10 years. These policies also need to look beyond economic growth as the principal priority driving Government, the policy formation process and society generally. Adopting this approach should ensure that short-term decisions being taken by Government do not work against the long-term interests of Irish society.

Address Inequality and Develop a Rights-Based Approach

Inequality is a key problem in Irish society. Inequality produces a whole range of negative outcomes for those who are poor and/or excluded. Increasing inequality, which has been the norm for some time, exacerbates the negative impacts on people who are poor and/or excluded. Reducing inequality must be a core objective of Government policy. *Social Justice Ireland* also believes strongly in the importance of developing a rights-based approach to social, economic and cultural issues. The need to develop these rights is becoming ever more urgent for Ireland in the context of achieving recovery. Such an approach would go a long way towards addressing the growing inequality Ireland has been experiencing.

Social, economic and cultural rights should be acknowledged and recognised just as civil and political rights have been. Among others, we believe that seven basic rights that are of fundamental concern to people who are socially excluded and/or living in poverty should be acknowledged and recognised. These are the rights to: sufficient income to live life with dignity; meaningful work; appropriate accommodation; relevant education; essential healthcare; cultural respect; and real participation. Until these rights are effectively recognised then Ireland and the EU will continue to have a major credibility problem, as they will be failing to match their commitment to civil and political rights with an equal commitment to social, economic and cultural rights.

To ensure that the recognition of social, economic and cultural rights goes beyond words, however, it is essential to address the question: how can such rights be made justiciable (capable of being vindicated in law)? In particular, how can this be done in a way that respects the political process and does not destroy the balance of power between the judicial and the governmental dimensions of society while also respecting the social, economic and cultural rights of people?

In previous publications we have developed a detailed proposal showing how this could be done[17]. We believe that movement in this direction would be a very progressive development and would make a major contribution to seeing the emergence of a New Ireland which would facilitate and support the well-being of all people equally.

Develop a 'Shared Social Responsibility' approach[18]

The current series of crises risks a regression in rights, social protection and democracy. On the one hand there is a danger that people put all their trust in the market as the only real source of solutions to the challenges being faced. On the other hand there is a danger that people expect Government to resolve all the challenges effectively and fairly. Both of these extremes must be resisted. As resources are scarce it is important that all stakeholders recognise the importance of securing the wellbeing of all. There must also be recognition of the need for social, environmental and intergenerational justice. To be effective an approach is required that is characterised by a spirit of reciprocity, mutual accountability and a shared commitment to reducing social inequalities and inequalities of influence.

We live in a world in which no-one is totally independent or immune from the damaging consequences of other people's actions or failure to act. The most advantaged population groups must not ignore their interdependencies and responsibilities vis-à-vis the rest of society. This is especially important when the least advantaged see their achievements in terms of access to rights, public services and common goods placed under threat. It is very important that all sectors of society work together and share responsibility for combating the causes of inequalities, poverty, insecurity and discrimination.

Taking a 'shared social responsibility' approach would mean that individuals and institutions (public and private) would be required to be accountable for the consequences of their actions or omissions. This would apply to the impact on areas such as the protection of human dignity, the environment and common good, poverty and discrimination and the pursuit of justice, development and social cohesion. It is clear that all individuals and institutions do not have equal responsibility in the various areas addressed. Some have much greater resources, power or capacity and, consequently, have greater responsibility. But all have some capacity and, consequently, some responsibility.

---

[17] For a further discussion of this issue see Healy and Reynolds (2003).
[18] Work is currently underway in the Council of Europe on this issue. It is likely to lead to publication of material in the course of 2011.

For such an approach to work effectively would require much greater transparency and accountability, much greater access to knowledge and a deliberative approach to decision-making. It would require a new approach to responsibility in a context of interdependence.

Avoid Upwards Redistribution
An unavoidable element of Ireland's recovery is the need to address the mess created by the incompetent management and regulation of our banking institutions. A similar, and related, mess needs to be cleaned up following the illogical behaviour of numerous property developers (big and small); ranging from those who built unwanted housing to those who dramatically over-paid, and over-borrowed, to buy development land. In addressing both these related problems Government must avoid adopting policies where the exchequer, representing society as a whole, provides huge resources to bail out a few companies, individuals and bondholders while inequality is allowed to continue growing and the most vulnerable are left further behind. Overpaying for bank assets as they transfer to state control or allowing broke developers keep 'performing assets' while the state carries the burden for their un-performing assets is simply unacceptable. Similarly, burdening society with the debts of wreckless banks while not sharing some of that burden with all bondholders who financed it is unfair and irresponsible. As we rebuild the financial system of this country we must avoid upwards redistribution in supporting banks, bondholders and developers.

2.5 Focusing on Specific Issues

In 2011, the challenges facing Irish society are among the greatest in living memory. As we have outlined in this chapter, it is necessary to face these challenges strategically; not with piecemeal policy initiatives to cope with the short–term, but with thought-through integrated policy initiatives that plan for the longer-term.

In the following sections of this review, we outline in greater detail what this would entail and how, through making better choices, Ireland can recover to become a fairer society. The specific issues we address are:

- Income
- Taxation
- Work
- Public Services

- Housing and Accommodation
- Healthcare
- Education and Education Disadvantage
- Intercultural & Migration issues
- Participation
- Sustainability and the Environment
- Rural Development
- The Developing World

On each of these issues, we propose a core policy objective. We also provide an analysis of the present situation, review relevant initiatives and outline key policy priorities aimed at securing a new and fairer Ireland. In doing this, we clearly indicate the choices *Social Justice Ireland* believes should be made in the years immediately ahead.

3. A NEW AND FAIRER IRELAND
Objectives, Analysis and Policy Proposals

3.1 Income

> **CORE POLICY OBJECTIVE: INCOME**
> To provide all with sufficient income to live life with dignity. This would involve enough income to provide a minimum floor of social and economic resources in such a way as to ensure that no person in Ireland falls below the threshold of social provision necessary to enable him or her to participate in activities that are considered the norm for society generally

High rates of poverty and income inequality in Ireland require greater attention. Tackling these problems effectively is a multifaceted task. It requires action on many fronts ranging from healthcare to education, from accommodation to employment. However, the most important requirement in tackling poverty is the provision of sufficient income to people to enable them to live life with dignity. No anti-poverty strategy can possibly achieve any success without an effective approach to addressing low incomes.

This section addresses the issue of income in four parts. The first examines the extent and nature of poverty in Ireland today while the second profiles our income distribution. The final two sections address potential remedies to these problems by outlining the issues and arguments surrounding achieving and maintaining an adequate social welfare income and the introduction of a basic income.

(a) Poverty
While the phenomenon of poverty remains large, there has been major progress on this issue over recent years.[19] Driven by increases in social welfare payments, in particular payments to the unemployed, the elderly and people with disabilities, the rate of poverty has significantly declined. Latest data, analysed in this section,

---

[19] This section of the *Socio Economic Review* complements our January 2011 *Policy Briefing* on Poverty and Income Distribution which is available from www.socialjustice.ie

reports that poverty has remained at the lowest level on record.[20] However, as we outline later, recent Budgets have reversed some of these increases and are likely to drive poverty upwards in the years to come

Data on Ireland's income and poverty levels are now provided by the annual *SILC* survey *(Survey on Income and Living Conditions)*. This survey replaced the *European Household Panel Survey* and the *Living in Ireland Survey* which had run across the 1990s. Since 2003 the *SILC / EU-SILC* survey has collected detailed information on income and living conditions from up to 130 households in Ireland each week; giving a total sample of between 5,000 and 6,000 households each year.

Social Justice Ireland welcomes this survey and in particular the speed and accessibility of the data produced. As this survey is conducted simultaneously across all of the EU states its results possess significant potential to inform the ongoing debate on relative income and poverty levels across the EU member states. It also provides the basis for informed analysis of the relative position of the citizens of member states. In particular, this analysis is informed by a set of agreed indicators of social exclusion which the EU Heads of Government adopted at Laeken in 2001. These indicators (known as the updated-Laeken indicators) are calculated from the survey results and cover four dimensions of social exclusion: financial poverty, employment, health and education.[21]

These changes are outlined below before we review the results from the most recent report which deals with data from 2009.

What is poverty?
The National Anti-Poverty Strategy (NAPS) published by government in 1997 adopted the following definition of poverty:

> *People are living in poverty if their income and resources (material, cultural and social) are so inadequate as to preclude them from having a standard of living that is regarded as acceptable by Irish society generally. As a result of inadequate income and resources people may be excluded and marginalised from participating in activities that are considered the norm for other people in society.*

This definition has been reiterated in the 2007 *National Action Plan for Social Inclusion 2007-2016 (NAPinclusion).*

---

[20] Irish household Income data has been collected since 1973 and all surveys up to 2009 and 2010 have recorded poverty levels above 15 per cent.

[21] For more information on these indicators see Nolan (2006:171-190).

Income

Where is the poverty line?
How many people are poor? On what basis are they classified as poor? These and related questions are constantly asked when poverty is discussed or analysed.

In trying to measure the extent of poverty, the most common approach has been to identify a poverty line (or lines) based on people's incomes. In recent years the European Commission and the UN among others have begun to use a poverty line located at 60 per cent of median income. The median income is the income of the middle person in society's income distribution; in other words it is the middle income in society. This poverty line is the one adopted in the *SILC* survey and differs from the previous Irish poverty line (prior to 2003) which was set at 50 per cent of mean (average) income. This switch to using median income is to be welcomed as it removes many of the theoretical and technical criticisms that had been levelled against using relative income measures to assess poverty.[22] In cash terms there is very little difference between the poverty line drawn at either 60 per cent of median income or 50 per cent of mean income.[23] While the 60 per cent median income line has been adopted as the primary poverty line, alternatives set at 50 per cent and 70 per cent of median income are also used to clarify and lend robustness to assessments of poverty.

The most up-to-date data available on poverty in Ireland comes from the 2009 *SILC* survey, conducted by the CSO. In that year the CSO gathered data from a statistically representative sample of 5,183 households and 12,641 individuals. The data gathered by the CSO is very detailed incorporating income from work, welfare, pensions, rental income, dividends, capital gains and other regular transfers. It is subsequently anonymously verified using PPS numbers to ensure the accuracy and reliability of the data.

According to the CSO the median disposable income per adult in Ireland during 2009 was €20,107 per annum or €385.61 per week. Consequently, the income poverty lines for a single adult derived from this were:

        50 per cent line - €192.81 a week
        60 per cent line - €231.37 a week
        70 per cent line - €269.93 a week

---

[22] In particular the use of median income ensures that it is possible to eliminate poverty (a rate of 0 per cent), a feature that was theoretically impossible when poverty lines were calculated using mean income.
[23] For example in 2003 the CSO reported that the 60 per cent median income line was €14 higher than the 50 per cent mean income line. In some other European countries the opposite situation was found.

Updating the 60 per cent median income poverty line to 2011 levels, using the ESRI's predicted changes in wage levels for 2010 (-3 per cent) and 2011 (-1 per cent), produces a relative income poverty line of €222.18 for a single person. In 2011, any adult below this weekly income level will be counted as being at risk of poverty. It is worth noting that the value of the 2011 poverty line is lower than the 2009 figure (above) because wages have fallen and are projected to decline further while taxes have increased and most social welfare rates of pyment have also decreased. Collectively, these impact on disposable income and as the poverty line is a relative measure it adjusts accordingly.

Table 3.1.1 applies this poverty line to a number of household types to show what income corresponds to each household's poverty line. The figure of €222.18 is an income per adult equivalent figure. This means that it is the minimum weekly disposable income (after taxes and including all benefits) that one adult needs to receive to be outside of poverty. For each additional adult in the household this minimum income figure is increased by €146.64 (66 per cent of the poverty line figure) and for each child in the household the minimum income figure is increased by €73.32 (33 per cent of the poverty line).[24] These adjustments are made in recognition of the fact that as households increase in size they require more income to keep themselves out of poverty. In all cases a household below the corresponding weekly disposable income figure is classified as living at risk of poverty. For clarity, corresponding annual figures are also included.

Table 3.1.1: The Minimum Weekly Disposable Income Required to Avoid Poverty in 2011, by Household Types

Household containing:	Weekly poverty line	Annual poverty line
1 adult	€222.18	€11,585
1 adult + 1 child	€295.50	€15,408
1 adult + 2 children	€368.82	€19,231
1 adult + 3 children	€442.14	€23,054
2 adults	€368.82	€19,231
2 adults + 1 child	€442.14	€23,054
2 adults + 2 children	€515.46	€26,877
2 adults + 3 children	€588.78	€30,701
3 adults	€515.46	€26,877

---

[24] For example the poverty line for a household with 2 adults and 1 child would be calculated as €222.18 + €146.64 + €73.32 = €442.14.

One immediate implication of this analysis is that most weekly social assistance rates paid to single people are €34.18 below the poverty line.

How many have incomes below the poverty line?

Table 3.1.2 outlines the findings of various poverty studies since 1994 (when detailed poverty studies commenced). Using the EU poverty line set at 60 per cent of median income, the findings reveal that in 2009 approximately 14 out of every 100 people in Ireland were living in poverty. However, the table also indicates that in recent years the rates of poverty have decreased significantly to record levels (there is no statistically significant difference between the levels recorded for 2008 and 2009). These recent decreases in poverty levels must be welcomed. They are directly related to the increases in social welfare payments delivered over the Budget's spanning these years.[25]

Table 3.1.2: Percentage of population below various relative income poverty lines, 1994-2009

	1994	1998	2001	2005	2006	2007	2008	2009
50% line	6.0	9.9	12.9	10.8	8.9	★	★	6.9
60% line	**15.6**	**19.8**	**21.9**	**18.5**	**17.0**	**15.8**	**13.9**	**14.1**
70% line	26.7	26.9	29.3	28.2	26.7	★	★	24.5

Source: CSO (2010:45, 46) and Whelan et al (2003:12), using national equivalence scale.
Notes: All poverty lines calculated as a percentage of median income.
★ Data not published for 2007 and 2008

As it is sometimes easy to overlook the scale of Ireland's poverty problem it is useful to translate the poverty percentages into numbers of people. Using the percentages for the 60 per cent median income poverty line and population statistics from CSO population projections and Census results we can calculate the numbers of people in Ireland who have been in poverty for the years 1994, 1998, 2001, 2003-2009 (CSO 2004:48, 2006:52, 2007:37, 2009:7, 2010:45). These calculations are presented in table 3.1.3. The results give a better insight into how large the phenomenon of poverty is.

---

[25] See table 3.1.14 below for further analysis of this point.

Table 3.1.3: The numbers of people below relative income poverty lines in Ireland, 1994-2009

	% of persons in poverty	Population of Ireland	Numbers in poverty
1994	15.6	3,585,900	559,400
1998	19.8	3,703,000	733,194
2001	21.9	3,847,200	842,537
2003	19.7	3,978,900	783,843
2004	19.4	4,045,200	784,769
2005	18.5	4,133,800	764,753
2006	17.0	4,239,800	720,766
2007	15.8	4,339,000	685,562
2008	13.9	4,422,100	614,672
2009	14.1	4,459,300	628,761

Source: Calculated using CSO (2008:11), Whelan et al (2003:12), using national equivalence scale and CSO (2004:48, 2006:52, 2007:37, 2010:35).

The table's figures are telling. Over the past decade more that 213,000 people have been lifted out of poverty. Furthermore, over the period from 2004-2008, the period corresponding with consistent Budget increases in social welfare payments, over 170,000 people left poverty.

However, the fact that there are now almost 630,000 people in Ireland living life on a level of income that is this low must be a major concern. As we have shown earlier (see table 3.1.1) these levels of income are low and those below them clearly face difficulty in achieving what the NAPS described as "*a standard of living that is regarded as acceptable by Irish society generally*".

Who are the poor?

In recent years two interchangeable phrases have been used to describe those who are living on incomes below the poverty line, namely those *'living in poverty'* and those *'at risk of poverty'*. The latter of these terms is the most recent, introduced following a European Council meeting in Laeken in 2001. There it was proposed that those with incomes below the poverty line should be termed as being 'at risk of poverty'.

The results of the *SILC* survey provided a breakdown of those below the poverty line. This section reviews those findings, starting with a broad overview in table

3.1.4 and then proceeding to a detailed assessment of the different groups in poverty.

Table 3.1.4 presents figures for the risk of poverty facing people when they are classified by their principal economic status (the main thing that they do). These risk figures represent the proportion of each group that are found to be in receipt of a disposable income that is less than the 60 per cent median income poverty line. In 2009 the groups within the Irish population that were at highest risk of poverty included the unemployed and those not at work due to illness or a disability. Almost one in five classified as on home duties, mainly women, live with an income below the poverty line. The student and school attendees' category represents a combination of individuals living in poor families while completing their secondary education and those attending post-secondary education but with low incomes. The latter element of this group are not a major policy worry given that they are likely to be experiencing poverty in the short-term, while they gain education and skills which should ensure they live with sufficient income subsequently. Those still in school and experiencing poverty are more aligned to the issue of child poverty which is examined later in this chapter.

The table also reveals the groups which have driven the reduction in poverty over the past few years. While the poverty rate has fallen for all groups other than students, there have been pronounced falls among the welfare-dependent groups namely the unemployed, retired and those not at work due to illness or a disability.

Table 3.1.4: Risk of poverty among all persons aged 16yrs + by principal economic status, 2003-09

	2003	2006	2009
At work	7.6	6.5	5.5
Unemployed	41.5	44.0	24.8
Students and school attendees	23.1	29.5	25.9
On home duties	31.8	23.8	19.1
Retired	27.7	14.8	9.6
Unable to work as ill/disabled	51.7	40.8	21.7
Total	**19.7**	**17.0**	**14.1**

Source: CSO (2005:11, 2007:15, 2010:45), using national equivalence scale

One obvious conclusion to draw from table 3.1.4 is that further progress to reduce poverty should be driven by continuing to enhance the adequacy of welfare

The working poor

The growth in jobs over the years leading up to the collection of this data in 2009 was dramatic (the subsequent increase in unemployment will only begin to become visible in the next set of poverty figures to be released in late 2011). However, it is important to realise that having a job is not, of itself, a guarantee that one lives in a poverty-free household. As table 3.1.4 indicates 5.5 per cent of those who are employed are living at risk of poverty. Translating this into numbers of people suggests that among Ireland's workers in 2009 at least 90,000 were at risk of poverty.[26]

This is a remarkable statistic and it is important that policy begin to address this problem. Policies which restore and protect the value of the minimum wage and attempt to keep those on that wage out of the tax net are relevant policy initiatives in this area. Similarly, attempts to increase awareness among low income working families of their entitlement to the Family Income Supplement (FIS) are also welcome; although evidence suggests that FIS is experiencing dramatically low take-up and as such has questionable long-term potential. However, one of the most effective mechanisms available within the present system to address the problem of the working poor would be to make tax credits refundable. We will address this proposal later.

Child poverty

One of the most vulnerable groups in any society are children and consequently the issue of child poverty is one that deserves particular attention. Child poverty is measured as the proportion of all children aged 17 years or younger who live in households that have an income below the 60 per cent of median income poverty line. The 2009 *SILC* survey indicates that 18.6 per cent were at risk of poverty and as table 3.1.5 shows in recent years the rate of child poverty has begun to increase (2010:45).

Table 3.1.5: Child Poverty – % Risk of Poverty Among Children in Ireland.				
	2006★	2007★	2008	2009
Children, 0-18 yrs	19.0	17.4	18.0	18.6

Source: CSO (various editions of SILC)
Note: ★ 2006 and 2007 data exclude SSIA effect.

---

[26] See table 3.1.13.

Translating the data in table 3.1.5 into numbers of children implies that in 2009 between 210,000–220,000 children lived in households that were experiencing poverty. The scale of this statistic is alarming. Given that our children are our future, this situation is not acceptable. Furthermore, the fact that such a large proportion of our children are living below the poverty line has obvious implications for the education system, for the success of these children within it, for their job prospects in the future and for Ireland's economic potential in the long-run.

Child benefit remains a key route to tackling child poverty and is of particular benefit to those families on the lowest incomes. Similarly, it is a very effective component in any strategy to improve equality and childcare. Consequently, it is of some concern that Government has cut child payments in recent Budgets. On foot of these policies, it is likely that over the next few years child poverty will increase further – something that will represent a major step backwards for Ireland's children and our record on child poverty.

Older people
According to the *Statistical Yearbook 2010* 11.1 per cent of the Irish population are aged over 65 years – some 495,000 people (CSO, 2010:11). Earlier data from the 2006 Census also indicated that just over a quarter of this group live alone (CSO, 2007: 36). When poverty is analysed by age group the 2009 figures show that 9.6 per cent of those aged between 65-74 years and 10.6 per cent of those older than 75 years live in relative income poverty (CSO, 2010:45).

Among all those in poverty, it is the retired that have experienced the greatest volatility in their poverty risk rates. As table 3.1.6 shows in 1994 some 5.9 per cent of this group were classified as poor, by 1998 the figure had risen to 32.9 per cent and in 2001 it peaked at 44.1 per cent. The most recent data record a decrease in poverty rates. Comparable figures for 2009 have not been published by the CSO although it is likely that the rate is approximately 10 per cent.[27] While these recent decreases are to be welcomed, it remains a concern that so many of this county's senior citizens are living on so little.

---

[27] Based on the published CSO data for the number of retired people in poverty at 9.6 per cent.

Table 3.1.6: Percentage of older people (65yrs+) below the 60 per cent median income poverty line.

	1994	1998	2001	2003	2004	2005	2006	2009*
Aged 65 +	5.9	32.9	44.1	29.8	27.1	20.1	13.6	10.0

Source: Whelan et al (2003: 28) and CSO (various editions of SILC)
Note: * approximate figure as comparable figure not published by CSO.

The Ill /Disabled

As table 3.1.4 showed those not employed due to illness or a disability are one of the groups at highest risk of poverty with 21.7 per cent of this group classified in this category. Much like the experience of Ireland's older people, the situation of this group has varied significantly over the last decade and a half. The group's risk of poverty climbed from approximately three out of every ten persons in 1994 (29.5 per cent) to over six out of every ten in 2001 (66.5 per cent) before decreasing to approximately two out of every ten in 2008/09. As with other welfare dependent groups, these fluctuations parallel a period where policy first let the value of payments fall behind wage growth before ultimately increasing them to catch-up.

Overall, although those not at work due to illness or a disability only account for a small proportion of those in poverty, among themselves their experience of poverty is high. Furthermore, given the nature of this group *Social Justice Ireland* believes there is an ongoing need for targeted policies to assist them. These include job creation, retraining (see section on work) and further increases in social welfare supports. There is also a very strong case to be made for introducing a non-means tested cost of disability allowance. This proposal, which has been researched and costed in detail by the National Disability Authority (NDA, 2006) and advocated by Disability Federation of Ireland (DFI), would provide an extra weekly payment of between €10 and €40 to somebody living with a disability (calculated on the basis of the severity of their disability). It seems only logical that if people with a disability are to be equal participants in society then the extra costs generated by their disability should not be borne by them alone, but rather society at large should act to level the playing field by covering those extra but ordinary costs. The *NESC Strategy 2006* also supported this policy development urging that "the Government strongly consider the case for a separate 'cost of disability payment' that, in line with its analysis in the Developmental Welfare State, would be personally tailored and portable across the employment/non-employment divide" (NESC, 2005:168). In their *2008 Pre-Budget Submission* (for Budget 2008) DFI anticipate such a scheme would cost €183m per annum (DFI, 2007). *Social Justice Ireland* believes the introduction of this payment is long overdue.

Poverty and education

The 2009 *SILC* results provide an interesting insight into the relationship between poverty and completed education levels. Table 3.1.7 reports the risk of poverty by completed education level and shows, as might be expected, that the risk of living on a low income is strongly related to low education levels. These figures underscore the relevance of continuing to address the issues of education disadvantage and early-school leaving (see section 3.7). Government education policy should ensure that these high risk groups are reduced. The table also suggests that when targeting anti-poverty initiatives, a large proportion should be aimed at those with low education levels, including those with low levels of literacy (we address the issue of adult literacy in section 3.7).

Table 3.1.7: Risk of poverty among all persons aged 16yrs + by completed education level, 2007-2009

	2007	2008	2009
Primary or below	24.0	20.4	18.6
Lower secondary	20.7	16.4	19.7
Higher secondary	13.8	12.4	12.8
Post leaving certificate	10.9	10.9	9.1
Third level non-degree	8.4	5.4	4.9
Third level degree or above	4.2	5.5	4.8
Total	**15.8**	**13.9**	**14.1**

Source: CSO (2008:15; 2009:45, 2010:45), using national equivalence scale and excluding SSIA effect for 2007 and 2008.

Poverty and Nationality

A feature of the last decade has been the growth in the number of people living in Ireland but born outside the state. The CSO refers to this group as "non-Irish nationals" and the 2006 *SILC* report presented data on poverty levels among this group vis-à-vis "Irish Nationals". For sampling reasons subsequent surveys did not publish an update of this figure. The definitions used by the CSO in examining this issue are necessarily broad given the difficulty associated with collecting accurate statistical samples among nationals of individual countries.

A New and Fairer Ireland

Table 3.1.8: Risk of poverty by nationality, 2005-2006			
	2005	2006	Change
Irish Nationals	18.0	16.6	-1.4
Non-Irish Nationals	26.9	23.5	-3.4
Overall Population	**18.5**	**17.0**	**-1.5**

Source: CSO (2007:15), using national equivalence scale.

The findings, reported in table 3.1.8, reveal a stark contrast between the poverty risk levels of the two groups. Non-Irish nationals face a much higher risk of poverty, overall and by gender. As the data does not allow for a more detailed breakdown of these figures by nationality we cannot conclusively say who these non-Irish nationals in poverty are and where they have originated from. However, it is likely that many of those experiencing poverty are recent migrants, many from the new member states of the EU.

Social Justice Ireland welcomed the provision of this new data although it is of some concern that the data was excluded from the most recent reports. The poverty data suggests that migration issues, including issues with regard to the participation of migrants in Irish society, deserve greater attention. We will consider many of these issues later in section 3.8.

Poverty by region and area
The 2009 *SILC* results have provided a detailed regional breakdown of poverty levels. The data, presented in table 3.1.9 below, suggests a very uneven national distribution of poverty. In Dublin less than one in ten people live in poverty while the figures are twice this in the Mid-West, South-East and the Midlands. As this is new data (first produced in the 2008 SILC report) the explanations to accompany them, other than that there are a higher percentage of people with lower incomes in these areas, is not yet clear. However, the analysis does underscore the need to think about poverty in both national and regional terms - a perspective absent from analysis in this area heretofore.

The table also reports that poverty is more likely to occur in rural areas than urban areas. The risk of poverty in rural Ireland was 6 per cent higher than in urban Ireland with at risk rates of 17.8 per cent and 11.8 per cent respectively.

Table 3.1.9: Risk of poverty by region and area, 2005-2009

	2005	2007	2008	2009
Border	–	17.8	16.6	14.1
Midlands	–	29.7	22.7	23.5
West	–	19.4	16.1	14.1
Dublin	–	11.5	9.3	8.3
Mid-East	–	8.1	10.2	14.6
Mid-West	–	19.0	21.3	18.9
South-East	–	18.0	15.4	18.3
South-West	–	17.1	13.0	14.7
Urban Areas	16.0	14.3	11.3	11.8
Rural Areas	22.5	18.4	18.2	17.8
Overall Population	**18.5**	**15.8**	**13.9**	**14.1**

Source: CSO (2008:15; 2009:45, 2010:45), using national equivalence scale and excluding SSIA effect for 2007 and 2008.
Note: Regional data only available for 2007 onwards

The poverty gap

As part of the 2001 Laeken indicators the European Union requested that all member countries begin to measure the relative at-risk-of poverty gap. This indicator assesses how far below the poverty line the income of the median (middle) person in poverty is. The size of that difference is calculated as a percentage of the poverty line and therefore represents the gap between the income of the middle person in poverty and the poverty line. The higher the percentage figure gets the greater the poverty gap and the further people are falling beneath the poverty line. As there is a considerable difference between being 2 per cent and 20 per cent below the poverty line this approach is significant.

Table 3.1.10: The Poverty Gap, 2003-2009

	2003	2004	2005	2006	2007*	2008*	2009
Poverty gap size	21.5	19.8	20.8	17.5	17.4	19.2	16.2

Source: CSO (2008:16; 2010:46)
Note: * Data for 2007 and 2008 not excluding SSIA effect as not published by CSO.

The *SILC* results for 2009 calculated that the poverty gap was 16.2 per cent a decrease from 19.2 per cent in 2008. Over time the gap had decreased from a figure of 21.5 per cent in 2003. In 2009 the poverty gap figure implies that 50 per cent of those in poverty had an equivalised income below 83.8 per cent of the poverty line. As the depth of poverty is an important issue, we look forward to monitoring the movement of this indicator throughout future editions of the *SILC*. It is crucial that as part of Ireland's approach to addressing poverty that this figure decline.

The incidence of poverty
Figures detailing the incidence of poverty reveal the proportion of all those in poverty that belong to particular groups in Irish society. Tables 3.1.11 and 3.1.12 report all those below the 60 per cent of median income poverty line classifying them by their principal economic status. The first table examines the population as a whole, including children, while the second table focuses exclusively on adults (using the ILO definition where adults are considered all those aged 16 years and above).

Table 3.1.10 shows that in 2009, the largest group of the population who are poor are children accounting for 27.6 per cent of the total. The second largest group are those working in the home (18 per cent). Of all those who are poor, 27.2 per cent are in the labour force and the remainder (72.8 per cent) are outside the labour market[28]

Table 3.1.11: Incidence of persons below 60% of median income by principal economic status, 2003-2009

	2003	2005	2006	2007★	2008★	2009
At work	16.0	15.7	16.1	16.8	19.0	14.3
Unemployed	7.6	7.5	8.3	9.2	8.1	12.9
Students/school	8.6	13.4	15.0	14.1	13.1	14.6
On home duties	22.5	19.7	18.4	18.7	18.9	18.0
Retired	9.0	7.5	5.8	7.1	4.9	4.7
Ill/disabled	9.1	7.9	8.0	7.4	6.5	6.4
Children (under 16 years)	25.4	26.8	26.6	25.9	27.4	27.6
Other	1.9	1.6	1.8	0.8	2.1	1.5
Total	**100.0**	**100.0**	**100.0**	**100.0**	**100.0**	**100.0**

Source: Collins (2006:141), CSO (2007:19; 2008:25; 2009:48; 2010:48).
Note: ★ Data for 2007 and 2008 not excluding SSIA effect as not published by CSO.

---

[28] This does not include the ill and disabled, some of whom will be active in the labour force. The SILC data does not distinguish between those are temporally unable to work due to illness and those permanently outside the labour market due to their illness or disability.

Table 3.1.12 offers a more informed assessment of the nature of poverty given that it looks at adults only. This is an important perspective as children depend on adults for their upbringing and support. Irrespective of how policy interventions are structured it is through adults that any attempts to reduce the number of children in poverty must be directed. The calculations show that almost one-fifth of Ireland's adults who have an income below the poverty line are employed. Overall, 37 per cent of adults who are at risk of poverty in Ireland are associated with the labour market.

The most alarming statistic here is that almost one in five adults at risk of poverty is in employment. This group's plight is consistently ignored. Many of this group do not benefit from Budget changes in welfare or tax. They would be the main beneficiaries of making tax credits refundable, a topic we will address in section 3.2.

Table 3.1.12: Incidence of adults (16yrs+) below 60% of median income by principal economic status, 2003-2009

	2003	2005	2006	2007*	2008*	2009
At work	21.4	21.4	21.9	22.7	26.2	19.8
Unemployed	10.2	10.2	11.3	12.4	11.2	17.8
Students/school	11.5	18.3	20.4	19.0	18.0	20.2
On home duties	30.1	26.9	25.1	25.2	26.0	24.9
Retired	12.0	10.2	7.9	9.6	6.7	6.5
Ill/disabled	12.2	10.8	10.9	10.0	9.0	8.8
Other	2.5	2.2	2.5	1.1	2.9	2.1
Total	100.0	100.0	100.0	100.0	100.0	100.0

Source: Collins (2006:141), CSO (2007:19; 2008:25; 2009:48; 2010:48).
Note: * Data for 2007 and 2008 not excluding SSIA effect as not published by CSO.

Finally, table 3.1.13 examines the composition of poverty by household type. Given that households are taken to be the 'income receiving units' (income flows into households who then collectively live off that income) there is an attraction in assessing poverty by household type. *Social Justice Ireland* welcome the fact that the CSO have, at our suggestion, begun to publish the *SILC* poverty data broken down by household category. From a policy making perspective, having this information is crucial as anti-poverty policy is generally focused on households (households with children, pensioner households, single person households etc). This data shows that in 2009 22.8 per cent of households who were at risk of poverty were headed by somebody who was employed. Almost 44 per cent of households at risk of poverty were found to be headed by a person outside the labour force.[29]

---

[29] Those on home duties, students and school attendees, retired plus a proportion of the ill and disabled.

Table 3.1.13: Households below 60% of median income classified by principal economic status of head of household, 2004-2009

	2004	2006	2007*	2008*	2009
At work	29.8	29.5	31.3	39.6	22.8
Unemployed	12.0	14.7	12.3	11.5	26.0
Students/school	2.8	4.6	5.1	4.1	5.4
On home duties	28.0	30.7	28.7	25.7	26.7
Retired	13.5	8.5	10.9	7.9	6.6
Ill/disabled	12.0	11.5	11.2	10.1	10.9
Other	1.9	0.7	0.4	1.1	1.6
Total	**100.0**	**100.0**	**100.0**	**100.0**	**100.0**

Source: CSO (2007:39; 2008:36; 2009:49; 2010:49)
Note: * Data for 2007 and 2008 not excluding SSIA effect as not published by CSO.

The Scale of Poverty - Numbers of People

As the three tables in the last section deal only in percentages it is useful to transform these proportions into numbers of people. Earlier, table 3.1.3 identified that in 2009 628,761 people were living below the 60 per cent of median income poverty line. Using this figure, table 3.1.14 presents the number of people in poverty in that year broken down into various categories. Comparable figures are also presented for 2005 2007 and 2008.

The data in table 3.1.14 is particularly useful in the context of framing anti-poverty policy. Groups such as the retired and the ill/disabled, although carrying a high risk of poverty, involve much smaller numbers of people than groups such as adults who are employed (the working poor), people on home duties and children/students. Over the years of data, it is interesting to track how the numbers living below the poverty line have changed within each group. The primary drivers of the recent poverty reductions have been increasing incomes among those who are on home duties, those who are classified as ill/disabled, the retired and children. Between 2008 and 2009 the numbers of workers in poverty declined while the numbers of unemployed people in poverty notably increased; a trend reflective of the changing labour market during that year as job losses occurred and the numbers unemployed rapidly increased (see Section 3.3).

Income

Table 3.1.14: Poverty Levels Expressed in Numbers of People, 2005-2009

	2005	2007	2008	2009
Overall	764,753	685,562	614,672	628,761
Adults				
On home duties	150,656	128,200	116,173	113,177
At work	120,066	115,174	116,788	89,913
Students/school	102,477	96,664	80,522	91,799
Unemployed	57,356	63,072	49,788	81,110
Ill/disabled	60,415	50,732	39,954	40,241
Retired	57,356	48,675	30,119	29,552
Other	12,236	5,484	12,908	9,431
Children				
Children (under 16 yrs)	204,954	177,561	168,420	173,538
Children (under 18 yrs)	n/a	224,179	200,998	219,438
Nationality				
Non-Irish	58,886	n/a	n/a	n/a

Source: Calculated using CSO (2010:48; 2009:48, 2008:25, 2007:19, 2006:13) and data from table 3.1.3.

Moving to Persistent Poverty

Social Justice Ireland is committed to using the best and most up-to-date data in its ongoing socio-economic analysis of Ireland. We believe that to do so is crucial to the emergence of accurate evidence-based policy formation. It also assists in establishing appropriate and justifiable targeting of state resources. At the intergovernmental conference in Laeken during 2001, the EU adopted a set of commonly measured indicators to monitor socio-economic progress across all of the member states. Data for these measures is to be collected annually in the *SILC* survey. The availability of annual data on poverty, incomes and living conditions is an important move. It facilitates a more informed and timely assessment of these issues than was achievable in the past. It will also allow us to track changes more closely over time and to make accurate comparisons across all 27 EU member states.

Among the Laeken indicators is an indicator of persistent poverty. This indicator measures the proportion of those living below the 60 per cent of median income poverty line in the current year and for two of the three previous years. Persistent poverty therefore identifies those who have experienced sustained exposure to poverty which is seen to harm their quality of life seriously and increase their levels of deprivation. To date the *SILC* survey has not produced any detailed results and breakdowns for this measure (although the survey has run for more than four full years and it is therefore possible to provide this insight). The CSO had indicated that it would publish such a breakdown during 2009; however this did not occur. We regret this delay and hope that the technical impediments to the publication of this data are overcome so that it can be made available. Once this data becomes available *Social Justice Ireland* believes that it should be used as the primary basis for setting poverty targets and monitoring changes in poverty status. Existing measures (relative and consistent poverty) should be maintained as secondary indicators. As the persistent poverty indicator will identify the long-term poor, we believe that the CSO should produce comprehensive breakdowns of those in persistent poverty, similar to the approach they currently take with relative income poverty.

However, the available *SILC* data has given some insight on the likely persistent poverty numbers. In the 2009 SILC report the CSO presented '*tentative estimates for persistent poverty*' which reported that in 2009 the persistent poverty rate was 7.7 per cent and that this figure had decreased from 9.5 per cent in 2008 and 15.5 per cent in 2007 (2010:123-124). These figures, while preliminary, are worryingly high. Using the 2009 figure it implies that more than half of all those in poverty (the overall population figure was 14.1 per cent) have been in poverty for a number of years. They also imply that most of Ireland's poor are long-term poor and that poverty in Ireland is a structural problem which requires focused policies to address and reduce it.

Poverty and social welfare recipients

Social Justice Ireland believes in the very important role that social welfare plays in addressing poverty. As part of the *SILC* results the CSO has provided an interesting insight into the role that social welfare payments play in tackling Ireland's poverty levels. They have calculated what the levels of poverty are before and after the payment of social welfare benefits.

Table 3.1.15 presents these results and shows that without the social welfare system Ireland's poverty rate in 2009 would have been 46.2 per cent. The actual poverty figure of 14.1 per cent reflects the fact that social welfare payments reduced poverty by 32.1 percentage points.

Looking at the impact of these payments on poverty over time it is clear that the recent increases in social welfare have yielded noticeable reductions in poverty levels. The small increases in social welfare payments in 2001 are reflected in the smaller effects achieved in that year. Conversely, the larger increases, and therefore higher levels of social welfare payments, in recent years have delivered greater reductions. This has occurred even as poverty levels before social welfare have increased. *Social Justice Ireland* has warmly welcomed these social welfare increases and the CSO's data proves the effectiveness of this policy approach.

Table 3.1.15: The role of social welfare (SW) payments in addressing poverty

	2001	2005	2006	2007*	2008*	2009
Poverty pre SW	35.6	40.1	40.3	41.0	43.0	46.2
Poverty post SW	21.9	18.5	17.0	16.5	14.4	14.1
The role of SW	-13.7	-21.6	-23.3	-24.5	-28.6	-32.1

Source: CSO (2006:7; 2007:13; 2010:46), using national equivalence scale.
Note: * Data for 2007 and 2008 not excluding SSIA effect as not published by CSO.

As social welfare payments do not flow to everybody in the population it is interesting to examine the impact they have on alleviating poverty among certain groups such as older people. Without any social welfare payments 88 per cent of all those aged over 65 years would be living in poverty. Benefit entitlements reduce the poverty level among this group to 9.6 per cent. Similarly, social welfare payments (including child benefit) reduce poverty among those under 18 years from 47.3 per cent to 18.6 per cent – a 60 per cent reduction in poverty risk (CSO, 2009:47). Both these findings underscores the importance of social transfer payments in addressing poverty; a point that needs to be bourn in mind as Government continues to address Ireland's ongoing crisis.

Table 3.1.4 and the subsequent analysis has shown that many of the groups in Irish society who experienced increases in their poverty levels over the last decade have been dependent on social welfare payments. These include pensioners, the unemployed, lone parents and those who are ill or disabled. Table 3.1.16 presents the results of an analysis of five key welfare recipient groups performed by the ESRI using poverty data for five of the years between 1994 and 2001. These are the years that the Irish economy grew fastest and the core years of the famed 'Celtic Tiger' boom. Between 1994 and 2001 all categories experienced large growth in their poverty risk. For example, in 1994 only 5 in every 100 old age pension recipients were in poverty; in 2001 this had increased ten-fold to almost 50 in every 100. The experience of widow's pension recipients is similar.

Table 3.1.16: Percentage of persons in receipt of welfare benefits/assistance who were below the 60 per cent median income poverty line, 1994/1997/1998/2000/2001

	1994	1997	1998	2000	2001
Old age pension	5.3	19.2	30.7	42.9	49.0
Unemployment benefit/assistance	23.9	30.6	44.8	40.5	43.1
Illness/disability	10.4	25.4	38.5	48.4	49.4
Lone Parents allowance	25.8	38.4	36.9	42.7	39.7
Widow's pension	5.5	38.0	49.4	42.4	42.1

Source: Whelan et al (2003: 31)

The lesson to be learnt from table 3.1.16 centres on the inadequacy of social welfare payments. Over the period covered by these studies groups similar to *Social Justice Ireland* repeatedly pointed out how these payments failed to rise in proportion to earnings elsewhere in society. The primary consequence of this was that recipients slipped further and further back and as a consequence more and more fell into poverty. It is clear that adequate levels of social welfare need to be maintained and we outline our proposals for this later in this chapter.

Poverty and deprivation
Income, alone, does not tell the whole story concerning living standards and command over resources. As we have seen in the NAPS definition of poverty it is necessary to look more broadly at exclusion from society because of a lack of resources. This would involve looking at other areas where "as a result of inadequate income and resources people may be excluded and marginalised from participating in activities that are considered the norm for other people in society" (NAPS, 1997). Although income is the principal indicator used to assess well-being and ability to participate in society there are other measures used. In particular these measures assess the standards of living people achieve by assessing deprivation through use of different indicators. To date assessments of deprivation in Ireland have been limited and confined to a small number of items. While this is regrettable, the information gathered is worth considering.

Deprivation in the SILC survey

Social Justice Ireland, among others, has continued to express its discomfort with the range of deprivation measures provided by the CSO in the *SILC* survey; although since 2007 the data presents a larger set of deprivation items than in previous years (eleven rather than eight). Looking forward we believe that a whole new approach to measuring deprivation needs to be taken. Continuing to collect information on a limited number of static indicators is problematic and not a true representation of the dynamic nature of Irish society and the ever changing set of items needed to participate in Irish society.

The details presented in table 3.1.17 should be interpreted in the context of the above reservation. It shows that the rates of deprivation recorded across a set of eleven items varied between 1 and 16 per cent of the Irish population. Overall 71.4 per cent of the population were not deprived of any item while 11.5 per cent were deprived of one item, 7.4 per cent were without two items and 9.7 per cent were without three or more items (CSO, 2010:67).

Table 3.1.17: Levels of deprivation for eleven items among the population in 2008 and 2009 (%)

	2008	2009
Without heating at some stage in the past year	6.3	7.3
Unable to afford a morning, afternoon or evening out in the last fortnight★	11.1	14.9
Unable to afford two pairs of strong shoes	2.7	2.1
Unable to afford a roast once a week	3.8	3.4
Unable to afford a meal with meat, chicken or fish every second day	3.0	2.1
Unable to afford new (not second-hand) clothes	5.6	4.5
Unable to afford a warm waterproof coat	2.6	1.1
Unable to afford to keep the home adequately warm★	3.7	4.1
Unable to replace any worn out furniture★	13.3	16.3
Unable to afford to have family or friends for a drink or meal once a month★	9.1	9.4
Unable to afford to buy presents for family or friends at least once a year★	2.3	3.4

Source: CSO (2009:66; 2010:71)
Note: ★ New deprivation indicator, used from 2007 onwards.

Deprivation and poverty combined: consistent poverty

'Consistent poverty' combines deprivation and poverty into one indicator. It does so by calculating the percentage of the population who are simultaneously experiencing poverty and are also registering as being deprived of two or more of the items in table 3.1.17. As such it captures a sub-group of the poor.

The 2007 *SILC* data marked an important change for this indicator. Coupled with the expanded list of deprivation items the definition of consistent poverty was changed such that individuals must now be below the poverty line and experiencing deprivation of at least two items to be counted as experiencing consistent poverty. Prior to the 2007 survey the indicator measured those below the poverty line and experiencing deprivation of at least one item. This change in definition also makes comparison with previous years inappropriate.[30] The *National Action Plan for Social Inclusion 2007-2016* (*NAPinclusion*) published in early 2007 set its overall poverty goal using this consistent poverty measure. It set an aim to reduce the number of those experiencing consistent poverty to between 2 per cent and 4 per cent by 2012, with the aim of eliminating consistent poverty by 2016.

Using these new indicators and definition, the 2009 *SILC* data indicates that 5.5 per cent of the population experience consistent poverty, an increase from 4.2 per cent in 2008 (CSO, 2010:86). Interpreting this in terms of the population, the 2009 figures indicate that 245,261 people live in consistent poverty.

Deprivation of food: food poverty

A report on the nature and extent of income-related constraints on food consumption in Ireland entitled *Food Poverty and Policy* defined food poverty as "the inability to access a nutritionally adequate diet and the related impacts on health, culture and social participation" (Society of St.Vincent de Paul et al, 2004). It found that among those living in poverty three main constraints were imposed on their food consumption. These were: (i) it affects food affordability through the choice and quantity of food that can be bought and the share of the household budget that is allocated to food; (ii) it impacts on access to food through the retail options available and the capacity to shop in terms of transport and physical ability; (iii) issues such as personal skills and knowledge, social pressure and cultural norms interact with structural and economic constraints to produce a complex set of factors contributing to food poverty. Consequently, the experience of food poverty

---

[30] The CSO have produced new and comparable figures for the 2005 and 2006 surveys. However, previously published consistent poverty indicators from these and earlier years are not comparable with the 2007 data.

among poor people was that they: eat less well compared to better off groups; have difficulties accessing a variety of nutritionally balanced good quality and affordable foodstuffs; spend a greater proportion of their weekly income on food; and know what is healthy but are restricted by a lack of financial resources to purchase and consume it.

The report found that those most at risk of food poverty were low-income households as well as the unemployed, older people, the homeless, Travellers and refugees/asylum-seekers.

Deprivation of heat in the home: fuel poverty
Another area of deprivation that has received attention in recent times is deprivation of heat in the home often labelled as fuel poverty. A 2007 policy paper from the Institute for Public Health (IPH) entitled "*Fuel Poverty and Health*" highlighted the sizeable direct and indirect effects on health of fuel poverty. Overall the IPH found that the levels of fuel poverty on the island of Ireland remain "unacceptably high" and that they are responsible for "among the highest levels of excess winter mortality in Europe, with an estimated 2,800 excess deaths on the island over the winter months" (2007:7). They also highlighted the strong links between low income, unemployment and fuel poverty with single person households and households headed by lone parents and pensioners found to be at highest risk. Similarly, the policy paper shows that older people are more likely to experience fuel poverty due to lower standards of housing coupled with lower incomes. More recently, The Society of St Vincent de Paul's (SVP) work on this area has defined energy poverty as the inability to attain an acceptable level of heating and other energy services in the home due to a combination of three factors: income; energy price and energy efficiency of the dwelling. The EU SILC study 2009 identifies 7.3% of households in the country are without heating at some stage of the year. The SVP points out that households in receipt of energy-related welfare supports account for less than half of the estimated energy poor households. Clearly, welfare payments need to address energy poverty. Other proposals made by the SVP include detailed initiatives on issues such as: the prevention of disconnections; investing in efficiency measures in housing; education and public awareness to promote energy saving; and the compensation of Ireland's poorest households for the existing carbon tax. *Social Justice Ireland* supports the IPH's call for the creation of a national fuel poverty strategy similar to the model currently in place in Northern Ireland. Addressing this issue, like all issues associated with poverty and deprivation, requires a multi-faceted approach. The proposals presented by the SVP should form the core of such a fuel poverty strategy.

The experience of poverty

For some years there existed a lack of information on the life experiences of those families living on a low income. Fortunately a number of recent publications have addressed this void and provided an insight that further underscores the extent and implications of poverty.

Two research reports from the Vincentian Partnership for Social Justice (VPSJ, 2006, 2010) cast new light on the challenges faced by people living on low incomes in urban and rural Ireland. Current debates about the extent of poverty and whether or not it can be reduced or eliminated suffer from the absence of agreed empirically based income standards. What is the minimum essential amount of money a person or household needs to enable them to have an acceptable standard of living? The VPSJ reports addressed this question. The results of this research show for the first time the income needed for a household to have a minimum essential lifestyle in modern Ireland. The households studied included: 2 parents and 2 children (aged 3 & 10); 2 parents and 2 children (aged 10 & 15); a lone parent and 2 children (aged 3 & 10); a pensioner couple, a single female pensioner and a single adult male. They find that most households on social welfare or the minimum wage do not have enough income to sustain a basic standard of living. The gap between the basic standard of living and the actual incomes of these households varied by between €10 and €150 a week. The only group judged to meet a basic standard of living were pensioner couples on a contributory pension but without the cost of running a car.

The studies also found and quantified the additional costs associated with meeting a minimum essential standard of living in rural Ireland. When compared to similar households in urban areas, the VPSJ report found that it cost between €69 and €108 extra per week to live in rural areas. This finding derives from higher food costs associated with more limited availability of supermarkets, higher transport costs and, in particular for working families and those with children, the additional costs associated with a need for at least one, if not two, cars (2010:33). Overall these studies carry major implications for government policy if poverty is to be eliminated. These include the need to address child poverty, the income levels of adults on social welfare, the 'working poor' issue and access to services ranging from social housing to fuel for older people and the distribution of resources between urban and rural Ireland.[31]

---

[31] Data from this study is available at www.budgeting.ie

Poverty: a European perspective

A European perspective on poverty is of interest and to facilitate this Eurostat, the European Statistics Agency, produce comparable 'at risk of poverty' figures (proportions of the population living below the poverty line) for each EU member state. The data is calculated using the 60 per cent of median income poverty line in each country and use comparable EU wide definitions of income and equivalence scales.[32] The latest data available is for the year 2008 and offer a useful point in time comparison of the relative performance of Ireland vis-à-vis other EU states.

As table 3.1.18 shows, in 2008 Irish people experienced a below average risk of poverty when compared to all other EU member states. The 2008 figures mark the first time Ireland's poverty levels have fallen below average EU levels; a phenomenon driven, as we outlined earlier, by sustained increases in welfare payments in the years prior to 2008. Across the EU the highest poverty levels are in the recent accession countries of Latvia, Romania and Bulgaria while the lowest levels are in countries such as Austria, Slovakia, Denmark and the Netherlands.

Table 3.1.18: The risk of poverty in the European Union in 2008

Country	Poverty Risk	Country	Poverty Risk
Latvia	25.6	Belgium	14.7
Romania	23.4	Malta	14.6
Bulgaria	21.4	Finland	13.6
Greece	20.1	Luxembourg	13.4
Lithuania	20.0	France	13.3
Spain	19.6	Hungary	12.4
Estonia	19.5	Austria	12.4
United Kingdom	18.8	Slovenia	12.3
Italy	18.7	Sweden	12.2
Portugal	18.5	Denmark	11.8
Poland	16.9	Slovakia	10.9
Cyprus	16.2	Netherlands	10.5
Ireland	**15.5**	Czech Rep	9.0
Germany	15.2	**EU-27 average**	**16.5**

Source: CSO, 2010:97
Notes: Table uses the most up-to-date comparable data available for countries and corresponds to the year 2008.

---

[32] Differences in definitions of income and equivalence scales result in slight differences in the poverty rates reported for Ireland when compared to those reported earlier which have been calculated by the CSO using national definitions of income and the Irish equivalence scale.

A New and Fairer Ireland

The average risk of poverty in the EU-27 for 2008 was 16.5 per cent. Chart 3.1.1 develops the findings in table 3.1.18 further and calculates the difference between national poverty risk levels and the EU-25 average.

Chart 3.1.1: Percentage difference in National Poverty risk from EU-25 average

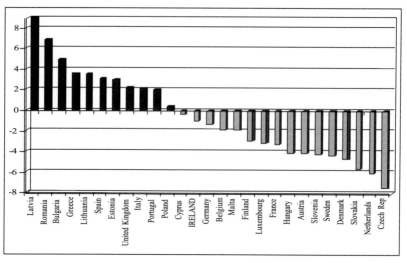

Source: CSO, 2010:97
Notes: Chart uses the most up-to-date comparable data available for countries and corresponds to the year 2008.

While there have been some reductions in poverty in recent years across the EU, though few as sizeable as the reductions achieved in Ireland, the above data does suggest that poverty remains a large and ongoing EU wide problem. *Social Justice Ireland* welcomed the EU decision to focus on poverty and exclusion issues during 2010, the *Year Against Poverty and Social Exclusion*, and we have strongly supported the EU-wide 'zero-poverty' campaign. However, despite this progress the EU needs to face up to the fact that more than half a century after the EU was established it has never come remotely close to full employment or eliminating poverty. If they are to do more than make statements on these issues, the EU (and all its member countries) needs to adopt a credible poverty reduction target to be achieved by 2020. This would show that they are serious about building a different world in the 21st century – one characterised by all people having the resources to live with dignity.

NAP*inclusion* (2007-2016)
A *National Action Plan for Social Inclusion 2007-2016* (*NAPinclusion*) was published in February 2007. It set out Government proposals to address social exclusion over the following decade.

Social Justice Ireland considers that the *NAPinclusion* contained a number of positive initiatives that are welcome such as the benchmarking of the lowest social welfare rates, the tackling of social housing problems and the provision of 500 primary care teams. However, we believe that the Plan completely failed to address the 'working poor' issue which is one of the major challenges facing Ireland if social exclusion is to be addressed effectively. To date, progress has been limited.

Following the agreement at EU level on the new *Europe 2020* strategy, the Irish Government is due to produce a *National Reform Programme* with new targets on poverty, education, environment and employment. As we go to print this programme has yet to be published. Once it has been, our response to this plan will be available on our website (www.socialjustice.ie).

(b) Income Distribution
As we have already outlined, despite some improvements, poverty remains a significant problem. The purpose of economic development should be to improve the living standards of all of the population. A further loss of social cohesion will ensure that large numbers of people continue to experience deprivation, and the gap between them and the better off will widen. This has implications for all of society and not just for those who are poor.

Analysing the annual accounts of income and expenditure provides us with some information on trends in the distribution of national income. However, the limitations of this accounting system need to be acknowledged. Measures of income are far from perfect gauges of a society. They ignore many relevant non-market features such as volunteerism, caring and environmental protection to name but a few. Many environmental factors, such as the depletion of natural resources, are registered as income but not seen as a cost. Pollution is not registered as a cost but cleaning up after pollution is seen as income. Increased spending on prisons and security, which are a response to crime, are seen as increasing national income but not registered as reducing human well-being.

The point is, of course, that national accounts do not include items that cannot easily be assigned a monetary value. Progress cannot be measured by economic growth alone. Many other factors are required as we highlight elsewhere in this review.[33] However, when judging economic performance and making judgements about how well Ireland is really doing, it is important to look at the distribution of national income as well as its absolute amount.[34]

Ireland's income distribution: current situation

The most recent data on income distribution, from the 2009 SILC survey, is summarised in chart 3.1.2. It examines the income distribution by household deciles starting with the 10 per cent of households with the lowest income (the bottom decile) up to the 10 per cent of households with the highest income (the top decile). The data presented is for disposable income which captures the amount of money households have in their pocket to spend after they have received any employment/pension income, paid all their income taxes and received any welfare entitlements.

Chart 3.1.2: Ireland's Income Distribution by 10% (decile) group, 2009

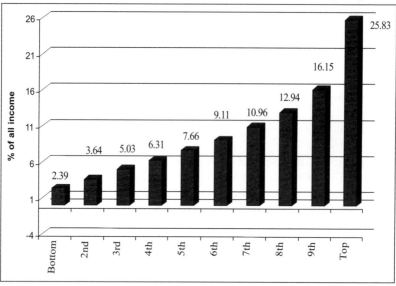

Source: Calculated from CSO, 2010:24-25

---

[33] We return to critique National Income statistics in section 3.10. There, we also propose some alternatives.
[34] We examine the issue of the world's income and wealth distribution in Section 3.12.

In 2009, the top 10 per cent of Irish households received 25.83 per cent of the total disposable income while the bottom decile received 2.39 per cent. Collectively, the poorest 50 per cent of households received a very similar share (25.02 per cent) to the top 10 per cent. Overall the share of the top 10 per cent is nearly 11 times the share of the bottom 10 per cent. Table 3.1.19 outlines the cash values of these income shares in 2009. It shows that the top 10 per cent of households receive an average weekly disposable income (after all taxes and having received all benefits) of €2,276 while the bottom decile receives €210 per week. In 2010 the average household disposable income was €880 a week / €45,926 per annum (CSO, 2010: 24-25).

Table 3.1.19: Amounts of disposable income, by decile in 2009.

	Decile Weekly disposable income	Annual disposable income
Bottom	€210.45	€10,973
2nd	€320.37	€16,705
3rd	€443.07	€23,103
4th	€555.88	€28,985
5th	€675.19	€35,206
6th	€802.53	€41,846
7th	€965.83	€50,361
8th	€1,140.49	€59,468
9th	€1,422.84	€74,191
Top	€2,276.00	€118,677

Source: Calculated from CSO (2010:24-25)
Note: Annual figures are rounded to the nearest Euro to ease interpretation.

Ireland's income distribution: trends from 1987-2009

The results of studies by Collins and Kavanagh (1998, 2006) combined with the recent CSO income figures provide a useful insight into the pattern of Ireland's income distribution over 22 years. Table 3.1.20 combines the results from these studies and reflects the distribution of income in Ireland as tracked by five surveys. Across the entire period the income distribution is very static. However, within the period there are notable changes with shifts in the distribution towards higher deciles during the decade from 1995 onwards.

Table 3.1.20: The distribution of household disposable income, 1987-2009 (%)

Decile	1987	1994/95	1999/00	2004	2009
Bottom	2.28	2.23	1.93	2.10	2.39
2nd	3.74	3.49	3.16	3.04	3.64
3rd	5.11	4.75	4.52	4.27	5.03
4th	6.41	6.16	6.02	5.69	6.31
5th	7.71	7.63	7.67	7.43	7.66
6th	9.24	9.37	9.35	9.18	9.11
7th	11.16	11.41	11.20	11.11	10.96
8th	13.39	13.64	13.48	13.56	12.94
9th	16.48	16.67	16.78	16.47	16.15
Top	24.48	24.67	25.90	27.15	25.83
Total	100.00	100.00	100.00	100.00	100.00

Source: Collins and Kavanagh (2006:156) and CSO (2006:18-19, 2010: 24-58).
Note: Data for 1987, 1994/95 and 1999/00 are from various Household Budget Surveys. 2004 and 2009 data from SILC.

Using data from the two ends of this period, 1987 and 2009, chart 3.1.3 examines the change in the income distribution over the intervening 22 years. Over that time a lot changed in Ireland; however, the income distribution did not change substantially. Compared with 1987, only two deciles saw their share of the total income distribution increase - the bottom decile and the top decile. However, the change for the former is small (+0.11 per cent) while the change for the latter is more notable (+1.34 per cent). All other deciles witnessed a decrease in their share of the national income distribution.

Looking at just the last six SILC surveys (2004-2009) the CSO found that the bottom two deciles saw their share of income increase. Similar to the earlier changes in the poverty figures, it is likely that these improvements are related to the budgetary policy over that period which increased social welfare payments. The CSO data show that households in these deciles receive a large proportion of their income from social welfare payments (CSO, 2010: 24-25). As we have shown earlier, during this period they experienced increases in welfare payments representing a partial catch-up in their relative income position given the declines experienced in the late 1990s.

Chart 3.1.3: Change in Ireland's Income Distribution, 1987-2009

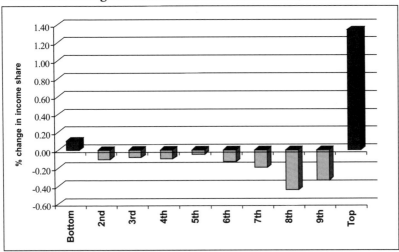

Source: Calculated from CSO, 2010:24-25

Income distribution: a European perspective

Another of the eighteen indicators adopted by the EU at Laeken assesses the income distribution of member states by comparing the ratio of equivalised disposable income received by the bottom quintile (20 per cent) to that of the top quintile. As such, this indicator reports how far away from each other the shares of these two groups are – the higher the ratio the greater the income difference. Table 3.1.21 presents the most up-to-date results of this indicator for the 27 states that were members of the EU in 2008. The 2008 data indicate that the Irish figure has fallen below the EU average for the first time; a factor driven by the aforementioned rise in the share of the bottom deciles following budgetary policy in recent years and the impact of the recession on the incomes of the most prosperous Irish households. Overall, the greatest differences in the shares of those at the top and bottom of the income distribution are found in many of the new and poorer member states. However, some EU-15 members including the UK, Italy, Spain, Greece and Portugal also record large differences.

Table 3.1.21: Ratio of Disposable Income received by bottom quintile to that of the top quintile in the EU-25.

Country	Ratio	Country	Ratio
Latvia	7.3	Belgium	4.1
Romania	7.0	Cyprus	4.1
Bulgaria	6.5	Luxembourg	4.1
Portugal	6.1	Malta	4.0
Greece	5.9	Netherlands	4.0
Lithuania	5.9	Finland	3.8
United Kingdom	5.6	Austria	3.7
Spain	5.4	Denmark	3.6
Italy	5.1	Hungary	3.6
Poland	5.1	Sweden	3.5
Estonia	5.0	Czech Republic	3.4
Germany	4.8	Slovenia	3.4
IRELAND	**4.4**	Slovakia	3.4
France	4.2	**EU-27 average**	**5.0**

Source: CSO (2010:97)

Note: Data is the most up-to-date available for all EU countries and corresponds to the year 2008.

Income Distribution and Budget 2011

Budget 2011 was one of the unfairest Budgets in the history of the Irish State; it followed an equally unfair and unjust Budget in 2010. As our *Analysis and Critique of Budget 2011* (available from our website) pointed out the Budget targeted Ireland's poorest through welfare cuts while protecting bondholders and financial market gamblers. The scale of the Budget's adjustments also raised serious questions for the stability of the economy and its ability to absorb and recover from the Budget's impacts.

Income tax and Social Welfare changes

When assessing the change in people's incomes following any Budget, it is important that wage and tax changes be included as well as changes to basic social welfare payments. Unemployed people, for example, do not experience any wage or income taxation changes while those with jobs may experience both. In assessing Budget 2011 our calculations have not included any income changes beyond those signalled in the Budget; therefore possible alterations to private sector pay levels during 2011 are not included. Chart 3.1.4[35] reports the findings of our analysis and

---

[35] This analysis was first published in our analysis and critique of the Budget, issued the day after the Budget 2011 was presented by the Minister for Finance.

Income

quantifies the implications of the Budget announcements on various household groupings in 2011. The additional impact of changes to child benefit are explored in more detail below.

Following Budget 2011, single people who are long-term unemployed will be €8 per week (€417 per year) worse off while couples who are long term unemployed will be €13.30 per week (€691 per year) worse off. Those on €25,000 a year will see a reduction of €17.80 a week (€929 a year) in their take home pay while those on €75,000 a year will be €22.71 a week (€1,185 a year) worse off. Couples with one income on €25,000 a year will be €11.86 a week (€619 a year) worse off while those on €50,000 will be €21.36 a week (€1,115 a year) worse off. Couples with two incomes on €25,000 a year will be €10.90 a week (€569 a year) worse off while those on €50,000 will be € 10.33 a week (€539 a year) worse off in 2011. Overall, the impact of Budget 2011 on the distribution of income in Ireland can be further assessed by examining the rich-poor gap. This measures the gap between the disposable income of a single person on long-term unemployment and a single person on €50,000 per annum. Budget 2011 reduced the rich-poor gap by €9.91 to €485.31 per week.

Chart 3.1.4: Income Distribution and Budget 2011

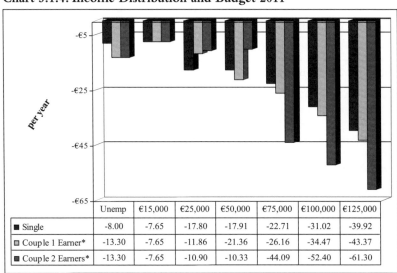

	Unemp	€15,000	€25,000	€50,000	€75,000	€100,000	€125,000
■ Single	-8.00	-7.65	-17.80	-17.91	-22.71	-31.02	-39.92
▫ Couple 1 Earner*	-13.30	-7.65	-11.86	-21.36	-26.16	-34.47	-43.37
■ Couple 2 Earners*	-13.30	-7.65	-10.90	-10.33	-44.09	-52.40	-61.30

Notes: * Except in the case of the unemployed where there is no earner.
Unemp = Unemployed
Couples with 2 earners are assumed to have equal shares of income

A New and Fairer Ireland

To extend this income distribution analysis, two further perspectives are worth exploring:

Child Benefit and Budget 2011
The changes to child benefit announced in Budget 2011 carry further income distribution implications, over and above those outlined above, for families with children. The Budget cut €10 from the payment for the first and second child, €20 from the payment for a third child and €10 from the payment for the fourth and subsequent child. These changes add to a series of reductions to child benefit introduced over the last five budgets (from 2008 onwards including the 2009 supplemental budget). Table 3.1.22 summarises these changes and shows how child benefit payments have been reduced over that period. For a family with one child, income support via child benefit has fallen by €26 per month (€312 per annum). The table does not take account of the additional reduction in income associated with the removal of the early childhood supplement payment which in 2008 was worth in excess of €1,000 per annum for families with young children. Taken together, these reductions have had a serious impact on the living standards of low income families and further exacerbate the child poverty problem outlined earlier in this chapter. For such families, child benefit acts as an essential income support payment and its decrease will continue to drive up the child poverty figures which are already worryingly high.

Table 3.1.22: Monthly Child Benefit Rates and Overall Change, 2008-2011

	2008	2009	2010	2011	2008-11
1 child	€166	€166	€150	€140	- €26
2 children	€332	€332	€300	€280	- €52
3 children	€535	€535	€487	€447	- €88
4 children	€738	€738	€674	€624	- €114

Low income families and Budget 2011
Among those who will feel the impact of Budget 2011 most will be low income families. Families, who are ending up paying a large price for the banking and fiscal misadventures of recent years – something for which they had no responsibility. The combined effect of a reduction in the minimum wage (by €1 per hour), a reduction in tax credits (of 10 per cent), the new universal social charge (USC) and a cut to child benefit payments means that these families experience large reductions in

their disposable income. Table 3.1.23 illustrates this effect through an examination of the pre and post Budget situation of a low income family on an income of €30,000 per annum in 2010. The analysis distinguishes between a couple with 1 earner and a couple with 2 earners. In both cases, we consider the situation of a family with three children and we assume that their wages are linked to the minimum wage (i.e. as it reduces their pay rates will also reduce by the same amount - €1 per hour).[36] The collective impact of the Budget 2011 changes sees these households experience significant reductions in income. (Not included in these calculations are the Budget's decision to increase charges paid for some services and to introduce charges where they had not previously been imposed.)

A reversal of the minimum wage reduction, something promised by the new government but now postponed, may reduce the scale of this impact for low income families. However, the table's calculations exclude the impact of new charges (e.g. primary school buses) and increases charges (e.g. prescription charges) in the Budget.

Table 3.1.23: Impact on Low Income Family with €30,000 per annum, 2 Adults and 3 Children

	Couple 1 Earner		Couple 2 Earners	
	2010	2011	2010	2011
Employment Income	€30,000	€27,920	€30,000	€26,880
- Tax, PRSI & USC	€2,730	€2,126	€900	€806
TAKE HOME PAY	€27,270	€25,794	€29,100	€26,074
+ Child Benefit	€5,844	€5,304	€5,844	€5,364
DISPOSABLE INCOME	€33,114	€31,158	€34,944	€31,438
Change 2010-2011	-	- €1,956	-	-€3,506
Change per week	-	- €37.51	-	- €67.24

Note: Wages linked to National Minimum Wage; Couple 2 earners with 65%/35% income division and 60 hours work per week.

---

[36] While the minimum wage reduction was not immediate or applied across all employees linked to that wage rate, anecdotal evidence suggests that these reductions have occurred.

(c) Maintaining an Adequate Level of Social Welfare

Over the latter half of the last decade there was major progress on benchmarking social welfare payments. As we detail below, Budget 2007 benchmarked the minimum social welfare rate at 30 per cent of Gross Average Industrial Earnings (GAIE). This was a key achievement and one that we predicted would lead to further reductions in poverty rates, complementing those already achieved and detailed earlier. We also note the comments of the Minister for Finance Brian Cowen T.D. who stated the morning after Budget 2007 that:

> We've hit a landmark-type point in relation to social welfare in this respect, that we have in the last three budgets had unprecedented increases, particularly on the lowest rate, in order to get it to the point where the social partnership commitment required us to do, something around 30 per cent of the gross average industrial earnings
>
> (Minister for Finance Brian Cowen T.D. on Today with Pat Kenny RTE Radio 1, 7th December 2006)

The process of benchmarking social welfare payments has centred on three elements: the 2001 *Social Welfare Benchmarking and Indexation Working Group* (SWBIG), the 2002 *National Anti-Poverty Strategy (NAPS) Review* and the *Budgets 2005-2007*.

Social welfare benchmarking and indexation working group

In its final report the SWBIG agreed that the lowest social welfare rates should be benchmarked. A majority of the working group, which included a director of *Social Justice Ireland*, also agreed that this benchmark should be index-linked to society's standard of living as it grows, and that the benchmark should be reached by a definite date. The working group chose Gross Average Industrial Earnings (GAIE) to be the index to which payments should be fixed.[37] The group further urged that regular and formal review and monitoring of the range of issues covered in its report should be provided for. The group expressed the opinion that this could best be accommodated within the structures in place under the NAPS and the *National Action Plan for Social Inclusion* (now combined as *NAPinclusion*). The SWBIG report envisaged that such a mechanism could involve

- the review of any benchmarks/targets and indexation methodologies adopted by government to ensure that the underlying objectives remain valid and are being met

---

[37] The group recommended a benchmark of 27 per cent although we argued for 30 per cent.

- the assessment of such benchmarks/targets and indexation methodologies against the various criteria set out in the group's terms of reference to ensure their continued relevance
- the assessment of emerging trends in the key areas of concern - e.g. poverty levels, labour market performance, demographic changes, economic performance, competitiveness, etc.
- identification of gaps in the area of research and assessment of any additional research undertaken in the interim.

National Anti-Poverty Strategy (NAPS) review 2002
In 2002, the NAPS review set the following as key targets:

> *To achieve a rate of €150 per week in 2002 terms for the lowest rates of social welfare to be met by 2007 and the appropriate equivalence level of basic child income support (i.e. Child Benefit and Child Dependent Allowances combined) to be set at 33 per cent - 35 per cent of the minimum adult social welfare payment rate.*

We, among others, welcomed this target. It was a major breakthrough in social, economic and philosophical terms. We also welcomed the reaffirmation of this target in *Towards 2016*. That agreement contained a commitment to "achieving the NAPS target of €150 per week in 2002 terms for lowest social welfare rates by 2007" (2006:52). The target of €150 a week was equivalent to 30 per cent of Gross Average Industrial Earnings (GAIE) in 2002.[38]

In response to this commitment we calculated the projected growth in €150 between 2002 and 2007 when it is indexed to the estimated growth in GAIE. Table 3.1.24 outlines these expected growth rates and calculates that the lowest social welfare rates for single people should have reached €185.80 by 2007.

---

[38] GAIE is calculated by the CSO on the earnings of all individuals (male and female) working in all industries. The GAIE figure in 2002 was €501.51 and 30 per cent of this figure equals €150.45 (CSO, 2006: 2).

A New and Fairer Ireland

Table 3.1.24: Estimating growth in €150 a week (30% GAIE) for 2002-2007

	2002	2003	2004	2005	2006	2007
% Growth of GAIE	-	+6.00	+3.00	+4.50	+3.60	+4.80
30% GAIE	150	159.00	163.77	171.14	177.30	185.80

Source: GAIE growth rates from CSO Industrial Earnings and Hours Worked (September 2004:2) and ESRI Medium Term Review (Bergin et al, 2003:49).

Budgets 2005-2007

The NAPS commitment was very welcome and was one of the few areas of the anti-poverty strategy that was adequate to tackle the scale of the poverty, inequality and social exclusion being experienced by so many people in Ireland today.

In 2002, we set out a pathway to reaching this target by calculating the projected growth of €150 between 2002 and 2007 when it is indexed to the estimated growth in GAIE. Progress towards achieving this target had been slow up until Budget 2005. At its first opportunity to live up to the NAPS commitment the government granted a mere €6 a week increase in social welfare rates in Budget 2003. This increase was below that which we proposed and also below that recommended by the government's own tax strategy group. In Budget 2004 the increase in the minimum social welfare payment was €10. This increase was again below the €12 a week we sought and at this point we set out a three-year pathway (see table 3.1.25).

Table 3.1.25: Proposed approach to addressing the gap, 2005-2007

	2005	2006	2007
Min. SW. payment in €'s	148.80	165.80	185.80
€ amount increase each year	14.00	17.00	20.00
Delivered	✓	✓	✓

Following Budget 2004 we argued for an increase of €14 in Budget 2005. The Government's decision to deliver an increase equal to that amount in that Budget marked a significant step towards honouring this commitment which we warmly welcomed. Budget 2006 followed suit, delivering an increase of €17 per week to those in receipt of the minimum social welfare rate. Finally, Budget 2007's decision to deliver an increase of €20 per week to the minimum social welfare rates brought the minimum social welfare payment up to the 30 per cent of the GAIE benchmark.

Social Justice Ireland believes that these increases, and the achievement of the benchmark in Budget 2007, marked a fundamental turning point in Irish public policy. Budget 2007 was the third budget in a row where the government delivered on its NAPS commitment. In doing so the government moved to meet the target such that in 2007 the minimum social welfare rate increased to €185.80 per week; a figure equivalent to the 30 per cent of GAIE.

We warmly welcomed its achievement. It marked major progress and underscored the delivery of a long overdue commitment to sharing the fruits of this country's economic growth since the mid 1990s. An important element of the NAPS commitment to increasing social welfare rates is the acknowledgement that the years from 2002-2007 marked a period of 'catch-up' for those in receipt of welfare payments. Now that this income gap has been bridged, the increases necessary to keep social welfare payments at a level equivalent to 30 per cent of GAIE become much smaller. In that context we welcomed the commitment by Government in *NAPinclusion* to "maintain the relative value of the lowest social welfare rate at least at €185.80, in 2007 terms, over the course of this Plan (2007-2016), subject to available resources" (2007:42). Whether or not 30 per cent of GAIE is adequate to eliminate the risk of poverty is an issue to be monitored through the SILC studies and in particular to be addressed when data on persistent poverty emerges.

Setting a Benchmark: 2011 onwards

In late 2007 the CSO discontinued their *Industrial Earnings and Hours Worked* dataset and replaced it with a more comprehensive set of income statistics for a broader set of Irish employment sectors. The end of that dataset also saw the demise of the GAIE figure from Irish official statistics; it has been replaced with a series of measures including a new indicator measuring average earnings across all the employment sectors now being measured. While the improvement to data sources is welcome, the end of the GAIE figure poses problems for continuing to calculate the social welfare benchmark. To this end, *Social Justice Ireland* commissioned a report in late 2010 to establish an appropriate way of continuing to calculate this benchmark.

A report entitled *'Establishing a Benchmark for Ireland's Social Welfare Payments'* was completed by economist Dr Micheál Collins of Trinity College Dublin in February

2011 and we have made this report available on our website. It established that 30 per cent of GAIE is equivalent to 27.5 per cent of the new average earnings data being collected by the CSO. A figure of 27.5 per cent of average earnings is therefore the appropriate benchmark for minimum social welfare payments and reflects a continuation of the previous benchmark using the new CSO earnings dataset.

Table 3.1.26 applies this benchmark using CSO data for quarter 2 2010 (published December 2010). The data is updated to 2011 and 2012 using ESRI projections for wage growth in 2011 (-1 per cent) and 2012 (0 per cent). In 2011 and 2012, 27.5 per cent of average weekly earnings equal €188.80; marginally more than the current minimum social welfare rate (€180). As a consequence of this benchmark, *Social Justice Ireland* believes that the appropriate Budgetary policy in 2012 is to leave minimum social welfare rates static at €188 per week. While such a figure is challenging for individuals to survive on, it would be completely unacceptable to reduce this payment below its current level. In that regard we welcome the commitment from the new Government not to reduce these rates further.

Table 3.1.26: Benchmarking Social Welfare Payments for 2011 and 2012 (€)

Year	Average Weekly Earnings	27.5% of Average Weekly Earnings
2010	693.58	190.73
2011	686.64	188.83
2012	686.64	188.83

Notes: 2010 data from Quarter 2 2010 (CSO, December 2010).
Earnings Growth rates for 2011 and 2012 from ESRI QEC Winter 2010.

Individualising social welfare payments

The issue of individualising payments so that all recipients receive their own social welfare payments has been on the policy agenda in Ireland and across the EU for several years. We welcomed the report of the Working Group, *Examining the Treatment of Married, Cohabiting and One-Parent Families under the Tax and Social Welfare Codes*, which addressed some of the individualisation issues. Recent Budgets have also made welcome progress on the individualisation of contributory State Pension payments.

At present the welfare system provides a basic payment for a claimant whether a pension, a disability payment or a job-seeker's payment etc. It then adds an additional payment of about two-thirds of the basic payment for the second person. For example, following Budget 2011 a couple on the lowest social welfare rate will receive a payment of €312.80 per week. This amount is approximately 1.66 times the payment for a single person (€188). Were these two people living separately they would receive €188 each; giving a total of €376. Thus by living as a household unit such a couple lose out and receive a lower income.

Social Justice Ireland believes that this system is unfair and inequitable. We also believe that the system as currently structured is not compatible with the Equal Status Acts (2000-2004); a point we strongly made in a submission to the *Department of Social and Family Affairs Review of the Social Welfare Code* with regard to its compatibility with the Equal Status Acts. People, often women, are disadvantaged, through the receipt of a lower income, for living as a household unit. We believe that where a couple are in receipt of welfare payments, the payment for the second person should be increased to equal that for the first person. Such a change would remove this disadvantage and bring the current social welfare system in line with the terms of the Equal Status Acts (2000-2004). We urge progress on this issue in the coming years and believe such a policy development would go some way towards delivering the equality that should be the hallmark of all systems.

(d) Basic Income

Over the past number of years major advances have been achieved in the case for introducing a basic income in Ireland. These include the publication of a *Green Paper on Basic Income* by the government in September 2002 and the publication of a book by Clark entitled *The Basic Income Guarantee* (2002). A major international conference on Basic income was also held in Dublin during Summer 2008; more than 70 papers from 30 countries were presented at that conference. These are available on our website.

The case for a basic income

Social Justice Ireland has argued for a long time that the present tax and social welfare systems should be integrated and reformed to make them more appropriate to the changing world of the twenty-first century. To this end we have argued for the introduction of a basic income system. This proposal is especially relevant at the present moment of economic upheaval.

A basic income is an income that is unconditionally granted to every person on an individual basis, without any means test or work requirement. In a basic-income system every person receives a weekly tax-free payment from the Exchequer, and all other personal income is taxed, usually at a single rate. For a person who is unemployed, the basic-income payment would replace income from social welfare. For a person who is employed the basic-income payment would replace tax credits in the income-tax system.

Basic income is a form of minimum income guarantee that avoids many of the negative side effects inherent in social welfare payments. A basic income differs from other forms of income support in that

- it is paid to individuals rather than households
- it is paid irrespective of any income from other sources
- it is paid without conditions. It does not require the performance of any work or the willingness to accept a job if offered one
- it is always tax free.

There is real danger that the plight of large numbers of people excluded from the benefits of the modern economy will be ignored. Images of rising tides lifting all boats are often offered as government's policy makers and commentators assure society that prosperity for all is just around the corner. Likewise, the claim is often made that a job is the best poverty fighter and consequently all priority must be given to getting everyone a paid job. These images and claims are no substitute for concrete policies to ensure that all are included. Twenty-first-century society needs a radical approach to ensure the inclusion of all people in the benefits of present economic growth and development. Basic income is such an approach.

As we have designed it, a basic income system would replace social welfare and income tax credits. It would guarantee an income above the poverty line for everyone. It would not be means tested. There would be no "signing on" and no restrictions or conditions. In practice a basic income recognises the right of every person to a share of the resources of society.

The Basic Income system ensures that looking for a paid job and earning an income, or increasing one's income while in employment, is always worth pursuing, because for every euro earned the person will retain a large part. It thus removes the poverty traps and unemployment traps in the present system. Furthermore, women and men get equal payments in a basic income system. Consequently the basic income system promotes gender equality because it treats every person equally.

It is a system that is altogether more guaranteed, rewarding, simple and transparent than the present tax and welfare systems. It is far more employment friendly than the present system. It also respects other forms of work besides paid employment. This is crucial in a world where other forms of work need to be recognised and respected. It is also very important in a world where paid employment cannot be permanently guaranteed for everyone seeking it. There is growing pressure and need in Irish society to ensure recognition and monetary reward for such work. Basic income is a transparent, efficient and affordable mechanism for ensuring such recognition and reward.

Basic income also lifts people out of poverty and the dreadful dependency mode of survival. In doing this it also restores their self-esteem and broadens their horizons. Poor people however are not the only ones who should welcome a basic income system. Employers for example should welcome it because its introduction would mean they would not be in competition with the social welfare system. Since employees would not lose their basic income when taking a job, there would always be an incentive to take up employment.

A basic income system would create a platform for meaningful work. It would benefit paid employment as well as other forms of work. It would also have a substantial impact on reducing income poverty. The present tax and welfare systems were designed for a different era. They have done well in addressing major problems of the second half of the twentieth century. The world however is changing radically. A new system is required for the twenty-first century. Basic income is such a system.

Ten reasons to introduce basic income

i   It is work and employment friendly.
ii   It eliminates poverty traps and unemployment traps.
iii   It promotes equity and ensures that everyone receives at least the poverty level of income.
iv   It spreads the burden of taxation more equitably.
v   It treats men and women equally.
vi   It is simple and transparent.
vii   It is efficient in labour-market terms.
viii   It rewards types of work in the social economy that the market economy often ignores, e.g. home duties, caring, etc.
ix   It facilitates further education and training in the labour force.
x   It faces up to the changes in the global economy.

Key Priorities on Income

- If poverty rates are to fall in the years ahead, *Social Justice Ireland* believes that the following are required:
  - benchmarking of social welfare payments,
  - equity of social welfare rates,
  - adequate payments for children,
  - refundable tax credits,
  - a universal state pension and
  - a cost of disability payment.

- *Social Justice Ireland* believes that in the period ahead Government and policy-makers generally should:

- **Acknowledge that Ireland has an ongoing poverty problem.**

- **Assess the impact on society's most vulnerable people of any proposed policy initiatives aimed at achieving the required fiscal adjustments required by the EU/IMF bailout and the Government's 4-year plan.**

- **Change the ratio of expenditure cuts to tax increases in forthcoming budgets. Tax increases should account for two thirds of the required fiscal adjustment.**

- **Examine and support viable, alternative policy options aimed at giving priority to protecting vulnerable sectors of society.**

- **Provide substantial new measures to address long-term unemployment. This should include programmes aimed at re-training and re-skilling those at highest risk.**

- **Recognise the problem of the 'working poor'. Make tax credits refundable so as to address the situation of the 22.8 per cent of all households in poverty which are headed by a person with a job.**

- **Introduce a cost of disability allowance to address poverty and social exclusion of people with a disability.**

- Poverty-proof all public policy initiatives and provision.

- Recognise the new problems of poverty among migrants and adopt policies to assist this group. In addressing this issue also reform and increase the 'direct provision' allowances paid to asylum seekers.

- Accept that persistent poverty should be used as the primary indicator of poverty measurement once this data becomes available.

- Move towards introducing a basic income system. No other approach has the capacity to ensure all members of society have sufficient income to live life with dignity.

3.2 Taxation

> **CORE POLICY OBJECTIVE: TAXATION**
>
> To collect sufficient taxes to ensure full participation in society for all, through a fair tax system in which those who have more, pay more, while those who have less, pay less

It has become increasingly apparent in recent years that the issue of taxation is central to budget deliberations and to policy development at both macro and micro level. It plays a key role in shaping Irish society through: (i) funding public services; (ii) supporting economic activity; and (iii) redistributing resources to enhance the fairness of society. Consequently it is crucial that clarity exist with regard to both the objectives and instruments aimed at achieving these goals. To ensure the creation of a fairer and more equitable tax system, policy development in this area should adhere to our core policy objective outlined above. In that regard, *Social Justice Ireland* is committed to increasing the level of detailed analysis and debate addressing this area.

The need for a wider tax base is a lesson painfully learnt by Ireland during the past three years. A disastrous combination of a naïve housing policy, a failed regulatory system and foolish fiscal policy and economic planning combined to cause a collapse in exchequer revenues. The narrowness of the Irish tax base resulted in almost 25 per cent of expected tax revenues disappearing thereby plunging the exchequer and the country in a series of fiscal policy crises. As we have already shown in section 2.3, tax revenues collapsed from over €47 billion in 2007 to an expected level of €34.9 billion in 2011. It is only through a determined effort to reform Ireland's taxation system that these mistakes can be addressed and avoided in the future. We have earlier identified this issue as one of the reforms needed for Ireland to achieve recovery.

The remainder of this section outlines Ireland's relative taxation position, the anticipated future taxation needs, further approaches to reforming and broadening the tax base and proposals for building a fairer tax system.

Ireland's total tax take up to 2008

The most recent comparative data on the size of the Irish tax burden has been produced by Eurostat (2010) and is detailed alongside that of 26 other EU states in table 3.2.1. The definition of taxation employed by Eurostat incorporates all compulsory payments to central government (direct and indirect) alongside social security contributions (employee and employer) and the tax receipts of local authorities.[39] The tax burden of each country is established by calculating the ratio of total taxation revenue to national income as measured by gross domestic product (GDP). Table 3.2.1 also compares the tax burdens of all EU member states against the average tax burden of 37 per cent.

Of the EU-27 states, the highest tax ratios can be found in Denmark, Sweden, Belgium, Finland and France while the lowest appear in Romania, Latvia, Slovakia, Lithuania, Estonia, Greece and Ireland. Overall, Ireland possesses the fourth lowest tax burden at 29.3 per cent, some 7.7 per cent below the EU average.

Table 3.2.1: Total tax revenue as a % of GDP, for EU-27 Countries in 2008

Country	% of GDP	+/- from average	Country	% of GDP	+/- from average
Denmark	48.2	+11.2	Czech Rep	36.1	-0.9
Sweden	47.1	+10.1	Luxembourg	35.6	-1.4
Belgium	44.3	+7.3	Malta	34.5	-2.5
Finland	43.1	+6.1	Poland	34.3	-2.7
France	42.8	+5.8	**Ireland GNP**	**34.1**	**-2.9**
Italy	42.8	+5.8	Bulgaria	33.3	-3.7
Austria	42.8	+5.8	Spain	33.1	-3.9
Hungary	40.4	+3.4	Greece	32.6	-4.4
Germany	39.3	+2.3	Estonia	32.2	-4.8
Cyprus	39.2	+2.2	Lithuania	30.3	-6.7
Netherlands	39.1	+2.1	**Ireland GDP**	**29.3**	**-7.7**
Slovenia	37.3	+0.3	Slovakia	29.1	-7.9
United Kingdom	37.3	+0.3	Latvia	28.9	-8.1
Portugal	36.7	-0.3	Romania	28.0	-9.0

Source: Eurostat (2010:28) and CSO National Income and Expenditure Accounts (2010:4)
Notes: All data is for 2008. EU average is 37 per cent.

---

[39] See Eurostat (2004:32-34) for a more comprehensive explanation of this classification.

GDP is accepted as the benchmark against which tax levels are measured in international publications. However, in Ireland some suggestions have been made to the effect that gross national product (GNP) should be used. This argument is based on the fact that Ireland's large multinational sector is responsible for significant profit outflows which if counted (as they are in GDP but not in GNP) exaggerate the scale of Irish economic activity.[40] Commenting on this Collins stated that "while it is clear that multinational profit flows create a considerable gap between GNP and GDP, it remains questionable as to why a large chunk of economic activity occurring within the state should be overlooked when assessing its tax burden" and that "as GDP captures all of the economic activity happening domestically, it only seems logical, if not obvious, that a nations' taxation should be based on that activity" (2004:6).[41] He also noted that using GNP will understate the scale of the tax base and overstate the tax rate in Ireland because it excludes the value of multinational activities in the economy but does include the tax contribution of these companies. As such, the size of the tax burden carried by Irish people and firms is exaggerated.

Social Justice Ireland believes that it would be more appropriate to calculate the tax burden by comparing GNP and an adjusted tax-take figure which excludes the tax paid by multi-national companies. As figures for their tax contribution are currently unavailable, we have simply used the unadjusted GNP figures and presented the results in table 3.2.1. In 2008 this stood at 34.1 per cent. This also suggests to international observers and internal policy makers that the Irish economy is not as tax-competitive as it truly is. This issue should be addressed by Government and appropriate adjustments made when calculating Ireland's tax-take as a percentage of GNP.

In the context of these figures, the question needs to be asked: if we expect our economic and social infrastructure to catch up to that in the rest of Europe, how can we do this while simultaneously gathering less taxation income than it takes to run the infrastructure already in place in most of those other European countries? Simply, we will never bridge the social and economic infrastructure gaps unless we gather a larger share of our national income and invest it in building a fairer and more successful Ireland.

---

[40] Collins (2004:6) notes that this is a uniquely Irish debate and not one that features in other OECD states such as New Zealand where noticeable differences between GDP and GNP also occur.

[41] See also Bristow (2004:2) who makes a similar argument.

Social Justice Ireland believes that Ireland should increase its tax take towards that of other European countries. Prior to the recent recession (see below) the Irish tax take had begun to increase. Using the GDP benchmark, it has climbed from 28.5 per cent in 2002 to 30.3 per cent in 2004 and to 30.8 per cent in 2005 (Eurostat, 2010:28). The 2006 figure climbed further to 32.3 per cent of GDP but this increase principally reflected large inflows of transaction taxes from stamp duty, VRT and construction/housing related VAT – the taxes that have since collapsed. However, the fact remains that increases towards the European average are certainly feasible and are unlikely to have any significant negative impact on the economy in the long term. We have proposed that over the next few years Ireland increase its total tax take to 34.9 per cent of GDP - a proposal explored further in the next section of this chapter.

Table 3.2.2: The changing nature of Ireland's current tax revenues

	Estimated Outturn 2007 €m	Estimated Outturn 2008 €m	Estimated Outturn 2009 €m	Estimated Outturn 2010 €m
Customs	285	255	209	230
Excise Duties	5,815	5,581	4,575	4,620
Capital Gains Tax	3,145	1,710	385	400
Capital Acquis. Tax	383	320	260	240
Stamp Duties	3,195	1,780	900	975
Income Tax *	13,605	13,200	11,810	11,125
Corporation Tax	6,349	6,000	3,790	3,775
Value Added Tax	14,545	13,525	10,640	10,165
Other Levies	3	1	1	0
Total Tax Receipts**	47,325	42,372	32,570	31,530

Source: Department of Finance, Budget Documents 2007-2011
Notes: *Including income levy in 2009 and 2010.
**These figures do not incorporate other tax sources including revenues to the social insurance fund, the health levy and local government charges. These are incorporated into the totals reported in table 3.2.4 below.

Ireland's total tax take 2010-14

Despite significant increases in the tax-take from the PAYE sector in the last three Budgets, the scale of collapse in Ireland's tax revenues has been dramatic. National taxes (those announced in the Budget and collected centrally – as detailed in table 3.2.2) have fallen by almost €16b since 2007 with the largest fall in areas such as capital gains taxes, stamp duties, corporation taxes and VAT. Decreases in income taxes have been somewhat offset by increased revenues from the income levy (2009-2010). Overall, total tax receipts have fallen from in excess of €47 billion in 2007 to €31.5 billion in 2010.

As we have shown earlier, the impact of these declines in taxation income, reflecting the scale of the national and international recession and the instability and narrowness of the national tax base, have had dramatic effects on the overall tax burden. Looking to the years immediately ahead, Budget 2011 provided some insight into the expected future shape of Ireland's current taxation revenues and this is reported in table 3.2.3. Over the next four years, assuming the policies announced in the National Recovery Plan and the EU/IMF deal are followed, overall current revenue will climb to €44.4b mainly driven by increases in income, corporation and consumption taxes. A new property tax, a site-value tax, will also yield revenues from 2012 onwards.

Table 3.2.3: Projected current tax revenues, 2010-2014

	2010 €m	2011 €m	2012 €m	2013 €m	2014 €m
Customs	230	235	240	250	260
Excise Duties	4,620	4,675	4,930	5,105	5,280
Capital Gains Tax	400	410	480	510	530
Capital Acquis. Tax	240	250	305	330	345
Stamp Duties	975	955	990	885	755
Income Tax *	11,125	14,125	16,245	18,040	19,930
Corporation Tax	3,775	4,020	4,460	4,665	4,895
Value Added Tax	10,165	10,230	10,485	11,120	11,895
Site Value Tax	0	0	180	355	530
Total Tax Receipts**	**31,530**	**34,900**	**38,315**	**41,260**	**44,420**

Source: Department of Finance, Budget 2011: D18, D24
Notes: *Including income levy in 2010 and USC from 2011 onwards
**These figures do not incorporate other tax sources including revenues to the social insurance fund, the health levy (2010 only) and local government charges. These are incorporated into the totals reported in table 3.2.4 below.

Budget 2011 also set out projections for the overall scale of the national taxation burden (per cent GDP) to 2014. These figures are reproduced in table 3.2.4 and have been used to calculate the cash value of the overall levels of tax revenue expected to be collected. While the table is calculated based on the tax burden figures as published and estimated by the Department of Finance in Budget 2011 – that document provided limited details on the nature and composition of these figures. Estimates for *Social Justice Ireland* suggest that the actual 2009, 2010 and 2011 tax burden figures will be lower than those reported above. Indeed, the OECD Preliminary figure for 2009 is 27.8 per cent of GDP (OECD, 2010:19).

Table 3.2.4: Ireland's projected total tax take, 2009-2014 (% GDP)*

Year	GDP (nominal)	Tax as % GDP	Total Tax Receipts
2009	€159,647m	30.2	€48,213m
2010	€157,300m	30.2	€47,505m
2011	€161,200m	30.5	€49,166m
2012	€168,100m	31.5	€52,952m
2013	€175,400m	32.3	€56,654m
2014	€183,500m	33.0	€60,555m

Source: Department of Finance, Budget 2011: D9, D25; CSO (2010:4)
Notes: * Total tax take = current taxes (see table 3.2.2 and 3.2.3) + Social Insurance Fund income + health levy (2009 and 2010 only) + charges by local government.

While a proportion of the tax decline is related to the recession, a large part is structural and requires attention. As we have detailed in Section 2 of this review, *Social Justice Ireland* believes that over the next few years policy should focus on increasing Ireland's tax take to 34.9 per cent of GDP, a figure defined by Eurostat as 'low-tax' (Eurostat, 2008:5). As a policy objective, Ireland should remain a low-tax economy, but not one incapable of adequately supporting the economic, social and infrastructural requirements necessary to complete our convergence with the rest of Europe.

> The recent bank bailouts and rescues have further added to the debt levels being carried by Ireland. Associated with this debt are large and increasing annual debt servicing costs which may consume between 15-20 per cent of the Department of Finance's annual projected taxation revenues. Later in 2011, once the process of bank bailouts, interest rate adjustments and debt restructuring has completed, *Social Justice Ireland* will revisit our proposed taxation benchmark and test its adequacy. Subsequently, we will publish an analysis and revise the benchmark upwards if appropriate.

A New and Fairer Ireland

Effective tax rates

Central to the ongoing debate on personal/income taxation in Ireland are effective tax rates. These rates are calculated by comparing the total amount of income tax a person pays with their pre-tax income. For example, a person earning €50,000 who pays a total of €10,000 in tax, PRSI and levies will have an effective tax rate of 20 per cent. Calculating the scale of income taxation in this way provides a more accurate reflection of the burden of income taxation faced by earners.

Following Budget 2011 we have calculated effective tax rates for a single person, a single income couple and a couple where both are earners. Table 3.2.5 presents the results of this analysis. For comparative purposes, it also presents the effective tax rates which existed for people with the same income levels in 2000 and 2008.

In 2011, for a single person with an income of €15,000 the effective tax rate will be 2.7 per cent, rising to 14.0 per cent of an income of €25,000 and 42.7 per cent of an income of €120,000. A single income couple will have an effective tax rate of 2.7 per cent at an income of €15,000, rising to 7.2 per cent at an income of €25,000, 26.2 per cent at an income of €60,000 and 39.1 per cent at an income of €120,000. In the case of a couple where both are earning and their combined income is €40,000 their effective tax rate is 9.2 per cent, rising to 33.4 per cent for combined earnings of €120,000.

Table 3.2.5: Effective Tax Rates following Budgets 2000 / 2008 / 2011

Income Levels	Single Person	Couple 1 earner	Couple 2 Earners
€15,000	13.9% / 0.0% / 2.7%	2.5% / 0.0% / 2.7%	0.8% / 0.0% / 2.0%
€20,000	13.9% / 0.0% / 9.8%	8.3% / 2.7% / 6.3%	6.1% / 0.0% / 2.3%
€25,000	24.0% / 8.3% / 14.0%	12.3% / 2.9% / 7.2%	11.0% / 0.0% / 2.5%
€30,000	28.4% / 12.9% / 16.8%	5.0% / 5.1% / 8.6%	14.6% / 1.7% / 4.7%
€40,000	33.3% / 18.6% / 24.2%	20.2% / 9.4% / 14.2%	17.5% / 3.6% / 9.2%
€60,000	37.7% / 27.5% / 33.4%	29.0% / 19.8% / 26.2%	28.0% / 12.2% / 16.8 %
€100,000	41.1% / 33.8% / 40.9%	35.9% / 29.2% / 36.5%	35.9% / 23.8% / 29.7 %
€120,000	41.9% / 35.4% / 42.7%	37.6% / 31.6% / 39.1%	37.7% / 27.2% / 33.4 %

Source: Social Justice Ireland (2010:8).
Notes: Tax = income tax + PRSI + levies
Couples assume 2 children and 65%/35% income division

While these rates have increased since 2008 for almost all earners they are still low compared to the situation which prevailed in 2000. Then, few complained that tax levels were excessive and the recent increases should be seen in this context. Taking a longer view, chart 3.2.1 illustrates the downward trend in effective tax rates for three selected household types since 1997. These are a single earner on €25,000; a couple with 1 earner on €40,000; and a couple with 2 earners on €60,000. Their experiences are similar to those on other income levels and are similar to the effective tax rates of the self-employed over that period (see Budget 2011, annex A).

Chart 3.2.1: Effective tax rates in Ireland, 1997-2011

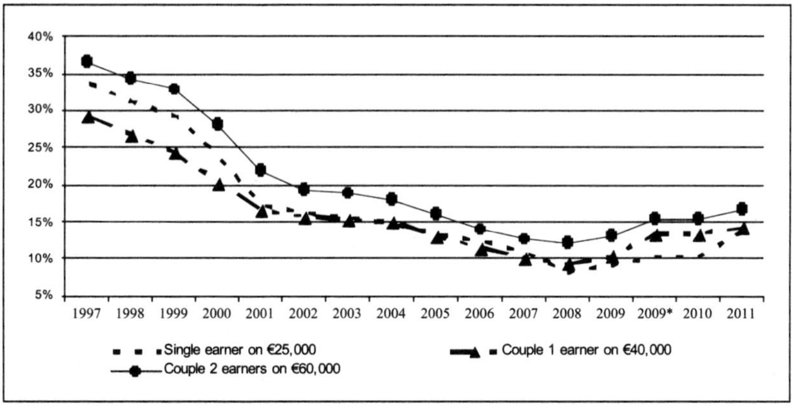

Source: Department of Finance, Budget 2011 (Annex A).
Notes: Tax = income tax + PRSI + levies
Couples assume 2 children and 65%/35% income division
2009★= Supplementary Budget 2009 (April 2009)

The two 2009 Budgets produced notable increases in these effective taxation rates. Both Budgets required government to raise additional revenue and with some urgency - increases in income taxes provided the easiest option. Similarly, the introduction of the Universal Social Charge (USC) in Budget 2011 increased these rates; most notably for lower income earners. However, income taxation is not the only form of taxation and, as the review below will suggest, there are many in Ireland not paying their fair share of tax and there are a number of available ways of substituting tax revenue from income for that raised through other taxation mechanisms.

Future taxation needs

Government decisions to raise or reduce overall taxation revenue needs to be linked to the demands on its resources. These demands depend on what Government is required to address or decides to pursue. The impacts of the current economic crisis, including the way it has been handled by Government, carries significant implications for our future taxation needs. The rapid increase in our national debt, driven by the need to borrow both to replace disappearing taxation revenues and to fund emergency 'investments' in the failing commercial banks, has increased the ongoing annual costs associated with servicing the national debt. The national debt has increased from a level of 25 per cent of GDP in 2007, low by international standards, to at least 100 per cent of GDP in 2011; it is projected to increase towards 115 per cent over the next three years with the final figure dependent on the scale of borrowing required to address the ongoing banking collapse. Data in Budget 2011 suggested that by 2014 approximately 20 per cent of annual taxation revenue will be required to service the national debt. Similarly, the erosion of the National Pension Reserve Fund (NPRF) through its use for funding various bank rescues has transferred the liability for future public sector pensions on to future exchequer expenditure. Again, this will require additional taxation resources.

These new future taxation needs add to those which already exist for funding local government, repairing our water infrastructure, paying for the health and pension needs of an ageing population, paying EU contributions, paying Kyoto protocol fines and purchasing any carbon credits that are required. Collectively, they necessitate that Ireland's overall level of taxation has to rise significantly in the years to come.

Research by Bennett et al (2003) has provided some insight into future exchequer demands associated with healthcare and pensions in Ireland in the years 2025 and 2050. As the population ages these figures will increase substantially, almost doubling between 2002 and 2050 from 8.9 to 16.7 per cent of GDP. Dealing purely with the pension issue, an ESRI study reached similar conclusions and projected that 'social welfare spending that is focused on older people' will rise from 3.1 per cent in 2004 to 5.5 per cent in 2030 and to 9.3 per cent in 2050. The 2008 OECD Economic Survey of Ireland reached similar conclusions suggesting a 2050 peak of 11.1 per cent of GDP (2008:80-84).[42]

---

[42] The 2010 National Pensions Strategy suggested a higher overall cost of pensions in 2050 as equivalent to 15.5% of GDP.

Table 3.2.6: Projected Costs of Healthcare and Pensions in Ireland, as % GDP			
	2002	2025	2050
Healthcare	6.0	6.3	8.8
Pensions	2.9	4.5	7.9
Healthcare + Pensions	**8.9**	**10.9**	**16.7**

Source: Bennett et al (2003)

Is a higher tax-take problematic?
Suggesting that any country's tax take should increase normally produces negative responses. People think first of their incomes and increases in income tax, rather than more broadly of reforms to the tax base. Furthermore, proposals that taxation should increase are often rejected by suggestions that they would undermine economic growth. However, a review of the performance of the British and US economies over recent years is interesting in light of this issue.

In the years prior to the current international economic crisis, Britain achieved low unemployment and higher levels of growth compared to other EU countries (OECD, 2004). These were achieved simultaneously with increases in its tax/GDP ratio. In 1994 this stood at 33.7 per cent and by 2004 it had increased 2.3 percentage points to 36.0 per cent of GDP. Furthermore, in his March 2004 Budget the then British Chancellor Gordon Brown indicated that this ratio would increase again to reach 38.3 per cent of GDP in 2008-09 (2004:262). His announcement of these increases was not met with predictions of economic ruin or doom for Britain and its economic growth remained high compared to other EU countries (IMF, 2004 & 2008).

Taxation and competitiveness
Another argument made against increases in Ireland's overall taxation levels is that it will undermine competitiveness. However, the suggestion that higher levels of taxation would damage our position relative to other countries is not supported by international studies of competitiveness. Annually the World Economic Forum publishes a *Global Competitiveness Report* ranking the most competitive economies across the world.

Table 3.2.7 outlines the top fifteen economies in this index for 2010-11 as well as the ranking for Ireland (which comes 29th). It also presents the difference between the size of the tax burden in these, the most competitive, economies in the world and Ireland for 2008.[43]

---

[43] This analysis updates that first produced by Collins (2004:15-18).

Table 3.2.7: Differences in taxation levels between the world's 15 most competitive economies and Ireland.

Competitiveness Rank	Country	Taxation level versus Ireland
1	Switzerland	+0.3%
2	Sweden	+17.5%
3	Singapore	*not available*
4	United States	-2.7%
5	Germany	+8.2%
6	Japan	-0.7%
7	Finland	+14.3%
8	Netherlands	+10.2%
9	Denmark	+19.4%
10	Canada	+3.5%
11	Hong Kong SAR	*not available*
12	United Kingdom	+6.9%
13	Taiwan, China	*not available*
14	Norway	+13.8%
15	France	+14.4%
29	**IRELAND**	-

Source: World Economic Forum (2010:15)
Notes: a) Taxation data from OECD for the year 2008 (2010:19)
b) For some countries comparable data is *not available*.
c) The OECD's estimate for Ireland in 2008 = 28.8 per cent of GDP

Only the US and Japan reports a lower taxation levels compared with Ireland. Of the other leading competitive economies all collect a greater proportion of national income in taxation. Over time Ireland's position on this index has varied, most recently falling from 22nd to 29th. When Ireland has slipped back the reasons stated for Ireland's loss of competitiveness included decreases in economic growth, poor performances by public institutions and a decline in the technological competitiveness of the economy (WEF, 2003: xv; 2008:193). Interestingly, a major factor in that decline is related to underinvestment in state funded areas: education; research; infrastructure; and broadband connectivity. Each of these areas is dependent on taxation revenue and they have been highlighted by the report as necessary areas of investment to achieve enhanced competitiveness.[44] As such, lower taxes do not feature as a significant priority; rather it is increased and targeted efficient government spending.

---

[44] A similar conclusion was reached in another international competitiveness study by the International Institute for Management Development (2007).

A similar point was expressed by the Nobel Prize winning economist Professor Joseph Stiglitz while visiting Ireland in June 2004. Commenting on Ireland's long-term development prospects he stated that "all the evidence is that the low tax, low service strategy for attracting investment is shortsighted" and that "far more important in terms of attracting good businesses is the quality of education, infrastructure and services." Professor Stiglitz, who chaired President Clinton's Council of Economic Advisors, added that "low tax was not the critical factor in the Republic's economic development and it is now becoming an impediment".[45]

Reforming and broadening the tax base
The methods by which the tax base should be reformed and broadened are an issue worth considering. *Social Justice Ireland* believes that there is merit in developing a tax package which places less of an emphasis on taxing people and organisations on what they earn by their own useful work and enterprise, or on the value they add or on what they contribute to the common good. Rather, the tax that people and organisations should be required to pay should be based more on the value they subtract by their use of common resources. Whatever changes are made should also be guided by the need to build a fairer taxation system, one which adheres to our core policy objective already stated.

There are a number of approaches available to Government in reforming the tax base. Recent Budgets have made some progress in addressing some of these issues while the 2009 Commission on Taxation Report has highlighted many areas that require further reform. A short review of the areas we consider a priority are presented below across the following subsections:

> ***Tax Expenditures / Tax Reliefs***
> ***Minimum Effective Tax Rates of Higher Earners***
> ***Corporation Taxes***
> ***Site Value Tax***
> ***Second Homes***
> ***Taxing Windfall Gains***
> ***Financial Speculation Taxes***

A separate and related section on environment taxes follows.

---

[45] In an interview with John McManus, Irish Times, June 2nd 2004.

Tax Expenditures / Tax Reliefs

A significant outcome from the Commission on Taxation is contained in part eight of their Report which details all the tax breaks or tax expenditures as they are referred to officially. For years we have sought to have a full list of these tax breaks and their actual cost published. However, despite our best endeavors, neither the Department of Finance nor the Revenue Commissioners were able to produce such a list. Subsequently, two members of the Commission have produced a detailed report for the Trinity College Policy Institute which offered further insight into this issue (Collins and Walsh, 2010). Table 3.2.8 reproduces their findings which highlight that the annual cost of tax expenditures in 2006 (the year where most data was available) totals in excess of €11.5b per annum and that of the 131 tax expenditures in the Irish system, cost estimates are only available for 89 of them (68 per cent). Given the scale of public expenditure involved, this is a bizarre and totally unacceptable situation.

Table 3.2.8: Estimate of the Annual Cost of Ireland's Tax Expenditures

Tax Expenditures relating to:	No. of tax expenditures	No. with available costs	Estimated Cost €m
Children	8	8	723
Housing	6	6	3,256
Health	10	7	579
Philanthropy	16	7	89
Enterprise	28	12	457
Employment	28	18	2,816
Savings and investment	8	6	2,995
Age-related and other	7	5	144
Property investment	20	20	435
Total	**131**	**89**	**11,494++**

Source: Collins and Walsh (2010:4).

Some progress has been made on addressing and reforming these tax breaks in recent Budgets, and we welcome this progress. However, there remains further potential to reduce the cost of this area; it is tax forgone as recipients of these tax expenditures reduce their tax bills via the use of these tax breaks. We have highlighted a number of these reforms in our pre-Budget Policy Briefings, *Budget Choices*, and will further address this issue in advance of Budget 2012; in particular with regard to the need to reform the most expensive tax break which is associated with pensions.[46] *Social Justice Ireland* believes that reforming the tax break system would make the tax system fairer. It would also provide substantial additional resources towards achieving the adjustment Government has proposed for the years to come.

Both the Commission on Taxation (2009:230) and Collins and Walsh (2010:20-21) have also highlighted and detailed the need for new methods for evaluation/introducing tax reliefs. We strongly welcome these proposals, indeed they are similar to the proposals the directors of *Social Justice Ireland* made to the Commission in written and oral submissions. The proposals focus on ex-ante (prior) evaluation of the costs and benefits of any proposed expenditure, the need to collect detailed information on each expenditure, the introduction of time limits for expenditures, the creation of an annual tax expenditures report as part of the Budget process and the regular scrutiny of this area by an Oireachtas committee. As part of the necessary reform of this area *Social Justice Ireland* believes that these proposals should be adopted.

Minimum Effective Tax Rates for Higher Earners
Evidence from both Department of Finance studies and Revenue Commissioner reports has shown that the major beneficiaries of the aforementioned tax breaks are those on the highest incomes.

In 2005 the Department of Finance commissioned a number of reports on the scale, extent, merit and distribution of the existing tax break schemes. The findings of these reports span some 1,000 pages and are of some interest (see Department of Finance 2006 Vols I, II, III). While it is impossible to summarise these findings over a few paragraphs, three examples provide a good indication of what the reports found. In 2000 the government introduced a tax relief scheme for capital investments in Hotels and Holiday Camps. An assessment by Indecon Consultants for the Department of Finance found that up to 2006 these schemes resulted in a net loss in tax revenue (revenue forgone) of €120.5m (Department of Finance, 2006 Vol. I: 73). The report recommended that the scheme now be abolished; a decision that Budget 2006 subsequently took. As part of this review Indecon also considered the distribution of these tax reliefs. Table 3.2.9 presents the results of a confidential survey of Ireland's accountancy and tax professionals carried out by the consultants. In the survey these professionals were asked to indicate where in the

---

[46] Relevant pre-Budget *Policy Briefings* for Budgets 2009, 2010 and 2011 are available on our website.

income distribution were the recipients of these schemes located. The figures therefore represent indicative views based on the judgement and expertise of these professionals.[47] They indicate that all these benefits flowed to investors with a gross income of over €100,000 per annum and that two-thirds of those who benefited had annual gross incomes in excess of €200,000. Table 3.2.9 also reports a similar distribution analysis of those investors who availed of tax reliefs for multi-storey car parks. It presents an even more skewed allocation to those with incomes in excess of €200,000. In terms of tax revenue forgone this scheme cost the exchequer €15.9m

Table 3.2.9: The % distribution of investors utilising two tax relief schemes according to the views of accountancy and tax professionals – by likely annual gross income

Gross Annual Income of Investors	Hotels and Holiday Camps	Multi-storey Car Parks
€200,000 +	66.7%	83.3%
€100,000 to €200,000	33.3%	16.7%
€50,000 to €100,000	0.0%	0.0%
Less than €50,000	0.0%	0.0%
Total	**100.0%**	**100.0%**
Net tax forgone up to 2006	**€120.5m**	**€15.9m**

Source: Department of Finance (2006, Vol I: 73-76, 297-298)

An assessment of the tax reliefs associated with the Urban renewal scheme by Goodbody Economic Consultants identified that between 1999 and mid-2006 the total cost of this scheme in terms of tax revenue forgone was €1,423m. When considering the equity implication of this scheme they concluded that "the tax benefits of the scheme have accrued to relatively few high income individuals" and that "it is difficult to escape the conclusion that the scheme has had very negative equity impacts" (Department of Finance, 2006 Vol. II: 84-86). Budget 2006 also abolished this scheme.

The suggestion that it is the better-off who principally gain from the provision of tax exemption schemes is underscored by a series of reports published by the Revenue Commissioners entitled *Effective Tax Rates for High Earning Individuals*

---

[47] Accurate income distribution figures are unavailable as the Revenue Commissioners did not collect detailed information on these schemes.

(2002, 2005, 2006 and 2007). These reports provided details of the Revenue's assessment of the top 400 earners in Ireland and the rates of effective taxation they faced.[48] The reports led to the introduction of a minimum 20 per cent effective tax rate as part of the 2006 and 2007 Finance Acts for all those with incomes in excess of €500,000. During 2009 the Revenue Commissioners published an analysis of the operation of this new minimum rate using data for 2007 – the first year the scheme applied (Revenue Commissioners, 2009). Table 3.2.10 reports the findings of that analysis for 214 individuals with income in excess of €500,000. The report also includes information on the distribution of effective tax rates among the 225 earners with incomes between €250,000 and €500,000.

Table 3.2.10: The Distribution of Effective Tax Rates among a sample of those earning in excess of €250,000 in 2007 (% of total)

Effective Tax Rate	Individuals with incomes of €500,000+	Individuals with incomes of €250,000 - €500,000
0%–5%	0%	19.6%
5% < 10%	0%	14.7%
10% < 15%	0%	27.1%
15% < 20%	77.6%	38.6%
20% < 25%	22.4%	0%
25% < 30%	0%	0%
30% +	0%	0%
Total Cases	**214**	**225**

Source: Revenue Commissioners (2009)

Social Justice Ireland welcomes the introduction of this scheme which marked a major improvement in the fairness of the tax system. However, it should be noted that a 20 per cent effective taxation rate in 2007 was equivalent to the amount of income tax paid by a single PAYE worker with a gross income of €40,000.

We also welcome the Budget 2010 decision and the commitment in the new Programme for Government (2011) to increase the minimum effective rate to 30 per cent (equivalent to the rate faced by a single PAYE worker on approximately

---

[48] The effective taxation rate is calculated as the percentage of an individual's total pre-tax income that they pay in taxation.

€55,000 gross) and to apply this to high earners; the precise income threshold has not been defined in the recent Programme for Government. We encourage the Government to continue to raise this minimum effective rate so that it is in-line with that faced by PAYE earners on equivalent high-income levels. Following Budget 2011 a single individual on an income of €120,000 gross will pay an effective tax rate of 42.7 per cent; a figure which suggests that the minimum threshold for high earners has potential to adjust upwards over the next few years.

Corporation Taxes

Following Budget 2003, the standard rate of corporation tax was reduced from 16 per cent to 12.5 per cent at a full year cost of €305m. This reduction followed another reduction in 2002 which brought the rate down from 20 per cent to 16 per cent. At the time, the total cost in lost revenue to the exchequer of these two reductions was estimated at over €650m per annum at the time. Serious questions remain concerning the advisability of pursuing this policy approach. Ireland's corporation tax rate is now considerably below the corresponding rates in most of Europe. Windfall profits are flowing to a sector that is already extremely profitable. Furthermore, Ireland's low rate of corporation tax is being abused by multi-national companies who are channelling profits through units, often very small units, in Ireland to avail of the lower Irish rate of tax. In many cases this is happening at a cost to fellow EU member's exchequers and with little benefit in terms of jobs and additional real economic activity in Ireland. Understandably, Ireland is coming under increasing pressure to reform this system.

Across the relevant literature no evidence of substance exists to support the contention that corporations would leave if the corporate tax rate were higher – at 17.5 per cent for example. Furthermore, the logic of having a uniform rate of corporation tax for all sectors is questionable. At a 2003 social policy conference which examined this issue David Begg (ICTU) stated, "there is no advantage in having a uniform rate of 12.5 per cent corporation tax applicable to hotels and banks as well as to manufacturing industry" (2003:12). In the last few years there has been some improvement in this situation with special, and higher, tax rates being charged on natural resource industries. *Social Justice Ireland* welcomes this as an overdue step in the right direction.

As the European Union expands corporation tax competition is likely to intensify. Already Estonia and the Isle of Man have put in place a zero per cent corporation tax rate, Cyprus has set its rate at 10 per cent and Hungary continues to reduce its rate; others are likely to follow.[49] Over the next decade Ireland will be forced to either ignore tax rates as a significant attraction/retention policy for foreign investors (this would be a major change in industrial policy) or to follow suit and compete by further cutting corporation tax further. Sweeney has warned of a dangerous situation where Ireland ends up "leading the race to the bottom" (2004:59). The costs of such a move, in lost exchequer income, would be enormous.

An alternative direction for corporation tax is to set a minimum rate for all EU countries. Given the international nature of company investment these taxes are fundamentally different from internal taxes, and the benefit of a European agreement which sets a minimum rate is clear. These would include protecting Ireland's already low rate from being driven down even lower, protecting the jobs in industries which might move to lower taxing countries and protecting the revenue generated for the exchequer by corporate taxes. *Social Justice Ireland* believes that an EU wide agreement on a minimum rate of corporation tax should be negotiated. We believe that the minimum rate should be set well below the 2009 EU-27 average rate of 23.5 per cent but above the existing low Irish level.[50] A rate of 17.5 per cent seems appropriate.

Site Value Tax
Taxes on wealth are minimal in Ireland. We are the exception to the rule among developed countries in having tax on immovable property. Revenue is negligible from capital acquisitions tax because it has a very high threshold where bequests and gifts within families are concerned and it treats family farms and firms very generously (see tax revenue tables at the start of this chapter). Following the publication of the Commission on Taxation Report (2009) much discussion has centered on their proposal for the introduction of a residential property tax. However, we believe that a Site Value Tax, also known as a Land Rent Tax, is a more appropriate and fairer approach. It would lead to a substantial broadening of the base at a single stroke and would also lead to a reduction of the tax-take required from other sources, thus providing an opportunity for Government to produce a just and fair tax system. In that context we welcome recent announcements in the National Recovery Plan (2010) and the 2011 Programme for Government that such a tax is to be introduced.

---

[49] It is worth noting that the Isle of Man has retained a 10 per cent rate on the profits of banking institutions.
[50] Data from Eurostat (2009:104).

The issue of site value taxation is one that has received ongoing attention over the past few years. Two papers at a 2004 Social Policy Conference directly addressed this issue (see O'Siochru, 2004:23-57; and Dunne, 2004:93-122) and the Chambers of Commerce of Ireland have published a report entitled *Local Authority Funding – Government in Denial* (2004) which called for an annual site tax.

A 'land value', 'land rent' or 'site-value' tax (all three names are used to describe the same concept) is based on the annual rental value of land. The annual rental site value is the rental value that a particular piece of land would have if there were no buildings or improvements on it. It is the value of a site, as provided by nature and as affected for better or worse by the activities of the community at large. The tax falls on the annual value of land at the point where it enters into economic activity, before the application of capital and labour to it.

The arguments for a land-rent tax are to do with fairness and economic efficiency. Most of the reward of rising land values goes to those who own land, while most of the cost of the activities that create rising land values does not. This is because rising land values - for example, in prosperous city centres or prime agricultural areas - are largely created by the activities of the community as a whole and by government regulations and subsidies, while the higher value of each particular site is enjoyed by its owner. This means that it often pays land owners to keep sites unused in order to sell them later when (they hope) land values will have risen. Speculation on rising land values distorts land prices, generally making them significantly higher than they would otherwise be. NESC (2003:96) points out that the introduction of a tax on development land would have minimal economic effects given the immobility of land.

A land value tax is positive on both efficiency and equity grounds. From an efficiency perspective a site value tax would be a major step toward securing the tax base as it could not move to any location providing greater tax reductions. In doing this it would move the tax away from a transaction (such as stamp duty) which can make the tax base vulnerable as it is dependent on maintaining and increasing the scale of the transactions and move it instead to an immovable physical asset which is a much securer base. It would have other efficiency impacts such as ensuring that derelict sites were developed and that land would not be held over, as appears to be the situation at present, in an attempt to increase its value by creating artificial scarcity of land for development.

A land value tax is also positive on equity grounds. High land values in urban areas of Ireland are mainly a product of the economic and social activity in those areas. Consequently, it can be argued that a substantial portion of the benefits of these land values should be enjoyed by all the members of the community and not just the site owners. As well as this the increasing site values are closely linked to the level of investment in infrastructure those areas have received. Much of that investment has been paid for by taxpayers. It can be argued that a substantial portion of the benefits of the increasing site value should go to the whole community through the taxation system and not just remain with the site owner who may well have made no contribution to the investment that produced the increased value.

In short, *Social Justice Ireland* believes that the introduction of a site value tax would lead to more efficient land use within the structure of social, environmental and economic goals embodied in planning and other legislation.

Second Homes
While addressing Ireland's housing problem, the *National Development Plan Mid-Term Review* (ESRI, 2003) pointed out the growing problem of second homes. It noted that a quarter of all houses built in 2003 were second (holiday) houses and would have nobody living in them for nine months of the year. Based on data collected by Census enumerators the CSO reported that on census night (April 23rd) 2006 there were 49,789 unoccupied holiday homes in Ireland representing approximately 3 per cent of the national housing stock. Their number has increased since then in many cases due to excess building at the peak of the housing boom; the results of Census 2011 will eventually provide a further insight. Table 3.2.11 outlines the county-by-county distribution of these holiday homes as found in 2006.

What is often overlooked when this issue is being discussed is that the infrastructure to support these houses is substantially subsidised by the tax-payer. Roads, water, sewage and electricity infrastructure are just part of this subsidy which goes, by definition, to those who are already better off as they can afford these second homes in the first place. *Social Justice Ireland* supports the views of the ESRI (2003) and the Indecon report (2005:183-186; 189-190) on this issue. We believe that people purchasing second houses should have to pay these full infrastructural costs, much of which is currently borne by society through the Exchequer and local authorities.

There seems something perverse in the fact that the taxpayer is providing substantial subsidies to the owners of these unoccupied (mostly holiday) houses while so many people do not have basic adequate accommodation. The second house issue should be addressed so that priority can be given to supplying accommodation which people need and will be lived in all year round. In that regard, the introduction of the Non Principal Private Residence (NPPR) charge in 2009 was a welcome step forwards. However, the charge is still very low relative to the benefits (previous and ongoing) that are derived from these properties. The charge should therefore be increased and the NPPR retained as a separate second homes payment once the system of site value taxes is introduced.

Table 3.2.11: The Number and Distribution of Holiday homes in Ireland, from Census 2006.

County	No. Holiday Homes	County	No. Holiday Homes
Donegal	8,275	Louth	575
Wexford	6,601	Dublin City and County	418
Cork City and County	6,561	Kilkenny	406
Kerry	5,990	Meath	346
Mayo	4,216	Limerick City and County	346
Clare	3,624	Carlow	308
Galway City and County	3,172	Westmeath	271
Sligo	1,540	Longford	261
Waterford City and County	1,326	Offaly	220
Leitrim	1,192	Monaghan	171
Wicklow	1,156	Kildare	116
Roscommon	942	Laois	103
Tipperary	874		
Cavan	779	**State**	**49,789**

Source: CSO (2007:92)

Taxing Windfall Gains

An undesirable feature of the recent economic boom was the vast profits being made by property speculators on the rezoning of land by local authorities. For some time we have called for a substantial tax to be imposed on the profits earned from such decisions. As rezonings are made by elected representatives in the interest of society generally, it seems appropriate that a sizeable proportion of the windfall gains they generate should be made available to local authorities and used to address the ongoing housing problems they face (see section 3.5). In that regard we welcome the recent decision to put such a tax in place. The windfall tax level of 80 per cent is appropriate and as table 3.2.12 shows this still leaves speculators and land owners with substantial profits from these rezoning decisions. We also believe that the profit from this process should then be targeted on funding local authorities.

Table 3.2.12: Illustrative examples of the Operation of an 80% Windfall Gain Tax on Rezoned Land

Agricultural Land Value	Rezoned Value	Profit	Tax @ 80%	Post-Tax Profit	Profit as % Original Value
€50,000	€400,000	€350,000	€280,000	€70,000	140%
€100,000	€800,000	€700,000	€560,000	€140,000	140%
€200,000	€1,600,000	€1,400,000	€1,120,000	€280,000	140%
€500,000	€4,000,000	€3,500,000	€2,800,000	€700,000	140%
€1,000,000	€8,000,000	€7,000,000	€5,600,000	€1,400,000	140%

Note: Calculations assume an eight-fold increase on the agricultural land value upon rezoning.

Financial Speculation taxes

As the international economic chaos of the past two years has shown the world is now increasingly linked via millions of legitimate, speculative and opportunistic financial transactions. Similarly, global currency trading has been increasing dramatically throughout the last few decades. It is estimated that a very high proportion of all financial transactions traded are speculative currency transactions – these speculative transactions are completely free of taxation.

There is growing support worldwide for the introduction of a tax on such speculative exchange transactions. The Tobin tax, proposed by the Nobel Prize winner James Tobin, provides a potential solution. It is a progressive tax, designed to target only those profiting from currency speculation. Therefore, it is neither a tax on citizens, nor on business. Given the recent world economic experience, the tax also has merit in assisting Governments and regulators to continually monitor the risk that financial institutions are taking. As the recent crisis has demonstrated, for the most part Central Banks and Governments are unable to adequately track and monitor these transactions.

The majority of foreign exchange dealings are done by one hundred of the world's largest commercial and investment banks. The scale of their dealings is estimated at US$1.5 trillion worth of currency every day; all this in essentially unregulated financial markets. In 1998 the financial institution with the largest share of this market, Citibank, engaged in foreign exchange transactions worth US$8.5 trillion, a value in excess of the corresponding US GDP for that same year. The scope of the Tobin tax varies. Initially, James Tobin suggested a tax on all purchases of financial instruments denominated in another currency. Since then, Canadian economist Rodney Schmidt has broadened the tax to include all foreign exchange transactions. These would include simple exchanges of one currency for another (spot transactions) as well as complex derivative financial instruments including forwards, swaps, futures and options if they involve two currencies. The recent proposals in the UK for a 'Robin-Hood Tax' represent a further development of these proposals.

The rate would be determined by each country enacting the tax, but the tax range recommended to produce moderate market calming and revenue-raising outcomes is between 0.1 and 0.25 per cent. While this may seem very small to consumers, relative to VAT rates and income taxes, the impact on the margins of currency speculators would be enough to curb their activities.

The revenue from the tax would be considerable - somewhere in the region of €50 -100 billion per year worldwide. Though the effect of the tax over time would be to reduce the volume of currency speculation and thus the potential revenue from the tax, nevertheless the intake will remain high. It is proposed that the revenue generated by this tax be used for national social development and international development co-operation purposes. According to the United Nations, the amount of annual income raised from the tax would be enough to guarantee to every citizen of the world basic access to water, food, shelter, health and education. Therefore, this tax has the potential to wipe out the worst forms of material poverty throughout the world.

When James Tobin first put forward his idea he envisaged the tax being adopted by every country in the world simultaneously. Otherwise, he argued, speculators would "flock" to those countries without Tobin tax laws. Since such international agreement seemed improbable, the tax was seen by many as a worthy but impracticable proposal. However, over recent years the work of economists and financial experts has demonstrated that universal simultaneous adoption is not vital for a successful implementation. Essentially, foreign currency markets are concentrated on a global scale and if the principal countries implement the tax, this would suffice to cover the planet as a whole. Eight major countries account for more than 80 per cent of world exchange transactions, the foremost four for 65 per cent. In the City of London, the largest financial centre with 33 per cent of the world total, the 10 biggest banks account for 50 per cent of transactions.

What is needed is for one major region of the world to implement the tax. Consequently, *Social Justice Ireland* welcomes the increasing attention this proposal has been receiving at European Inter-Governmental Level and the 2011 decision of the European Parliament to urge the EU to promote the introduction of a financial transaction tax. The Parliament encouraged the EU to promote the introduction of such a tax, even if it is alone in doing so, "as a first step", according to the resolution which was agreed by a vote of 529 to 127 on Tuesday March 8, 2011. The resolution argues that a tax of this kind can yield a "double dividend" by not only generating more funds (€200m per annum), but also making the financial sector safer and society greener. The plenary session of the parliament in Strasbourg, which approved this resolution, heard that the next step should see the European Commission produce a feasibility study and concrete legislative proposals. The German finance minister, Wolfgang Schäuble, has included a tax on financial transactions as part of his budget plan covering the period 2012-2015. Mr Shauble said he saw new momentum for a financial transactions tax in Europe and urged the European Commission to drop its "hesitant attitude" towards such an approach. The European Parliament has supported the introduction of such a tax. So too have the leaders of the 17 eurozone countries. Mr Shuble urged the European Commission to flesh out the details of such a tax. He rejected the argument that there was need for global agreement before implementing such a tax.

Social Justice Ireland believes that the time has come for such a tax, It would simultaneously facilitate, and perhaps fund, the required regulation of financial speculation while providing substantial funds to adequately address the world development issues highlighted in the Millennium Development Goals (see section 3.12). *Social Justice Ireland* urges the Commission to act swiftly on this issue which has so many positive aspects if it were introduced.

Introducing Environmental Taxes
Environmental taxes also have a role to play in broadening Ireland's tax base. We address this issue over the following two subsections:

    Carbon Taxes
    Cap and Share

Carbon Taxes

Budget 2010 announced the long-overdue introduction of a carbon tax – the tax had been promised since Budget 2003 and committed to in the *National Climate Change Strategy* and *Programme for Government*. The tax has been structured along the line of the proposal from the Commission on Taxation (2009: 325-372) and is linked to the price of carbon credits which was set at an initial rate of €15 per tonne of CO_2 with products taxed in accordance to the level of emissions they create. Oil and gas were subject to the charge from May 2010 and coal and peat from September 2010.

While we welcomed the development, we regret the lack of detail in Budget 2010 on the accompanying measures to protect low income households and rural dwellers. The Government should be more specific in defining how it will assist these households other than indicating possible future fuel vouchers and increase rural transport funding. Furthermore, there is a danger that recent announcements, in the National Recovery Plan (2010) and the Programme for Government (2011), to increase the carbon tax over the next few years may alleviate the intention of the tax as one intended to encourage behavioural change rather than simply raise revenue.

Cap and Share

Another approach in the area of environmental taxation is called 'Cap and Share'. This is a personal carbon trading scheme aimed at supporting the transition to a lower carbon intensity economy. Cap and Share (C&S) envisages the establishment of an overall cap on greenhouse gas emissions and, subsequently, the allocation of 'entitlements' to every resident based on an equal division of the overall cap. Upstream companies (fuel importers, refineries, etc.) would be required to purchase sufficient entitlements to match the emissions from their operations. C&S is founded on the philosophy of equal rights for all to emit to the atmosphere. At the downstream end, C&S rewards individuals who consume electricity and fuel at below average levels, whilst those with greater than average carbon intensity would be penalised. Design of the scheme needs to ensure that it does not result in disadvantaged sectors of society being made worse off.

At a 2004 Social Policy Conference Douthwaite provided some detail on this approach (2004: 125-137). He suggested that a tradable quota system could be introduced and to achieve this, Ireland would divide the total tonnage of carbon dioxide it is allowed to emit under the agreement it reached with its EU partners under the Kyoto arrangements – its 1990 emissions plus 13 per cent - by its current population and issue permits for that amount - roughly 15.5 tonnes of CO_2 per head - to the population, perhaps at the rate of 1.3 tonnes each month. Citizens could then sell on these permits, through the financial institutions, and polluters such as large firms and oil distribution companies would have to purchase them. The price received for these permits would vary according to the demand for fossil energy and just how well Ireland and the rest of the EU was doing in getting emission levels down. If the EU economy was booming and a lot of energy was being used, the price of the permits would be high but, equally, so would be the price of petrol, electricity and home-heating oil. If the economy was depressed, these prices, and the amount we got for our permits, would fall. This builds an automatic cushion against higher energy prices into the system, which protects, in particular, the least well-off who, although they spend a greater proportion of their incomes on energy, spend less on it in absolute terms. The provision of this cushion is very important since, as energy is used in the production of everything we use and consume, all prices will go up as a result of any restrictions on energy use. The proceeds from the permit sales would also provide the average person with enough extra purchasing power to cover the higher costs of the fuels and (because of the higher energy prices) the other goods and services they buy, provided that their purchases are not excessively energy-intensive. However, if some individuals were able to cut their direct and indirect fuel use below their entitlement, they would make themselves better off. On the other hand, if they continued to drive around in their SUVs, they would have to pay more frugal people for the privilege. The fact that fossil fuels themselves and goods made with significant amounts of fossil energy would cost more would encourage people to find lower-fossil-energy alternatives and enable the transition to renewable energy sources to gather pace. In short, a quota system would give people the price signals to move in the right direction.[51] A detailed report from Comhar (2008) has advanced a similar proposal.

Building a fairer taxation system
The need for fairness in the tax system was clearly recognised in the first report of the Commission on Taxation more than twenty-five years ago. In that volume it stated:

> "...in our recommendations the spirit of equity is the first and most important consideration. Departures from equity must be clearly justified by reference to the needs of economic development or to avoid imposing unreasonable compliance costs on individuals or high administrative costs on the Revenue Commissioners." (1982:29)

---

[51] A more comprehensive outline of this proposal is presented in Douthwaite (2004) and in Feasta/NEF (2006).

A New and Fairer Ireland

The need for fairness is very obvious today and *Social Justice Ireland* believes that this should be a central objective of the current reform of the taxation system. While we recognise that many of the reforms below can only occur once the current crisis in the exchequer's finances has been resolved, we include them here as they represent necessary reforms that would greatly enhance the fairness of Ireland's taxation system. This section is structured across eight parts:

> ***Standard Rating Discretionary Tax Expenditures***
> ***Keeping the Minimum Wage Out of the Tax Net***
> ***Favouring changes to tax credits rather than tax rates***
> ***Favouring changes to tax credits rather than tax bands***
> ***Introducing Refundable Tax Credits***
> ***Introducing a Refundable Tax Credit For Children***
> ***Reforming Individualisation***
> ***Making the taxation system simpler***

Standard rating discretionary tax expenditures
One crucial step towards achieving a fairer tax system is to standard rate all discretionary tax reliefs/expenditures, making them available at the 20 per cent rate only. If there is a legitimate case for making a tax relief/expenditure available then it should be made available in the same way to all. It is unfair that some people can claim certain tax reliefs at a rate of 20 per cent (the standard tax rate) and others with higher incomes can claim it at a higher rate. That unfairness is further exacerbated by the fact that it is those who are better off who can claim these reliefs at the upper rate. Standard rating tax expenditures offers the potential to simultaneously make the tax system fairer and fund these necessary developments without any significant macroeconomic implications.[52]

Keeping the minimum wage out of the tax net
A major achievement of Budget 2005 was the decision by the Minister of Finance to remove those on the minimum wage from the tax net. This decision had an important impact on the growing numbers of working-poor and addresses an issue with which *Social Justice Ireland* is highly concerned. The fiscal and economic crisis of 2008-11 lead to Government reversing this policy first via the income levy in Budget 2009 #2 and then via the Universal Social Charge (USC) in Budget 2011. In the case of the latter, the USC is charged on all the income of those who earner

---

[52] See O'Toole and Cahill (2006:215) who also reach this conclusion.

more than €4,004 per annum. Using the unadjusted minimum wage of €8.65 per hour, the thresholds implies that a low-income worker on the minimum wage and working more than 9 hours per week (earning €77.85 per week) is subject to the tax. *Social Justice Ireland* believes that this threshold is far too low and unnecessarily impacts on the income and living standards of the working poor. We welcome to commitment of the new Government to examine and reform this charge. It is likely that imposing the USC at such low income levels raises a very small amount of funds for the exchequer; perhaps less than the administrative costs associated with its imposition. We hope that the forthcoming review will raise the point at which the USC commences and in the years to come, as resources return, we will urge Government to restore the policy of keeping the minimum wage outside the tax net.

Favouring changes to tax credits rather than tax rates
Social Justice Ireland believes that any future income tax changes should be concerned with changes to either tax credits or tax bands rather than tax rates. In the context of achieving fairness in the taxation system, changes to tax credits rather than tax bands are more desirable.

To explain this point further, we start by comparing a change in tax credits against a change in tax rates (the next section makes a comparison with tax bands). One of the initiatives announced in Budget 2007 was a cut in the top tax rate of one per cent (from 42 to 41 per cent). In his Budget speech the Minister indicated that the full year cost of this change was €186m. The Budget documentation also indicated that the full-year cost of a €90 increase in the tax credits of every tax payer equalled €185m. Therefore, both policy changes have roughly the same exchequer cost. Chart 3.2.2 compares these two changes and the increased income they delivered to earners across the income distribution.

An increase in tax credits would provide the same value to all taxpayers across the income distribution; provided they are earning sufficient to pay more than €90 in income taxes. Therefore, the increased income received by an earner on €25,000 and on €80,000 is the same – an extra €90. However, a decrease in the top tax rate only benefits those paying tax at that rate. Therefore, the earner on €25,000 gains nothing from this change while those on €50,000 gain €160 per annum and those on €80,000 gain €460 per annum. The higher your income the greater the gain.

Chart 3.2.2: Budget 2007 comparison of a 1% cut in the top tax rate and an increase in tax credits of €90 for each taxpayer.

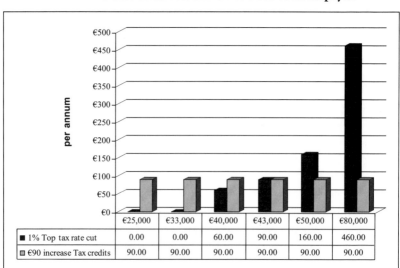

	€25,000	€33,000	€40,000	€43,000	€50,000	€80,000
■ 1% Top tax rate cut	0.00	0.00	60.00	90.00	160.00	460.00
□ €90 increase Tax credits	90.00	90.00	90.00	90.00	90.00	90.00

As chart 3.2.2 shows, in Budget 2007 all single people earning less than €43,000 would have gained more from an increase in tax credits rather than a decrease in the top tax rate. For a couple (not shown in the diagram), all those earning less than €86,000 would have been better off had the government used the same money to deliver an increase in tax credits rather than a decrease in the top tax rate.

In terms of fairness, changing tax credits is a fairer option than changing tax rates. Government should always take this option when it has money available to reduce income taxes.

Favouring changes to tax credits rather than tax bands

In reforming income taxation policy over the years and decades to come, Government must be conscious of always enhancing fairness. The following example based on numbers from Budget 2008 illustrates the choices between changing either tax credits or tax bands. If €535 million were available for distribution in a Budget it could be used to either (i) increase the 20 per cent tax band by €5,000 (full year cost €536.1m) or (ii) increase personal tax credits by

€250 a year (full-year cost €533.75m).[53] While the exchequer cost of these two alternatives is roughly the same, their impact is notably different:

(i) Increasing the tax band by €5,000 would be of no benefit to anyone with incomes at or below the top of the then tax band (i.e. €35,400 for a single person) but would provide a benefit of €1,000 a year to a single person earning more than €40,400. Single people with incomes in the €35,400-40,400 range would benefit by a proportion of the €1,000. (The thresholds for married people with one or two incomes are different but the impacts are along the same trajectory as identified for single people here).

(ii) Increasing the tax credit by €250 a year would mean that every earner with a tax bill in excess of €250 a year would benefit by that amount.

In terms of fairness, increasing tax credits is a fairer option than widening the standard rate tax band. Government should always take this option when it has money available to reduce income taxes. It has the additional advantage of helping to address the 'working poor' issue which, as we have highlighted earlier, is emerging as a growing problem that requires a policy response.

Introducing refundable tax credits

The move from tax allowances to tax credits was completed in Budget 2001. This was a very welcome change because it put in place a system that had been advocated for a long time by a range of groups. One problem persists however, a problem that the old system of tax allowances also had. If a low income worker does not earn enough to use up his or her full tax credit then he or she will not benefit from any tax reductions introduced by government in its annual budget. In effect this means that, under the present system, those with the lowest pay will not benefit in any way at budget time.

A simple solution exists to rectify this problem: make tax credits refundable. This would mean that the part of the tax credit that an employee did not benefit from would be "refunded" to him/her by the state.

The major advantage of making tax credits refundable would lie in addressing the disincentives currently associated with low-paid employment. The main

---

[53] Figures from Department pre-Budget 2008 income tax ready reckoner.

beneficiaries of refundable tax credits would be low-paid employees (full-time and part-time). Chart 3.2.3 displays the impacts of the introduction of this policy across various gross income levels. It clearly shows that all of the benefits from introducing this policy would go directly to those on the lowest incomes.

Chart 3.2.3: How much better off would people be if tax credits were made refundable?

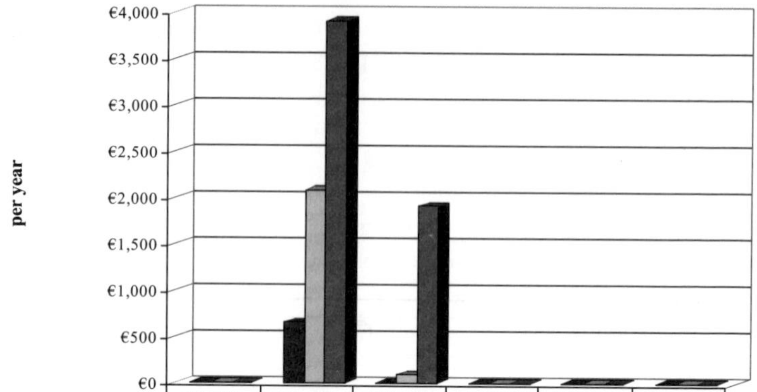

per year	LTU**	€15,000	€30,000	€50,000	€75,000	€100,000
■ Single	0	660	0	0	0	0
□ Couple 1 Earner*	0	2090	90	0	0	0
■ Couple 2 Earners*	0	3920	1920	0	0	0

Notes: * Except in LTU case where there is no earner
　　　　** LTU: Long Term Unemployed

As regards administering this reform the central idea recognises that most people with regular incomes and jobs would not receive a cash refund of their tax credit because their incomes are too high; they would simply benefit from the tax credit as a reduction in their tax bill. Therefore, as chart 3.2.3 shows no change is proposed for these people and they would continue to pay tax via their employers, based on their net tax liability after their employers have deducted tax credits on behalf of the Revenue Commissioners. For other people on low or irregular incomes, the refundable tax credit could be paid via a refund from the Revenue Commissioners at the end of the year

Following the introduction of refundable tax credits, all subsequent increases in the level of the tax credit would be of equal value to all employees.

Taxation

To illustrate the benefits of this approach, charts 3.2.4 and 3.2.5 compare the benefits of a €100 increase in tax credits before and after the introduction of refundable tax credits. Chart 3.2.4 shows the effect as the system is currently structured – an increase of €100 in credits, but these are not refundable. It shows that the gains are allocated equally to all categories of earners above €50,000. However, there is no benefit for these workers whose earnings are not in the tax net.

Chart 3.2.5 shows how the benefits of a €100 a year increase in tax credits would be distributed under a system of refundable tax credits. This simulation displays the equity attached to using the tax-credit instrument to distribute budgetary taxation changes. The benefit to all categories of income earners (single/couple, one-earner/couple, two-earners) is the same. Consequently, in relative terms, those earners at the bottom of the distribution do best.

Chart 3.2.4: How much better off would people be if tax credits were increased by €100 per person?

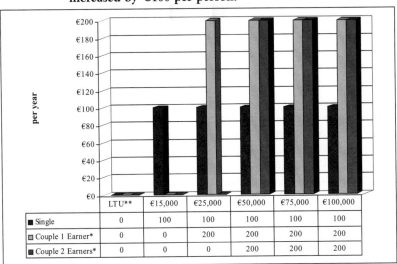

	LTU**	€15,000	€25,000	€50,000	€75,000	€100,000
Single	0	100	100	100	100	100
Couple 1 Earner*	0	0	200	200	200	200
Couple 2 Earners*	0	0	0	200	200	200

Notes: * Except in LTU case where there is no earner
       ** LTU: Long Term Unemployed

Chart 3.2.5: How much better off would people be if tax credits were increased by €100 per person and this was refundable?

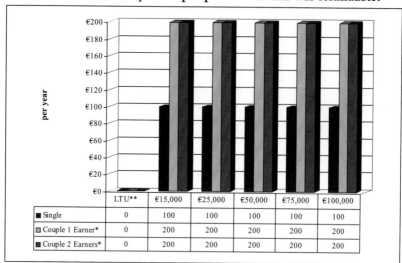

	LTU**	€15,000	€25,000	€50,000	€75,000	€100,000
■ Single	0	100	100	100	100	100
□ Couple 1 Earner*	0	200	200	200	200	200
■ Couple 2 Earners*	0	200	200	200	200	200

Notes: * Except in LTU case where there is no earner
** LTU: Long Term Unemployed

Overall the merits of adopting this approach are: that every beneficiary of tax credits could receive the full value of the tax credit; that the system would improve the net income of the workers whose incomes are lowest, at modest cost; and that there would be no additional administrative burden placed on employers. Outside Ireland, the refundable tax credits approach has gathered more and more attention over recent years including a detailed Brooking Policy Briefing on the issue published in the United States in late 2006 (see Batchelder et al, 2006). In reviewing this issue in the Irish context Rapple stated that "the change is long overdue" (2004:140).

During the past year *Social Justice Ireland* published a detailed study on the subject of refundable tax credits. Entitled '*Building a Fairer Tax System: The Working Poor and the Cost of Refundable Tax Credits*' the study identified that the proposed system would benefit 113,000 low-income individuals in an efficient and cost-effective manner.[54] When children and other adults in the household are taken into account

---

[54] The study is available from our website: www.socialjustice.ie

the total number of beneficiaries would be 240,000. The cost of making this change would be €140m. The *Social Justice Ireland* proposal to make tax credits refundable would make Ireland's tax system fairer, address part of the working poor problem and improve the living standards of a substantial number of people in Ireland. The following is a summary of our proposal:

Making tax credits refundable: the benefits
- Would address the problem identified already in a straightforward and cost-effective manner.
- No administrative cost to the employer.
- Would incentivise employment over welfare as it would widen the gap between pay and welfare rates.
- Would be more appropriate for a 21st century system of tax and welfare.

Details of Social Justice Ireland proposal
- Unused portion of the Personal and PAYE tax credit (and only these) would be refunded.
- Eligibility criteria in the relevant year:
- Individuals must have unused personal and/or PAYE tax credits (by definition).
- Individuals must have been in paid employment.
- Individuals must be at least 23 years of age.
- Individuals must have earned a minimum annual income from employment of €4,000.
- Individuals must have accrued a minimum of 40 PRSI weeks.
- Individuals must not have earned an annual total income greater than €15,600.
- Married couples must not have earned a combined annual total income greater than €31,200.
- Payments would be made at the end of the tax year.

Cost of implementing the proposal
- The total cost of refunding unused tax credits to individuals satisfying all of the criteria mentioned in this proposal is estimated at €140,051,823.

Major findings
- Almost 113,300 low income individuals would directly benefit from a refund and would see their disposable income increase as a result of the proposal.

- The majority of the refunds are valued at under €2,400 per annum (or €46 per week) with the most common value being individuals receiving a refund of between €800 to €1,000 per annum (or €15 to €19 per week).
- Considering that the individuals receiving these payments have incomes of less than €15,600 (or €299 per week), such payments are significant to them.
- Almost 40 per cent of refunds flow to low-income working poor households who live below the poverty line.
- A total of 91,056 individuals (men, women and children) below the poverty threshold benefit either directly (through a payment to themselves) or indirectly (through a payment to their household) from a refundable tax credit.
- Of the 91,056 individuals living below the poverty line that benefit from refunds, most (over 71 per cent) receive refunds of more than €10 per week with 32 per cent receiving in excess of €20 per week.
- A total of 148,863 individuals (men, women and children) above the poverty line benefit from refundable tax credits either directly (through a payment to themselves) or indirectly (through a payment to their household). Most of these beneficiaries have income less than €120 per week above the poverty line.
- Overall, almost 240,000 individuals (91,056 + 148,863) living in low-income households would experience an increase in income as a result of the introduction of refundable tax credits, either directly (through a refund to themselves) or indirectly (through a payment to their household).

Once adopted, a system of refundable tax credits as proposed in this study would result in all future changes in tax credits being equally experienced by all employees in Irish society. Such a reform would mark a significant step in the direction of building a fairer taxation system and represent a fairer way for Irish society to allocate its resources.

Reforming individualisation

Social Justice Ireland supports the individualisation of the tax system. However, the process of individualisation followed by government to date has been deeply flawed and unfair. The cost to the exchequer of this transition has been in excess of €0.75 billion, and almost all of this money has gone to the richest 30 per cent of the population. A significantly fairer process would have been to introduce a basic income system that would have treated all people fairly and ensured that a windfall of this nature did not accrue to the best off in this society (see section 3.1).

All the predictions currently indicate that there will be a future increase in the level of unemployment. Given the current form of individualisation, couples who see one partner lose his/her job will end up even worse off than they would have been had the current form of individualisation not been introduced.

Before individualisation was introduced, the standard-rate income-tax band was €35,553 for all couples. After that they would start paying the higher rate of tax. Now, the standard-rate income-tax band for single-income couples is €44,400, while the band for dual-income couples is €70,800. If one spouse (of a couple previously earning two salaries) leaves a job voluntarily or through redundancy, the couple loses the value of the second tax band.

Making the taxation system simpler
Our tax system is not simple. In a book reviewing Ireland's taxation system Bristow (2004) argues that "some features of it, notably VAT, are among the most complex in the world". The reasons given to support this complexity vary but they are focused principally around the need to reward particular kinds of behaviour which is seen as desirable by legislators. This, in effect, is discrimination in favour of one kind of activity or against another. There are many arguments against the present complexity and in favour of a simpler system.

Discriminatory tax concessions in favour of particular positions are often very inequitable. They often contribute far less to equity than might appear to be the case. On many occasions they fail to produce the economic or social outcomes which were being sought. Sometimes they generate very undesirable effects. At other times they may be a complete waste of money since the outcomes they seek would have occurred without the introduction of a tax incentive. Having a complex system also has other down-sides. It can, for example, have high compliance costs both for taxpayers and for the Revenue Commissioners who are responsible for collecting tax.

For the most part society at large gains little or nothing from the discrimination contained in the tax system. In some cases this discrimination causes very negative effects. Mortgage interest relief, for example, and the absence of any residential or land-rent tax have contributed to the rise in house prices. Complexity makes taxes easier to evade, invites consultants to devise avoidance schemes and greatly increases the cost of collection. It is also inequitable because those who can afford professional advice are in a far better position to take advantage of that complexity than those who cannot afford to do this. A simpler taxation system would serve Irish society and all individuals within it, irrespective of their means, better.

In conclusion, we outline our key policy proposals with regard to taxation.

Key Priorities on Taxation
Social Justice Ireland believes that Government should:
- increase the overall tax take
- adopt policies to broaden the tax base
- develop a fairer taxation system

We outline our policy proposals under each of these headings below.

Increase the overall tax take
- Move towards increasing the total tax take to 34.9 per cent of GDP – a level which will keep Ireland as a low tax economy.

Broaden the tax base
- Continue to reform the area of tax expenditures and put in place procedures within the Department of Finance and the Revenue Commissioners to monitor on an ongoing basis the cost and benefits of all current and new tax expenditures.

- Continue to increase the minimum effective tax rates on very high earners (those with incomes in excess of €125,000) so that these rates are consistent with the levels faced by PAYE workers.

- Move to negotiate an EU wide agreement on minimum corporate taxation rates (a rate of 17.5 per cent would seem fair in this situation).

- Introduce site-value tax.

- Impose charges so that those who construct or purchase second homes pay the full infrastructural costs of these dwellings.

- Retain the 80 per cent windfall tax on the profits generated from all land rezonings.

- Collaborate with other EU member states to introduce a tax on financial speculation and currency transactions such as the Tobin Tax.

- Move decisively to shift the burden of taxation from income tax to eco-taxes on the consumption of fuel and fertilisers, waste taxes and a land rent tax. In doing this, government should ensure that the impact of this on people with low incomes should not be negative.

- Successfully introduce the proposed carbon tax and investigate the Cap and Share approach as advocated by Comhar and Feasta among others.

Develop a fairer taxation system
- Standard rate all discretionary tax expenditures.

- Adjust tax credits and the USC so that the minimum wage returns to being out of the tax net.

- Make tax credits refundable.

- Ensure that individualisation in the income tax system is done in a fair and equitable manner.

- Integrate the taxation and social welfare systems.

- Begin to monitor and report tax levels (personal and corporate) in terms of effective tax rates.

- Develop policies which allow taxation on wealth to be increased.

- Ensure that the distribution of all changes in indirect taxes discriminate positively in favour of those with lower incomes.

- Adopt policies to simplify the taxation system.

- Poverty-proof all budget tax packages to ensure that tax changes do not further widen the gap between those with low income and the better off.

3.3 Work

> **CORE POLICY OBJECTIVE: WORK**
> To ensure that all people have access to meaningful work

The past three years have seen Ireland return to the phenomenon of widespread unemployment. Despite the attention given to the banking and fiscal collapse, the transition from near full employment to high unemployment has been the real characteristic of this recession. The implications for people, families, social cohesion and the exchequer's finances have been serious. CSO data and economic forecasts for the remainder of 2011 indicate that unemployment will stabilise at an annual rate of just over 14 per cent of the labour force for 2011 having been 4.6 per cent in 2007. There can be little doubt that we have entered a very challenging period where high levels of long-term unemployment once again become a characteristic of Irish society.

Having first reviewed the evolution of this situation, this section of the *Socio-Economic Review* considers the implications and challenges which arise for Government and society. We also review the impact on various sectors of the working-age population before outlining a series of proposals for responding to this unemployment crisis. Finally, we conclude the chapter by considering the narrowness of how we consider and measure the concept of 'work'.

The labour force
The recent dramatic turnaround in the labour market contrasts with the fact that one of the major achievements of the last twenty years had been the increase in employment and the reduction in unemployment, especially long-term unemployment. In 1991 there were 1,155,900 people employed in Ireland. That figure increased by almost one million to peak at 2,146,000 in mid-2007; during early 2006 the employment figure exceeded two million for the first time in the history of the state. Overall, the size of the Irish labour force has expanded significantly and today equals over 2.12 million people, almost one million more than in 1991 (see chart 3.3.1).

However, during the past two years emigration has returned resulting in a decline in the labour force (first recently arrived migrants returned home, then native Irish began to leave) employment has fallen and unemployment has dramatically increased. CSO figures indicate that during the first quarter of 2009 the numbers employed fell below two million and by late 2010 they had fallen further to reach 1.82m workers (CSO, 2011:9).

Chart 3.3.1: The Numbers of People in the Labour Force and Employed in Ireland, 1991-2010.

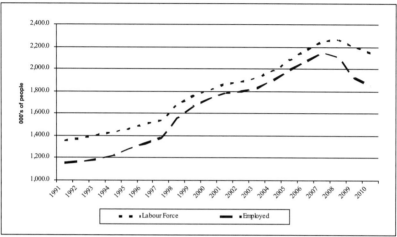

Source: CSO, QNHS various editions

The numbers unemployed

At the outset it is important to outline what the term 'unemployment' means. There are two measurement sources often quoted, the *Quarterly National Household Survey* (QNHS) and the *Live Register*. The former is considered the official and most accurate measure of unemployment although it appears only four times a year unlike the monthly live register data.

The CSO's QNHS unemployment data use the definition of 'unemployment' supplied by the International Labour Office (ILO). It lists as unemployed only those people who, in the week before the survey, were unemployed *and* available to take up a job *and* had taken specific steps in the preceding four weeks to find employment. Any person who was employed for at least *one hour* is classed as employed. By contrast, the live register counts everybody 'signing-on' and includes part-time employees (those who work up to three days a week), those working but on short weeks, seasonal and casual employees entitled to Unemployment Assistance or Benefit.

As chart 3.3.2 shows, the period from 1993 was one of decline in unemployment. During mid-2001 Irish unemployment reached its lowest level at 3.6 per cent of the labour force. Since then the international recession and domestic economic crisis have brought about increases in the rates. During 2006 unemployment exceeded 100,000 for the first time since mid-1999 with a total of 104,800 people recorded as unemployed in mid 2006.

Chart 3.3.2: The Numbers of Unemployed and Long-Term Unemployed in Ireland, 1991-2010.

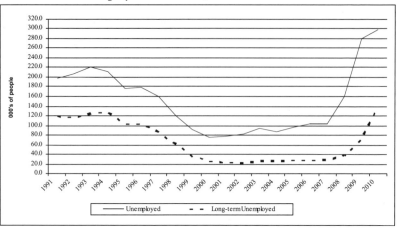

Source: CSO, QNHS various editions

While QNHS figures for early 2011 will not be available until mid-2011, table 3.3.1 gives some indication of the transformation that occurred between 2007 and late 2010. In that period both the numbers in the labour force and the numbers employed fell. Unemployment increased by almost 195,000 people bringing the unemployment rate up from 4.6 per cent to just over 14 per cent. By late 2010 almost 300,000 people were unemployed. The table also reports the rapid growth in the number of long-term unemployed (unemployed for more than 12 months). The CSO data report that there are now over 150,000 people in long-term unemployment and that this figure has doubled in one year; simply given the current crisis many of those who entered unemployment in 2007 and 2008 have remained unemployed for more than 12 months and have therefore become long-term unemployed. For the first time on record, the late 2010 figures indicated that long-term unemployment accounted for more than 50 per cent of the unemployed. It is expected that this figure will rise further, towards 200,000, during 2011.

Table 3.3.1: Labour Force Data, 2007 - 2010				
	Q3 2007	Q3 2008	Q3 2009	Q4 2010
Labour Force	2,253,100	2,266,600	2,202,300	2,122,200
In Employment	2,149,800	2,107,100	1,922,400	1,823,200
Unemployed	103,300	159,400	279,800	299,000
of whom LT Unemp	28,800	38,100	71,400	153,900
Unemployment Rate	4.6	7.0	12.7	14.1
LT Unemployment Rate	1.3	1.7	3.2	7.3

Source: CSO, QNHS March 2011
Note: LT = Long Term (12 months or more)

The *Live Register*

While the live register is not an accurate measure of unemployment it is a useful barometer of the nature and pace of change in employment and unemployment. Increases suggest a combination of more people unemployed, more people on reduced working weeks and consequently reductions in the availability of work hours to the labour force. Table 3.3.2 shows the number of people signing on the live register increased rapidly across 2008-2010. By January 2011 the numbers signing-on the live register had increased more than 240 per cent from three years earlier.

Table 3.3.2: Numbers on the Live Register (unadjusted), Jan 2008 - Jan 2011				
Year	Month	Males	Females	Total
2008	January	116,200	65,300	181,400
	May	130,700	71,100	201,800
	September	156,100	84,200	240,200
	December	194,600	95,400	290,000
2009	January	220,400	105,900	326,300
	May	265,500	128,700	394,100
	September	278,000	141,900	419,900
	December	282,900	140,700	423,600
2010	January	291,600	145,300	436,900
	May	290,400	147,500	437,900
	September	289,800	152,600	442,400
	December	288,800	148,300	437,100
2011	January	292,000	150,700	442,700

Source: CSO *Live Register*, February 2010 and March 2011

Youth unemployment

While the increase in unemployment has been spread across people of all ages and sectors, table 3.3.3 highlights the very rapid increase on the live register of those aged less than 25 years. Previous experiences, in Ireland and elsewhere, have found that many of those under 25 and over 55 find it challenging to return to employment after a period of unemployment. This highlights the danger of the major increases in long-term unemployment and suggests a major commitment to retraining and re-skilling will be required. In the long-run Irish society can ill afford a return to the long-term unemployment problems of the 1980s. In the short-run the new-unemployed will add to the numbers living on low-income in Ireland and will impact on future poverty figures.

Table 3.3.3: Persons under 25 yrs on the Live Register, Jan 2008 - Jan 2011

Month and Year	Numbers	Month and Year	Numbers
January 2008	36,900	December 2009	84,400
May 2008	42,700	January 2010	85,900
September 2008	53,700	May 2010	85,600
December 2008	62,000	September 2010	88,700
January 2009	70,300	December 2010	81,300
May 2009	83,900	January 2011	82,200
September 2009	89,800	February 2011	82,100

Source: CSO *Live Register*, March 2011

Responding to the unemployment crisis

The scale of these increases are enormous. However, it is crucial that Government, commentators and society in general remember that each of these numbers represents people who are experiencing dramatic and, in many cases, unexpected turmoil in their and their families' lives. As Irish society comes to terms with the enormity of this issue, this perspective should remain central.

In responding to this situation *Social Justice Ireland* believes that the Government should:
- Resource the upskilling of those who are unemployed and at risk of becoming unemployed through integrating training and labour market programmes.
- Maintain a sufficient number of active labour market programme places available to those who are unemployed.

- Adopt policies to address the worrying trend of youth unemployment. In particular, these should include education and literacy initiatives as well as retraining schemes.
- Recognise that many of the unemployed are skilled professionals who require appropriate support other than training.
- Prioritise initiatives that strengthen social infrastructure such as the school building programme and the social housing programme.
- Resource a targeted re-training scheme for those made unemployed from the construction industry in recognition of the fact that this industry is never likely to recover to the level of employment it had in recent years.
- Recognise the scale of the evolving long-term unemployment problem and adopt targeted policies to begin to address this.
- Ensure that the social welfare system is administered such that there is minimal delays in paying the newly unemployed the social welfare benefits to which they are entitled.
- Reverse the Budget 2011 cut of 15 per cent (15,410 places) to the FAS allocation for training the unemployed as indicated in the *Programme for Government*.

Part Time Job Opportunities Programme

In our pre-Budget 2011 *Policy Briefing* (Social Justice Ireland, 2010:10) we outlined a proposal for a *Part Time Job Opportunities Programme*. We proposed that the government introduce a new programme to ensure real employment at the going hourly rate for the job is available to 100,000 people currently long-term unemployed. Participation must be voluntary and the scheme should be modelled on the *Part-Time Job Opportunities Programme* that was piloted in the 1994-1998 period.[55] Details of that pilot programme are outlined in the box below.

The proposed programme:
- Would create 100,000 part-time jobs for unemployed people;
- Paid at the going rate for the job;
- Participants working the number of hours required to earn the equivalent of their social welfare payment and a small top-up
- Up to a maximum of 19.5 hours a week.
- Access on a voluntary basis only;
- Jobs would be created in the public sector and the community and voluntary sector;

---

[55] The current Directors of *Social Justice Ireland* led this pilot programme.

- Participants would be remunerated principally through the reallocation of social welfare payments.
- Working on these jobs participants would be allowed to take up other paid employment in their spare time without incurring loss of benefits and would be liable to tax in the normal way if their income was sufficient to bring them into the tax net.

Social Justice Ireland believes that a Part-Time Job Opportunities programme should be established along the lines of the programme piloted in the 1994-1998 period. Additional funding of €150m would be required and the funding currently being spent on social welfare payments to participants on this programme should be switched to their new employer.

Part Time Job Opportunities (PTJO) Pilot Programme, 1994-98

The early 1990s saw high unemployment levels in Ireland and little prospect of jobs being available for some time even though the economy was beginning to recover. Jobless growth was the reality. A proposal made by the current Directors of Social Justice Ireland was formally adopted by the Irish Government and announced in Budget 1994.

The proposal sought to create real part-time jobs in the community and voluntary sector principally. Long-term unemployed people could access these jobs on a voluntary basis. They were paid the going rate for the job and they worked the number of hours required to earn the equivalent of their social welfare payment with a small top up. The going rate for the job was agreed with the relevant trade unions and employers.

This programme was piloted in Finglas/Blanchardstown, Co. Laois, Waterford City, Four towns in South Tipperary (Clonmel, Carrick-on-Suir, Cashel and Tipperary Town), Co. Kerry and the offshore islands. It created 1,000 part-time jobs in community and voluntary organisations in those pilot areas within six months of its establishment. These jobs were sustained throughout the pilot period. More than 500 of the original participants departed to take up full-time employment or full-time education during those years and all were replaced by new participants.

The market economy is unable to provide anywhere near to the number of jobs required to reduce unemployment anytime soon. This programme contributes to Social Justice Ireland's view that public policy should change so that 1) it recognises that people have a right to work; 2) that unemployed people should not be forced to spend their lives doing nothing when jobs don't exist; and 3) that all meaningful work should be recognised.

Work and people with disabilities

The results of the 2004 QNHS special module on disability revealed that of all persons aged between 15 and 64, 10.9 per cent indicated that they had a longstanding health problem or disability (CSO, 2004). This equates to 298,300 people in Ireland, of whom 155,800 were male and 142,500 were female. Of those individuals only 37 per cent (110,800) were in employment. This is a figure considerably below the participation rate of the overall population which stood at 61 per cent. Furthermore, of those employed approximately one-quarter worked part-time while the remaining three-quarters were in full-time employment.[56]

This low rate of employment among people with a disability is of concern. Apart from restricting their participation in society it also ties them into state dependent low-income situations. Therefore it is not surprising that Ireland's poverty figures reveal that people who are ill or have a disability are the group with a very high risk of poverty (see table 3.1.4). *Social Justice Ireland* believes that further effort should be made to reduce the impediments faced by people with a disability in achieving employment. In particular consideration should be given to reforming the current situation where many such people face losing their benefits, in particular their medical card, when they take up employment. This situation ignores the additional costs faced by people with a disability in pursuing their day-to-day lives. For many people with disabilities the opportunity to work is denied to them and they are trapped in unemployment, poverty or both.

Some progress was made in Budget 2005 to increase supports intended to help people with disabilities access employment. However, sufficient progress has not been made. New policies, including that outlined above, need to be adopted if this issue is to be addressed successfully and is all the more relevant given the growing employment challenges of the past two years.

Asylum seekers and work

Social Justice Ireland remains very disappointed that the government continues to reject the proposal to recognise the right to work of asylum seekers. We along with others advocated that where government fails to meet its own stated objective of processing asylum applications in six months, the right to work should be automatically granted to asylum seekers. Detaining people for an unnecessarily prolonged period in such an excluded state is completely unacceptable.

---

[56] Census 2006 found comparable results, reporting that 9.3 per cent of the population had a disability – 393,785 people (CSO, 2007:13).

Recognising asylum seekers right to work would assist in alleviating poverty and social exclusion among one of Ireland's most vulnerable groups.

The need to recognise all work
A major question raised by the current labour-market situation concerns assumptions underpinning culture and policy making in this area. One such assumption concerns the priority given to paid employment over other forms of work. Most people recognise that a person can work very hard even though they do not have a conventional job. Much of the work carried out in the community and in the voluntary sector fits under this heading. So too does much of the work done in the home. *Social Justice Ireland*'s support for the introduction of a basic income system comes, in part, from a belief that all work should be recognised and supported.

The need to recognise voluntary work has been acknowledged in the Government White Paper, *Supporting Voluntary Activity* (Department of Social, Community and Family Affairs, 2000). The report was prepared to mark the UN International Year of the Volunteer 2001 by Government and representatives of numerous voluntary organisations in Ireland. The report made a series of recommendations to assist in the future development and recognition of voluntary activity throughout Ireland. The national social partnership agreement *Towards 2016* also contains commitments in this area. In that agreement the Government undertakes to:

> ... continue to develop policies on volunteering arising from the package of measures initiated in February 2005. A key principle underlying the Government's approach is that volunteering finds meaning and expression at a local level and that supports and funding should seek, as far as possible, to recognise this reality. The Government remains committed to further developing policy to support volunteering, drawing on the experience in delivering these measures and informed by the recommendations of the Task Force on Active Citizenship (*Towards 2016*:71).

An insight into this issue was also provided by a report presented to the Joint Oireachtas Committee on Arts, Sport, Tourism, Community, Rural and Gaeltacht Affairs. It established that the cost to the state of replacing the 475,000 volunteers working for charitable organisations would be a minimum of €205 million and could cost up to €485 million per year.

Social Justice Ireland believes that government should more formally recognise and acknowledge all forms of work. We believe that everybody has a right to work, i.e.

to contribute to his or her own development and that of the community and the wider society. However, we believe that policy making in this area should not be exclusively focused on job creation. Policy should recognise that w*ork* and a *job* are not always the same thing.

The Work of Carers

The work of Ireland's carers receives minimal recognition in spite of the essential role their work plays in society. According to the Carers Association people caring full-time for the elderly and people with disabilities are saving the state approximately €2.5 billion a year in costs which it would otherwise have to bear. In its Pre-Budget Submission in 2010 the Carers Association calculated there were 160,917 carers in Ireland providing 3,724,434 hours of care which was valued at more than €2.5bn.

Results from the 2006 Census give similar indications. It found that 4.8 per cent of the population aged over 15 provided some care for sick or disabled family members or friends on an unpaid basis. This figure equates to almost 161,000 people. The dominant caring role played by women was highlighted by the fact that 100,214 (62.25 per cent) of these care providers were female.[57] When assessed by length of time, the Census found that almost 41,000 people provide unpaid help to ill or disabled family members and friends for 43 hours a week or more, a working week considerably in excess of the standard working week for paid workers (CSO, 2007: 119-121).

Social Justice Ireland welcomes the ongoing examination of this area by the Oireachtas Joint Committee on Social and Family Affairs. We also welcomed the commitment in *Towards 2016* contained a welcome commitment to develop a National Carers Strategy. However, the March 2009 announcement by Government that they were to abandon the finalisation and publication of this strategy is shortsighted. We strongly urge the new Government to reverse this decision and complete the preparation of the strategy. It is crucial that policy reforms be introduced to reduce the financial and emotional pressures on carers. In particular these should focus on addressing the poverty experienced by many carers and their families alongside increasing the provision of respite care for carers and for those for whom they care. In that context, the twenty-four hour responsibilities of carers contrast with the recent improvements in employment legislation setting limits on working-hours of people in paid employment.

---

[57] A 2008 ESRI study entitled '*Gender Inequalities in Time Use*' reached similar conclusions (McGinnity and Russell, 2008:36, 70).

In conclusion, we outline key priorities with regard to work.

Key Priorities on Work
- Adopt the following policy positions in responding to the recent rapid increase in unemployment:
  - Resource the upskilling of those who are unemployed and at risk of becoming unemployed through integrating training and labour market programmes.
  - Maintain a sufficient number of active labour market programme places available to those who are unemployed.
  - Adopt policies to address the worrying trend of youth unemployment. In particular, these should include education and literacy initiatives as well as retraining schemes.
  - Recognise that many of the unemployed are skilled professionals who require appropriate support other than training.
  - Prioritise initiatives that strengthen social infrastructure such as the school building programme and the social housing programme.
  - Resource a targeted re-training scheme for those made unemployed from the construction industry in recognition of the fact that this industry is never likely to recover to the level of employment it had in recent years.
  - Recognise the scale of the evolving long-term unemployment problem and adopt targeted policies to begin to address this.
  - Ensure that the social welfare system is administered such that there is minimal delays in paying the newly unemployed the social welfare benefits to which they are entitled.
  - Reverse the Budget 2011 cut of 15 per cent (15,410 places) to the FAS allocation for training the unemployed as indicated in the *Programme for Government*.
- Introduce a *Part Time Job Opportunities Programme* to create 100,000 positions for long-term unemployed people.
- Funding for programmes supporting community should be expanded to meet the growing pressures arising from the current economic downturn.
- A new programme should be put in place targeting those who are very long-term unemployed (i.e. 5+ years).

- Seek at all times to ensure that new jobs have reasonable pay rates and adequately resource the inspectorate.
- As part of the process of addressing the working poor issue, reform the taxation system to make tax credits refundable.
- Develop employment-friendly income-tax policies which ensure that no unemployment traps exist. Policies should ease the transition from unemployment to employment.
- Adopt policies to address the obstacles facing women when they return to the labour force. These should focus on care initiatives, employment flexibility and the provision of information and training.
- Reduce the impediments faced by people with a disability in achieving employment. In particular address the current situation where many face losing their benefits when they take up employment.
- Recognise the right to work of all asylum seekers whose application for asylum is at least six months old (and who are not entitled to take up employment).
- Recognise work that is not paid employment. Everybody has a right to work, i.e. to contribute to his or her own development and that of the community and the wider society. This, however, should not be confined to job creation. *Work* and a *job* are not the same thing.
- Request the CSO to conduct an annual survey to discover the value of all unpaid work in the country (including community and voluntary work and work in the home). Publish the results of this survey as soon as they become available.
- Give greater recognition to the work carried out by carers in Ireland and introduce policy reforms to reduce the financial and emotional pressures on carers. In particular these should focus on addressing the poverty experienced by many carers and their families alongside increasing the provision of respite care for carers and for those for whom they care.
- Expand the Rural Social Scheme.

3.4 Public Services

> **CORE POLICY OBJECTIVE: PUBLIC SERVICES**
> To ensure the provision of, and access to, a level of public services regarded as acceptable by Irish society generally

Increasingly Ireland is being identified as a country whose public services are underdeveloped. Given that Ireland is not a poor country, this is a situation that is far from acceptable. Because poorer people rely on public services more than those who are better off, it is they who are most acutely affected by this shortage.

This issue was examined by the National Economic and Social Forum (NESF). In its report entitled *Improving the Delivery of Quality Public Services* it recommended a series of developments (2006:112-117). *Social Justice Ireland* believes that Government should implement the approach for the delivery of public services outlined in the NESF report.

We address public services over this section and the next three sections on housing & accommodation, healthcare and education. This section assesses public transport, library services, financial services, information and communications technology, telecommunications, free legal aid, sports facilities and regulation.[58]

Public transport
Transport remains a most problematic area. Bottlenecks throughout the country are adding to the difficulty and cost experienced by everybody in conducting their lives; although some of these have partially 'improved' in parallel with the recent recession. The rapid increase in the number of cars over the last decade has also added to problems of environmental destruction.[59]

Transport policy should seek to combine easy access, affordable, integrated and high-quality public transport with the high costs of ownership and use of private vehicles. While it may be necessary to re-schedule some public transport initiatives that had been planned as part of the National Development Plan it is crucial that Government give priority to public transport over private transport in allocating capital funding.

---
[58] Issues specifically related to the provision of public services in rural areas are examined in section 3.11.
[59] The environmental impact of cars is discussed in 3.10(b).

Continued support is also required for the development of public transport schemes in rural Ireland. For such a policy to be credible it must be comprehensive, adequately resourced and enhance the current provision. These schemes significantly increase the quality of life of those living in remote rural areas, particularly older people. The Rural Transport Initiative (RTI) has been very successful to date. However, increased funding which has been promised, is required if the full potential of the RTI is to be realised.[60]

It should also be recognised that public transport generally has a long way to go before it reaches the levels usually associated with a developed society. We urge Government to honour commitments already entered into and to implement a comprehensive, integrated and effective public transport strategy in consultation with stake-holders including the community and voluntary sector which has a vital contribution to make and role to play in local and rural transport services.

Library services
Libraries play an important role in Irish society. According to the Library Council there are over 14 million visits to public libraries annually. The Local Government Management Services Board (LGMSB) indicated that in 2007 on average 20.5 per cent of the population in each local authority area was a registered member of a public library; a figure corresponding to approximately 870,000 members (2008:29-30). They also reported that in 2008 there were on average 3.2 visits per person to libraries and an average of 3.13 books were issued per head of population (2009:29-32). These membership figures alone do not capture the increasing level of usage by adults of the reference, information and other services in public libraries, such as local history and exhibitions. Reflecting this, a 2003 survey by TNS (MRBI) found that 36 per cent of the adult population had used a public library recently. The same survey also found that 68 per cent of adults were or had been a member of a public library (Library Council, 2004). Clearly, public libraries play a strong and central role in Irish society. *Social Justice Ireland* believes that as part of our commitment to providing a continuum of education provision from early childhood to third level and throughout the life-cycle, Ireland needs to recognise the potential that the library service offers.

Central to such developments is information and easy access to this information. Coupled with information is the need for easy access to modern means of communication. Libraries are obvious centres with potential to support these objectives. To play this potential role, expansion of the library service is essential.

---
[60] The RTI is addressed in more detail in section 3.11.

Recent budgetary policy has been neglectful of this important role with significant cuts in recent Budgets. We regret this move and call for a sustained substantial investment in these facilities. In the long-term a failure to resource this service properly is short-sighted.

Financial Services

Financial exclusion refers to a household's difficulty accessing and using financial services. A 2011 study by the ESRI examined four dimensions of financial exclusion: access to a bank current account, access to credit, ability to save, and access to housing insurance (Russell et al, 2011). Of these, access to a bank current account was considered the most fundamental, as exclusion from basic banking services means that households can face difficulties carrying out everyday transactions such as paying bills, receiving earnings or welfare benefits, transferring funds, and purchasing goods and services.

The results of the research highlighted some serious deficiencies in the ability of Irish households to access these basic financial services. In 2008 it was found that 20 per cent of Irish households did not have a bank current account a figure that is almost three times higher than the average for the EU15. The proportion without a bank current account rose to 40 per cent among those with low education qualifications, 38 per cent in households in the bottom 20 per cent of the income distribution, 50 per cent among local authority tenants, 52 per cent among those who are ill or disabled and 27 per cent among those aged over 55 years (2011:126-127).

The research highlights the need for policy to encourage financial institutions, such as the banks and the Post Office, to provide people with easy to access and affordable basic bank accounts and financial facilities. This is an area where targeted action by the Department for Social Protection could have a speedy and significant impact.

Information and communications technology

Increasingly the ability to use information and communications technology (ICT) is becoming a central requirement in modern society. The phenomenon of a technological divide is becoming evident. In particular it is of concern that a number of young people, including early school-leavers (many of whom are now unemployed), have little or no skill in ICT. Consequently initiatives are necessary to improve information technology provision in schools, as well as to further increase its availability in areas such as public libraries and community centres.

While progress has been made, particularly as regards public libraries, Government needs to show greater commitment to this area.

It also needs to address the issue of including everybody in the information society. In addressing this issue it is crucial that priority is given to ensuring access is available to those who currently cannot afford the market costs. Ignoring this will ensure that the "digital divide" will widen social exclusion. More, targeted, resources are needed.

Telecommunications
Three issues arise within the topic of telecommunications. First, we are concerned by a request in March 2003, and repeated on a number of occasions since, by Eircom, Ireland's principal telecommunications company, that they be relieved of their universal public service obligation to provide a telephone for every house in the country. Instead they proposed sharing the annual cost of this obligation with other telecommunications companies and with consumers. The impact of such a change would be sizeable on the poor and on those living in rural areas. Both would experience an increase in the proportions of their incomes needed to be spent to ensure they had access at home to a telephone land line. We welcome the fact that this change was not introduced; however the fact that it was requested raises concerns that an attempt to revisit this issue may occur in the years ahead. Any such change which would impose additional costs on people who are already isolated from society, physically and financially, should be resisted. In considering any future decisions of this nature the Communications Regulator (ComReg) should take these societal points into account.

A second issue in the telecommunications area concerns one of the consequences of the growth in mobile phone usage over recent years. This has seen a decline in usage of public payphones. In response to this a large number of these payphones have been decommissioned. We urge care in any further decision to remove more payphones.

Finally, *Social Justice Ireland* believes it is important to explore technical options to address the requirements of people living in underserved areas, and remote rural areas. We believe that the use of technological advances offers a real method of addressing many of the inequities that exist in the allocation of, and access to, information and telecommunications resources. One obvious goal of public policy should be to ensure nationwide coverage for high-speed broadband and mobile phones. The ongoing failure in this context means that particular areas, especially in rural Ireland, are particularly disadvantaged.

A New and Fairer Ireland

Free legal aid

Citizens depend on the law and associated institutions to defend their rights and civic entitlements. A central element of this system, particularly for those with limited incomes, is the free legal aid system. The Legal Aid Board provides civic legal aid to people with incomes of less than €18,000 per annum; recipients contribute a nominal sum. In 2008 21,000 people availed of legal aid and the Board provided aid and advice in 17,900 cases. These figures include the Board's work on refugee legal services. The Board have also reported that waiting times to receive aid can be up to four months.

Social Justice Ireland believes that free legal aid is an important public service. In the current economic climate, with rising unemployment and decreasing income, it is likely that the demand on the Legal Aid Board will grow. The provision of, and adequate support for, this service is a basic requirement of governance. Government should continue to support and enhance this service.

Sports facilities

An insight into the role played by sport in Irish society was provided in an ESRI report entitled *The Social and Economic Value of Sport in Ireland* (Delaney and Fahey, 2005). Its findings indicated that: approximately 400,000 adults (15 per cent of the adult population) volunteer for sport in some way each year; 20 per cent of the adult population play sport; 30 per cent of adults are members of sports clubs; and the economic value of sport is between 1-2 per cent of GNP. In reaching its conclusions the report notes that current government policy commitments to promote social capital need to take account of the social aspects of sport and their potential contribution to the further development of social capital and volunteering in Ireland. Similarly it finds that there should be greater dialogue between those concerned with sports policy and those concerned with policy on social capital and volunteering; their common interest in sport should be recognised and explored; and their efforts to support social capital and volunteering should be co-coordinated.

However, recent studies have also indicated a declining level of participation by Irish people, and in particular young people, in sports activities. Long term this may have significant health consequences. There is a special case to be made for poor areas, most of which have limited, if any, sports facilities. The National Sports Council has developed a creative initiative of local sports partnerships. Some of these are working effectively and attempting to address this problem. Further funding for local sports partnerships should be made available. Given their huge potential such funding would be most worthwhile.

The national agreement, *Towards 2016*, contained a number of initiatives relating to sport and sports facilities which the new Government should implement. These include commitments to: (i) increasing support for sports infrastructure and sporting organisations recognising that sport has the potential to be a driver for social change and that targeting specific groups can address issues of exclusion and inequality; (ii) promoting sport in education settings; and (iii) achieving the Irish Sport Council target to increase by 3 per cent the numbers of children taking part in sport. *Social Justice Ireland* supports each of these commitments and looks forwards to seeing the implementation of various initiatives aimed at fulfilling them.

Consideration also needs to be given to the way in which exchequer funds are allocated towards sport. We note a recent ESRI study which concluded that public expenditure is skewed towards elite sport at the expense of grassroots activity, is too focused on new facilities and is biased towards traditional team games (Lunn, 2008). As we develop sports policy in the context of increasingly scarce public expenditure resources, *Social Justice Ireland* believes that more in-depth consideration needs to be given to how we maximise the returns to these investments. In many cases simple schemes to encourage participation and use of existing sports facilities are required; certainly these are currently lacking.

Regulation
Regulatory policy in Ireland has failed in many areas and requires significant reform over the next few years. This has been clearly demonstrated in the problems that have emerged in the financial services sector. A serious re-think is required to ensure that regulation plays a stronger and far more effective role to ensure there is no repetition of these huge failures.

Central to our opinion on how regulation should develop is the view that all regulators, be they currently in existence or established in the future, should be required to consider the societal impact of any reforms they propose before they are implemented. They should also have the capacity to monitor what is happening and to act effectively and quickly when negative impacts occur. There are a range of impacts that flow from decisions taken by people in the various areas where regulation applies. Regulation should be judged on how its outcome impacts on social, cultural and sustainability issues in society as well as on the economy. Implementing regulation with this as its central aim would certainly achieve better regulation for all. It would also ensure consistently better outcomes for consumers. Such an approach would have prevented the failure of the regulatory process in the current banking crisis.

We also believe that there should be solid and justifiable reasons for introducing regulation. It should not be introduced just to create choice/competition within the market. For example, to achieve competition in the electricity market the electricity regulator increased the price of electricity. While this may achieve competition we question the benefit to people. Furthermore assessment mechanisms should be established to allow an analysis of regulation pre and post its implementation. Central to such an assessment procedure should be an examination of its societal impacts. We also believe that, as part of the assessment procedure, inputs should be sought from interested parties including the community and voluntary sector.

A further important aspect is the need to consider the impact of regulation within the context of regional policy. Cross-subsidisation issues, in postal or electrical services, are important to retain equity between rural and urban dwellers. A further challenge for regulatory authorities must be to retain this inter-regional equity.

Regulation and regulatory law has profoundly failed Ireland in recent years. It should be framed in such a way as to ensure that it is effective, timely, accessible and interpretable. Currently regulatory law is complex and in many cases requires those being regulated to divert a considerable quantity of resources to keep up with it. Complex regulation will also make it difficult for interested parties to actively participate in the pre and post regulation assessment mechanisms. *Social Justice Ireland* believes it is important that where regulation has been judged to be a failure, government should reform it at the earliest opportunity.

Key Priorities for Public Services

- **Focus policy on ensuring that there is provision of, and access to, a level of public services regarded as acceptable by Irish society generally.**

- **Target funding strategies to ensure that far greater priority is given to providing an easy-access, affordable, integrated and high-quality public transport system. This should include adequate support for the Rural Transport Initiative which increases significantly the quality of life of those living in remote rural areas, particularly older people and women.**

- Support the further development of library services throughout the country including provision of open-access information technology.

- Adopt policies to encourage financial institutions, such as the banks and the Post Office, to provide people with easy to access and affordable basic bank accounts and financial facilities.

- Give more in-depth consideration to how public funds are used to encourage sport and sporting activity. In many cases simple schemes to encourage participation and use of existing sports facilities are required; certainly these are currently lacking.

- Adopt further information-technology programmes to increase the skills of schoolchildren, early school-leavers, unemployed and older people.

- Take action to address the huge failures identified in the regulatory process as clearly identified by the crisis in banking and financial services. This process should ensure that all types of regulation are judged against how they impact on social, cultural and sustainability issues within society as well as on the economy. Implementing regulation with this balance as its central aim would achieve better regulation for all.

- Ensure equality of access across all public services.

3.5 Housing and Accommodation

> **CORE POLICY OBJECTIVE:**
> **HOUSING & ACCOMMODATION**
> To ensure that adequate and appropriate accommodation is available for all people and to develop an equitable system for allocating resources within the housing sector

Housing and accommodation policy

Issues concerning housing and accommodation have had a major profile in recent years. Most of that profile, however, has been concerned with the provision and cost of privately owned accommodation and more recently the challenges associated with the large surplus housing stock that has appeared throughout the country on foot of foolish and reckless speculative investments and the economic collapse. A comparison of European housing tenures illustrates the existence of three main models of housing provision: an owner-occupier sector, a rental sector and a social housing sector. Table 3.5.1 gives details of how Irish tenure patterns have changed over time using data from various Censuses of Population. In 2006 77.2 per cent of households were owner-occupiers, a figure which gives Ireland one of the highest rates of owner occupation in the EU (CSO, 2009:61; 2003:55). Compared to other countries Irish housing policy supports owner occupation to the detriment of all other forms of housing tenure; a feature which reflects the policy choices of government.

Table 3.5.1: Nature of Occupancy of Private Households, Ireland 1961-2006

Year	Owner-occupied	Rented	Other
1961	59.8%	35.6%	4.6%
1971	68.8%	28.9%	2.3%
1981	74.7%	22.6%	2.6%
1991	80.0%	17.9%	2.1%
2002	79.8%	18.5%	1.7%
2006	77.2%	21.3%	1.5%

Source: CSO (2009:61)

Ireland's level of home ownership reflects the high value Irish people put on owning their own homes. It also reflects public policy which provided a variety of tax incentives to those who have the resources to invest in housing. Since the 1970s it has been the policy of successive Irish governments to subsidise owner occupation heavily. This has been achieved by the abolition of local rates on residential property and the subsequent failure to implement a system of residential property tax. More recently investment policies have been introduced that favour investment in residential development, for example investors in urban renewal schemes stood to gain over 419 per cent on their investment (Bacon, 1998). These policy developments, combined with policies of mortgage-interest tax relief and very favourable tenant purchase schemes have resulted in an extremely high level of home ownership. Owner-occupiers make up 77.2 per cent of the Irish households – this is considerably higher than the EU average of 63.4 per cent. Government housing policy has resulted in a housing system that is not tenure neutral and which has led to the residualisation of the rental sector, both public and private.

The down-the-line effect of this policy is the lack of adequate accommodation for larger and larger numbers of households. The value of home ownership should be discussed in the light of present realities. These include: the excessive prices paid for houses and for land rezoned for housing in recent years and the subsequent phenomenon of negative-equity and instability in the financial sector; the burden of mortgage repayments especially on young families; the ghettoisation of local authority housing because private owners object to developments which may seem to devalue their properties; difficulties in providing suitable accommodation for special groups including Travellers, homeless people, asylum-seekers, young offenders and drug abusers.

The housing crisis
During most of the last decade improved levels of economic growth combined with low interest rates resulted in high levels of housing inflation. This in turn resulted in a crisis in housing provision in both the public and the private sectors. In the private sector this crisis was evident from the rapid increase in house prices and from the severe difficulties currently being experienced by those who pay inflated prices for their homes (difficulties that are likely to persist for these households for most of the next decade). In the public sector the demand (waiting lists) for social housing has remained high and is increasing.

Housing: a new philosophy
A series of publications by the economist Professor PJ Drudy of Trinity College have offered an interesting new approach to how Irish society views housing. In his paper at a 2005 *Social Policy Conference*, in a co-authored book with Michael Punch

A New and Fairer Ireland

-entitled *Out of Reach* (2005) – and in a chapter in the *Social Policy in Ireland* book (Drudy, 2006) he has outlined these views.

The essence of Professor Drudy's proposal is to view housing as a home rather than as a market commodity. In his conference paper Professor Drudy stated that we should "place the emphasis on housing as a home – shelter, a place to stay, to feel secure, to build a base, find an identity and participate in a community and society". Therefore he continued: "housing thus becomes a central feature of 'development' – a process not simply comprising increases in economic growth, but containing positive actions to improve the quality of life and wellbeing for all" (2005: 44).

In concluding his paper, Drudy suggested that Irish society now needs to address "a fundamental philosophical question: is it the purpose of a housing system to provide investment, speculative or capital gains for those with the necessary resources or should the critical aim be to provide a home as a right for all citizens?" (2004: 46). In his view it is time now for Ireland to move away from seeing housing as a commodity to be traded on the market like any other tradable commodity; and to accept the latter opinion that views housing as a social requirement like health services or education.

Social Justice Ireland strongly welcomes and endorses these views. Had society adopted this approach over the past decade the Irish economy, and many Irish families, would not be in a precarious financial position. It is now time that we formally incorporate this approach into our national housing policy.

NESC report on housing in Ireland

At the end of 2004 the National Economic and Social Council (NESC) published a major report on housing. A central conclusion of the NESC housing report was that the supply of social housing will have to rise dramatically if the needs of Irish society are to be addressed in the years ahead. The main recommendation of the council on the issue of social housing is outlined in table 3.5.2. It calls on Government to "create an expanded and more flexible stock of social housing - adding in the order of 73,000 permanent social housing units to bring the stock to 200,000 dwellings by 2012 - in a manner that is consistent with other public investment needs and sound public finances" (2004:221).

Table 3.5.2: The role of social housing in Ireland in 2012	
	2012
Total number of dwellings	1,653,000
Social housing as a % of total	12.0
Number of social housing units	200,000
Population of Ireland	4,505,000
Social housing units per thousand	44.4

Source: Data are based on NESC projection (2004:152-153) and CSO (2004:26) projections for 2011 (assumption M1F1).

The figure of 200,000 social housing units had been calculated based on the projected increases in the Irish population over that period and in the context of limited responses to existing social housing needs (e.g. homelessness, community based accommodation for disabled and older persons). The scale of the challenge facing Irish society can be gauged from the fact that at the end of 2004 the total stock of social housing (including units managed by both local authorities and the voluntary and cooperative housing sector) stood at about 127,000.

NESC concluded that to achieve the target of 200,000 units over the eight year period between 2005 and 2012, an annual increase of in excess of 9,000 units is necessary. They also pointed out that an estimated capital investment of €1.4bn a year would be required to achieve a net increase of 73,000 units by 2012. Given the recent decreases in building costs, construction wages and the price of development land the figure is now likely to be considerably lower.

Social Justice Ireland believes that reaching this target is essential if Ireland is to achieve the goal of ensuring that everyone in the country has appropriate accommodation. However, in the current climate we must be careful not to chase simplistic solutions to the crisis through large-scale allocation of surplus housing stock (via NAMA and elsewhere) to local authorities for social housing. If such a model is to be adopted it should be careful to avoid the creating of large clusters of social housing and instead use this opportunity to integrate social housing throughout the housing stock. This may be a difficult solution in the short-run, but it is the better outcome for Ireland in the longer-term.

Waiting lists: how many and for how long?

The most recent assessment of local authority waiting lists, for which results have been published, occurred on the 31st of March 2008 and the results have been published by the Department of Environment, Heritage and Local Government. A further study was carried out in 2010 but its results have yet to be published. The 2008 study found that there was a total of 56,249 households on local-authority housing waiting lists (see table 3.5.3).[61] This figure represents an increase of over 30 per cent since the 2005 assessment. However, since 1996 waiting lists have more than doubled and the 2008 figure indicates that across Ireland about 150,000 people are in need of accommodation. Report from Local Authorities in 2009 and 2010 suggest that these waiting list have increased further as the impact of the recession has driven additional households on to these waiting lists.[62]

Table 3.5.3: The Need for and Supply of Local Authority (LA) Social Housing, 1996- 2008			
Year	Households on LA Waiting Lists	Stock of LA Housing Units	Waiting List as % of Rental Stock
1996	27,427	98,394	28
1999	39,176	99,163	40
2002	48,413	104,688	46
2005	42,946	109,779	39
2008	56,249	118,396	47

Source: Department of the Environment, Heritage and Local Government, *Housing Statistics Bulletin,* various issues.

It is worthwhile examining the composition of this total waiting list figure. Table 3.5.4 shows that in 2008 the largest category of households on the lists was those labelled as being not able to meet costs of existing accommodation. This group accounted for 53 per cent of the waiting list or 29,583 households. Comparing this figure to previous editions of the *Housing Statistics Bulletin* reveals that this figure increased from 34 per cent in 1999 (it reached 44 per cent in 2002) but that it decreased since 2005. A comparison with the 2005 figures also reveals that the other big increase is for those in housing need due to "medical or compassionate grounds" (+6 per cent).

---

[61] The published 2008 figures also included a revision to the figures published for 2005.
[62] A media report, in the Irish Examiner (April 26th, 2010) indicated that the waiting list had risen to 79,337 households by March 31st 2010.

Table 3.5.4: Breakdown of the Local Authority Housing Waiting List by Major Categories of Need, 2005 and 2008

Category of Need	% 2005	No. of Households 2008	% 2008
Homeless	4.5	1,394	3
Travellers	2	1,317	2
Existing accommodation unfit	4	1,757	3
Existing accommodation overcrowded	10	4,805	9
Involuntarily sharing of accommodation	8	4,965	9
Young persons leaving institutional care	0.5	715	1
Medical or compassionate grounds	8	8,059	14
Older persons	4	2,499	4
Disabled or handicapped	1	1,155	2
Not able to meet costs of existing accommodation	58	29,583	53
Total	**100.00**	**56,249**	**100.00**

Source: Calculated from Department of the Environment, Heritage and Local Government, *Housing Statistics Bulletin* (2009:99).

Analysis of the housing statistics also reveals that 46 per cent (25,550) of all those households on the waiting lists consist of single-person households. The majority of those waiting are Irish citizens (77 per cent) while a further 12 per cent are EU-citizens and the remainder are from elsewhere in the world. A further 6,299 individuals on the waiting lists were classified as either refugees or individuals who had been granted permission to remain in the state.

Table 3.5.5 indicates a clear association between being in housing need and low income. It reports household income (unadjusted for household composition) and finds that almost three-quarters of households possess an annual income of less than €15,000. Larger households are likely to have larger incomes (alongside larger living expenses), yet only 5 per cent recorded an income above €25,000.

When the 56,249 households on the 2008 waiting lists are classified by the length of time they have spent on the waiting list the figures reveal that 29 per cent of all households have been waiting for more than three years. A further 20 per cent are on the list for between 2-3 years while 20 per cent are waiting for between 1-2 years. The remaining 31 per cent have been waiting for less than a year.

Table 3.5.5: Breakdown of the Local Authority Housing Waiting List by Household Income, 2008

Household income band	Number of Households	% of Waiting List
Below €10,000	15,841	28
€10,001-€15,000	25,580	45
€15,001-€20,000	7,194	13
€20,001-€25,000	4,918	9
€25,001-€30,000	1,697	3
Over €30,000	1,019	2
Total	56,249	100

Source: Calculated from Department of the Environment, Heritage and Local Government, *Housing Statistics Bulletin* (2009:101).

In the context of all these figures it has to be acknowledged that more progress needs to be made. Achieving that progress requires a greater commitment to providing social housing. Implementing NESC's social housing recommendation (see table 3.5.2) will significantly address this problem and move Ireland closer to achieving *Social Justice Ireland's* core policy objective of ensuring that appropriate accommodation is available for all.

House completions

Table 3.5.6 shows the rate of house completions in the various sectors between 1993 and 2012. 2006 marked a peak in the levels of house completions with over 93,000 units completed. Since then the rate of dwelling completion has rapidly declined and projections suggest that it will decline further in 2011.

In 2009 the vast majority of new houses (80 per cent) were built by the private sector (down from 91 per cent in 2007). Local authorities built 3,362 new homes in 2009. The figures for 2009 also reveal a further growth in the levels of voluntary/non-profit and co-op housing. These organisations built 2,011 dwellings during that year and they now account for over a third of all publicly assisted housing completions. Currently they are managing a stock of approximately 27,000 dwellings. This trend is very welcome and underscores the growing role this sector is playing. *Social Justice Ireland* believes this sector has the capacity to make an even greater contribution to addressing the current housing crisis and that government must give further assistance to facilitating its continued growth.

Housing and Accommodation

Table 3.5.6: House Completions, 1993–2012				
Year	Local Authority Housing	Voluntary/Non Profit Housing	Private Housing	Total
1993	1,200	890	19,301	21,391
1994	2,374	901	23,588	26,863
1995	2,960	1,011	26,604	30,575
1996	2,676	917	30,132	33,725
1997	2,632	756	35,454	38,842
1998	2,771	485	39,093	42,349
1999	2,909	579	43,024	46,512
2000	2,204	951	46,657	49,812
2001	3,622	1,253	47,727	52,602
2002	4,403	1,360	51,932	57,695
2003	4,516	1,617	62,686	68,819
2004	3,539	1,607	71,808	76,954
2005	4,209	1,350	75,398	80,957
2006	3,968	1,240	88,211	93,419
2007	4,986	1,685	71,356	78,027
2008	4,905	1,896	44,923	51,724
2009	3,932	2,011	21,076	26,420
2010★	–	–	–	14,000
2011★	–	–	–	8,000
2012★	–	–	–	10,000

Source: Department of Environment, Heritage and Local Government, *Housing Statistics Bulletins (various editions)*.
Note: ★ figures for 2010-12 are projections as published by AIB (2011)

Table 3.5.7 also shows a welcome development in local authorities' response. The total number of local authority completions plus acquisitions increased substantially to almost 7,000 in 2007, after falling in 2003 and 2004, and progressing slowly or remaining static in 2005 and 2006. The economic crisis curtailed the number of local authority acquisitions in 2008 decreasing the overall annual number once again.

Table 3.5.7: Local Authority Completions and Acquisitions, 1995–2008			
Year	Local Authority Completions	Local Authority Acquisitions	Total
1995	2,960	882	3,842
1996	2,676	897	3,573
1997	2,632	585	3,217
1998	2,771	511	3,282
1999	2,909	804	3,713
2000	2,204	1,003	3,207
2001	3,622	1,400	5,022
2002	4,403	671	5,073
2003	4,516	456	4,972
2004	3,539	971	4,510
2005	4,209	918	5,127
2006	3,968	1,153	5,121
2007	4,986	2,002	6,988
2008	4,905	787	5,692

Source: Department of the Environment, Heritage and Local Government, *Housing Statistics Bulletin (various editions)*.

The Planning and Development (Amendment) Act, 2002.
Social Justice Ireland considered the decision by the Government to repeal section V of the Planning and Development Act 2000 to be most unwise and stated so at the time. This u-turn changed the 20 per cent rule which required all developers to allocate 20 per cent of all housing built for social and affordable housing. This policy was worthwhile for two reasons. First it facilitated a more speedy provision of housing for those on our ever-growing waiting lists (see table 3.5.2) and second it opened up the prospect of Ireland developing as a more socially integrated nation.

In the context of Ireland's social housing crisis, the decision to repeal this section of the Act was wrong. One of the major achievements of the government in the 1997-2002 period was that it showed a long-absent willingness to address the social housing and societal integration issue. Therefore it is particularly sad that within six months of re-assuming office it chose to cancel one of its most noteworthy previous achievements.

The private rented sector

Traditionally the private rented sector was the residual sector of the Irish housing system. The private rented sector is the "tenure of last resort for those unable to obtain local authority housing or not yet ready to enter owner-occupation" (McCashin, 2000:43). It was characterised by poor-quality accommodation and non-secure tenure at the lower end of the housing market. Today, this sector is highly differentiated, with high-quality housing and relatively secure tenure at the upper end of the market, and low-quality housing and insecurity of tenure at the lower end. Both ends of the market have experienced dramatic increases in rent over the last decade.

Table 3.5.8: Percentage distribution of housing units by occupancy status, 1961-2006.

Occupancy Status	1961	1971	1981	1991	2002	2006
LA Rented	18.4	15.9	12.7	9.7	6.9	7.5
Private Rented	17.2	10.9	8.1	7.0	11.1	10.3
Owner Occupied	53.6	60.7	67.9	80.2	77.4	77.2
Other	10.8	12.5	11.2	3.0	4.6	5.0
Total	100.0	100.0	100.0	100.0	100.0	100.0

Source: CSO (2003:28) and calculated from CSO (2007:48).

The percentage of the population dependent on this sector to meet their housing needs declined from 17.2 per cent in 1961 to 7 per cent in 1991 (see table 3.5.8). This compares with an EU average of 21 per cent. The results of Census 2006 indicate that the composition of the sector changed dramatically during the last 15 years. A combination of a growing population, changing household structure, and the increasing cost of owner-occupation has seen the number of households in the private rented sector increase by almost 50 per cent. As table 3.5.8 shows the private rented sector now accounts for 10 per cent of households. In total in 2006 there were 145,317 households living in the private rented sector. Of these 16,621 rented unfurnished dwellings and 128,696 rented furnished or part-furnished dwellings. The average weekly rents paid were €161.57 for unfurnished and €191.09 for part/fully furnished dwellings (CSO, 2009: 339–48).

Ensuring that the standard of accommodation offered by this sector is at an appropriate level is a task which falls to the Private Residences Tenancy Board (PRTB) and local councils. Despite legal requirements, and the linking of tax deductions to registration, it remains the case that a sizeable proportion of the privately rented residences in the country are not registered with the PRTB. As of 31st December 2009 there were 234,000 tenancies registered (PRTB, 2010).

The *Housing Statistics Bulletin* also reports on the level and geographical distribution of inspections of these registered properties. The data indicated that in some areas inspections are common while in others they are far lower. For example there were 703 inspections during 2007 in Cork city, 266 in Galway city, 26 in County Sligo and 30 in County Louth. Nationwide, in 2007 a total of 14,008 dwellings were inspected with 17 per cent being found to not meet the regulatory requirements (2008:93).

These 2007 figures marked important progress in this area as they indicate that for the first time all local authorities are carrying our inspections. *Social Justice Ireland* believes that as this sector continues to expand the government must take steps to ensure that all local authorities begin to carry out a reasonable number of inspections. Implementing such a policy would further enhance recent progress towards increasing standards in this sector. We also believe that it is important that further efforts are made to officially register more properties.

Rental Accommodation Scheme (RAS)

At the lower end of the housing market an increasing number of households are in receipt of a Supplementary Welfare Allowance in the form of rent supplement. There have been substantial changes to the rent supplement programme over the past number of years. Following on the furore caused by the changes introduced as part of Budget 2004, Government took a number of initiatives to address the concerns raised at that time. Of greater importance, however, Government now recognises that the rent supplement programme, originally designed as an emergency intervention, has expanded into a housing payment for a great many people who had spent several years in receipt of rent supplement. The introduction of the new Rental Accommodation Scheme (RAS) was a welcome move in the right direction.

By 2011 however there are major challenges. The rent supplement programme has been hugely expanded to cope with the difficulties in meeting housing costs being experienced by a rapidly expanding number of households. On the other hand while the Rental Accommodation Scheme is projected to expand to almost 18,000 units by the end of 2011 and been effective on a range of fronts there is no way this scheme is sufficient to address the rapid rise in social housing needs in Ireland.

Homelessness

It is possible to extract from the assessment of housing needs information about those most urgently in need of accommodation – the homeless. Data from the last three assessments has shown that the level of homelessness across the country has fallen from 2,468 in 2002 to 2,399 in 2005 and to 1,394 in 2008. A Homeless Agency (2008) study focused on Dublin entitled *Counted in 2008* found that there were 2,366 homeless adults comprising 2,144 households in the capital city. This figure represents a 4 per cent increase on the 2005 figure (2,066 households). Of the total homeless adults 68 per cent were male with the majority aged between 30-49 years (2008: 34). Almost half of the 2,366 adults in homeless services became homeless for the first time between March 2005 and March 2008.

Research has shown that there are three broad categories of homeless people. The first category consists of those who become homeless because of poverty combined with either eviction or a relationship breakdown. The second and growing category of homeless persons consists of those who have chronic disabilities or special needs as a result of alcoholism, mental illness or drug dependency. This group has multiple needs, of which housing is just one (Homeless Initiative, 1999). A report for the National Advisory Committee on Drugs in mid-2005 noted that the vast majority (87 per cent) of the homeless people they surveyed first used drugs before becoming homeless. It also noted that 74 per cent of homeless individuals reported lifetime use of an illicit drug (Lawless and Corr, 2005:95, 97). A third category of homeless persons has emerged in Ireland in recent years – this comprises asylum-seekers, migrants and refugees who have specific housing and other social-service needs. The association between homelessness and mental health problems was assessed in a study at the Mater Hospital in Dublin. It found that one-third of all referrals for psychiatric assessments from its A&E department were homeless people. In all it is estimated that about 40 per cent of Ireland's homeless have mental health difficulties. These facts underscore the vulnerability of the homeless and the need for ever greater efforts to continue to address this problem.

Over time the nature and scale of Ireland's homeless problem has changed significantly. *Social Justice Ireland* believes that the resources allocated to this area provide sufficient residential places for those who seek a place to stay and who in the past were refused because of the lack of available accommodation; often emergency accommodation. However, there remains homelessness related to mental health, drug and migration issues. These are problems that require solutions far beyond the simple provision of a bed. There is also a need for greater availability of transitional places. The current economic crisis has further increased the challenges in this area; reduced funding combined with increased demand ensured that the Government did not meet its target of eliminating homelessness by the end of 2010.

Traveller accommodation

Results from the 2006 Census of Population show that there were 22,435 members of the Travelling community in Ireland. These comprised 11,028 males and 11,407 females living in a total of 4,371 Traveller households. Of these households, 60 per cent (2,640) lived in a house, 6 per cent (260) in a flat or apartment and 28 per cent (1,221) in 'temporary housing units' such as a caravan or mobile home. The Census also reports that among adult Travellers (those aged 15 years and over) only 3.4 per cent had completed upper secondary (leaving certificate or equivalent) education (CSO, 2007: 32, 45, 61). As a minority group, Travellers have been very exposed to social exclusion and in particular have experienced continued problems with the provision of accommodation. Responding to the report of The National Traveller Accommodation Consultative Committee (published in January 2005) the then Minister of State for Housing, Noel Ahern, admitted that the pace at which Traveller accommodation is provided was too slow. A similar view was expressed by the Council of Europe in May 2004. Reform in this area is long overdue and necessary.

Housing and people with a disability

Social Justice Ireland welcomed the recognition by NESC in its review of housing policy that "a particular gap is the lack of a strategic framework to support the provision of tailored housing and housing supports for people with disabilities" (2004:157). A feature of having a disability is additional housing costs. Primarily these costs are for adjustments to residences to ensure access and continued use. For some years local authorities have provided a disabled persons housing grant to assist in the cost of these changes. However, during 2002 the Irish Wheelchair Association reported that an estimated six thousand people with disabilities across the state were waiting for these grants. Limited progress has been made since. Besides quality of life issues studies have shown that the cost of keeping people who are older or who have a disability in nursing care is almost eight times the cost of adapting and providing health care within their own homes.

The establishment a National Housing Strategy for People with Disabilities was welcome. Such a strategy can play an important part in enhancing the provision of tailored housing and housing support to people with disabilities. Funding this strategy adequately is a necessity and *Social Justice Ireland* believes that the government should allocate appropriate funding to reduce any unnecessarily long waiting lists. Furthermore, as a growing number of people with disabilities who have a housing need seek access to social housing and as the population ages the demands on this scheme will increase. Therefore we believe that the government should judge the value of the investments required under this strategy broadly.

Children and housing

Living in housing that is overcrowded, damp, in disrepair or in a poor neighbourhood can be damaging to people of all ages. However, its impact on children's welfare tends to be very significant. A study produced for the Children's Research Centre at Trinity College Dublin by Simon Brooke found that between 1991 and 2002 the numbers of children living in these conditions doubled. According to the report entitled *Housing Problems and Irish Children* there were some 50,000 children living in such conditions. The report found that these problems were concentrated among children in one-parent families and among those living in rented accommodation. In response to this problem the report suggested that local authorities need to create a specific fund to provide regular maintenance of their dwellings. Furthermore the report called for the current minimum standards set for the private rented sector to be raised and that these be enforced by local authorities. Finally the report suggested that the National Children's Strategy be revised to include housing as a 'basic need'. *Social Justice Ireland* welcomed the recommendations of this report. As we have previously highlighted Ireland has a serious problem with child poverty. Continually research has pointed out that low income and low accommodation standards are associated with poor health levels and poor future educational and life opportunities. More resources need to be allocated to this area.

Key Priorities on Housing and Accommodation

- **Adopt new social housing targets for the period from 2012 onwards that take account of the growing local authority housing waiting lists.**

- **Provide the budget allocation for social housing including co-op and voluntary/non-profit housing, on the scale required to eliminate local authority housing waiting lists.**

- Develop and support policies focused on mixed housing, mixed communities, choice of tenure, and mix of different-sized housing units.

- Provide sufficient resources to implement the commitment to eliminate homelessness.

- Actively implement and enforce the legislation on the private rented sector of housing.

- Ensure that nobody remains dependent on rent supplement for more than 18 months. To this end ensure prompt delivery and adequate resourcing of the Rental Accommodation Scheme (RAS).

- Provide the resources required to ensure implementation of the local authorities Travellers' Accommodation programmes.

- Integrate housing policy with other social and care supports to enable vulnerable people (e.g. disability, elderly, homeless) to live independent lives.

- Ensure that sufficient funds are made available to reduce the waiting lists for the disabled persons housing grant.

3.6 Healthcare

> **CORE POLICY OBJECTIVE: HEALTHCARE**
> To provide an adequate healthcare service focused on enabling people to attain the World Health Organisation's definition of health as a *state of complete physical, mental and social well-being and not merely the absence of disease or infirmity*

Healthcare is a social right that every person should enjoy. People should be assured that care in their times of vulnerability is guaranteed. The standard of care is dependent to a great degree on the resources made available which in turn are dependent on the expectations of the society. The obligation to provide healthcare as a social right rests on all people. In a democratic society this obligation is transferred through the taxation and insurance systems to government and other bodies who assume/contract this responsibility. These are very important considerations at this particular moment as a new Government proposes fundamental changes in Ireland's healthcare system. In the following pages we outline some of the major considerations *Social Justice Ireland* believes Government should bring to bear on its decision-making on these issues.

Health inequalities in Ireland

A very welcome insight into the extent of health inequalities in Ireland has been provided by the Public Health Alliance of the Island of Ireland (PHAI). This group, a north-south alliance of non-governmental organisations, statutory bodies, community and voluntary groups, advocacy bodies and individuals who are committed to work together for a healthier society by improving health and tackling health inequalities, has published two detailed reports in recent years: *Health in Ireland – An Unequal State* (2004) and *Health Inequalities on the island of Ireland: the facts, the causes, the remedies* (2007). These reports gather together the baseline information on health inequalities in Ireland and their findings are worthy of serious attention. These include:

- Between 1989 and 1998 the death rates for all causes of death were over three times higher in the lowest occupational class than in the highest
- The death rates for all cancers among the lowest occupational class is over twice as high for the highest class; it is nearly three times higher for strokes, four times higher for lung cancer, six times for accidents

- Perinatal mortality is three times higher in poorer families than in richer families
- Women in the unemployed socio-economic group are more than twice as likely to give birth to low birth weight children as women in the higher professional group
- The incidence of chronic physical illness has been found to be two and a half times higher for poor people than for the wealthy
- Men in unskilled jobs were four times more likely to be admitted to hospital for schizophrenia than higher professional workers
- The rate of hospitalisation for mental illness is more than 6 times higher for people in the lower socio-economic groups as compared with those in the higher groups
- The incidence of male suicide is far higher in the lower socio-economic groups as compared with the higher groups
- The 1998 and 2002 National Health and Lifestyle Surveys (SLAN) found that poorer people are more likely to smoke cigarettes, drink alcohol excessively, take less exercise, and eat less fruit and vegetables than richer people. Poorer people's lifestyle and behavioural choices are directly limited by their economic and social circumstances
- On average 39 per cent of people surveyed in 2003 identified financial problems as the greatest factor in preventing them from improving their health.

The reports also found that some groups experience particularly extreme health inequalities. These include:

- Members of the Traveller community live between 10 and 12 years less than the population as a whole.[63]
- The rate of sudden infant deaths among Travellers is 12 times higher than for the general population.
- Research has found that many expectant mothers among asylum seekers in direct provision suffer malnutrition, babies in these communities suffer ill-health because of diet, many adults experience hunger.

---

[63] For much greater detail on age-specific mortality rates among Travellers and a range of other Traveller health statistics cf. *All Ireland Traveller Health Study: Our Geels*, September 2010, published by the All Ireland Traveller Health Study Team, School of Public Health, Physiotherapy and Population Science, University College Dublin.

- Homeless people experience high incidence of ill-health – a 1997 report found that 40 per cent of hostel dwellers had a serious psychiatric illness, 42 per cent had problems of alcohol dependency, and 18 per cent had other physical problems.
- The incidence of injecting drug use is almost entirely confined to people from the lower socio-economic groups.

The PHAI also compared the health of people in Ireland against that of the 15 other EU states (pre-enlargement). They found that Irish people compare badly with the experience of citizens in other EU counties. These findings included:

- Mortality rates in Ireland are worse than the EU average for a range of illnesses, particularly diseases of the circulatory system, breast cancer and death from smoking related illnesses.
- Irish women have almost twice the rate of death from heart disease as the average European woman.
- The incidences of mortality for Irish women for cancers of the breast, colon, larynx and oesophagus and for ischaemic heart disease are among the highest in the EU.
- At the age of 65 Irish men have the lowest life expectancy in the EU. (PHAI, 2004:3-4).

In their 2007 study the PHAI summarised what the international research literature highlights as the most important influences on health and the causes of health inequalities. These are the economic, social and political environments in which people live including:

- Level of income;
- Early life experience;
- Access to education and employment;
- Food and nutrition;
- Work opportunities;
- Housing and environmental conditions;
- Levels of stress and social support.

Furthermore, they noted that "research has also established that the greatest determinant of health is the level of income equality in society. Societies with more equal distribution of income across the population have higher average life expectancies and better health outcomes than less equal societies" (PHAI, 2007:8).

It is the nature of these inequalities and the fact that they are so interconnected with the social, economic and political environment of Ireland that places this issue as central to the agenda of *Social Justice Ireland*. Throughout the various part of this *Socio-Economic Review* we address each of these issues.

Poverty and healthcare exclusion
The link between poverty and ill health has been well established by international and national research. The poor get sick more often and die younger than those in the higher socio-economic groups. Poverty directly affects the incidence of ill health; it limits access to affordable healthcare and reduces the opportunity for those living in poverty to adopt healthy lifestyles. Reflecting this, a 2006 study of the accessibility of health care found 18.9 per cent of Irish people indicated that cost had deterred them from visiting a GP and seeking medical advice (O'Reilly and Thompson, 2006). Healthcare exclusion is a major dimension of poverty and social exclusion.

Life expectancy and infant mortality
In 2008 Irish males had life expectancies of 76.8 years while Irish females were expected to live 4.8 years longer reaching 81.6 years. Based on these figures, Ireland's life expectancy performance is similar to the European average; the EU average, however, is dragged down by low life expectancies among men in Estonia, Latvia and Lithuania among others (see table 3.6.1). Relative to the older member states of the EU, the Irish figures are less impressive. The story behind Ireland's life expectancy figures incorporates many of the findings of the PHAI reports and the earlier poverty figures (see Section 3.1). Ireland's poverty problem has serious implications for health in light of the fact that there is a clear link between poverty and ill health, a relationship that has been well supported by international research. Thus, those in lower socio-economic groups have a higher percentage of both acute and chronic illnesses.

Table 3.6.1: EU-27 life expectancy at birth by sex in 2008, in years.			
Country	Males	Females	Difference
Spain	78.9	85.0	6.2
France	77.5	84.3	6.8
Italy	78.8	84.1	5.3
Belgium	77.5	83.5	6.1
Sweden	79.1	83.2	4.1
Finland	76.3	83.0	6.7
Austria	77.6	83.0	5.3
Luxembourg	77.6	82.7	5.1
Greece	77.5	82.5	4.9
Germany	77.2	82.4	5.2
Malta	76.7	82.3	5.6
Netherlands	78.3	82.3	4.0
Slovenia	75.4	82.3	6.8
Portugal	75.5	81.7	6.3
Cyprus	77.0	81.7	4.7
United Kingdom	77.6	81.7	4.1
IRELAND	**76.8**	**81.6**	**4.8**
Denmark	76.3	80.7	4.4
Czech Republic	74.0	80.1	6.2
Poland	71.3	80.0	8.7
Estonia	68.6	79.2	10.6
Slovakia	70.9	78.7	7.9
Latvia	67.2	77.9	10.7
Hungary	69.8	77.8	8.0
Lithuania	66.3	77.6	11.3
Bulgaria	69.5	76.6	7.1
Romania	69.2	76.1	7.0
EU 27	**76.1**	**82.2**	**6.1**

Source: CSO 2010:53

Health expenditure

Healthcare is a social right for all people. For this right to be upheld governments need to provide the required funding to ensure the relevant services and care are provided as required. In table 3.6.2 we see that Ireland spends 7.6 per cent of GDP on health; this is well below the EU-27 average of 9.3 per cent. Less is spent on public and private health as a proportion of GDP than the majority of other EU-27 countries. In Gross National Income (GNI) terms this expenditure translates into a figure of 8.8 per cent.[64] In comparison France spends 11 per cent; Germany spends 10.4 per cent and Austria 10.1 per cent. Ireland has the twelfth lowest expenditure on health (measured as a percentage of GDP) according to EU-27 data, although this ranking position has been improving over time. Healthcare costs tend to be higher in countries which have a higher old age dependency ratio. This is not yet so significant an issue for Ireland as the old age dependency ratio is extremely low (11.1 per cent are aged 65 yrs and over) compared to a much higher EU average. However, this level of funding must be seen as inadequate in light of the fact that waiting lists, bed closures, shortage of staff and long-term care requirements continue to be issues in the health service today. Clearly, there are significant efficiencies to be gained in a restructuring of the Irish health system, and in particular the HSE. However, as the population ages and demand for facilities increases funding as a percentage of national income will have to rise.[65]

Table 3.6.2: EU-27 health expenditure as a percentage of GDP, 2007			
Country	%	Country	%
France	11.0	Slovakia	7.7
Germany	10.4	**IRELAND (% GDP)**	**7.6**
Austria	10.1	Malta	7.5
Portugal	10.0	Hungary	7.4
Denmark	9.8	Bulgaria	7.3
Greece	9.6	Luxembourg	7.1
Belgium	9.4	Czech Republic	6.8
Sweden	9.1	Cyprus	6.6
Netherlands	8.9	Poland	6.4
IRELAND (% GNI)	**8.8**	Lithuania	6.2
Italy	8.7	Latvia	6.2
Spain	8.5	Estonia	5.4
United Kingdom	8.4	Romania	4.7
Finland	8.2		
Slovenia	7.8	**EU 27**	**9.3**

Source: CSO (2010:52)

---

[64] GNI is similar to the concept of GNP and has a similar value.
[65] This issue is also analysed in section 3.2 of this review.

The Model of Healthcare in Ireland
Community-based health and social services require a model of care that:

- Is accessible and acceptable to the community they serve;
- Is responsive to the local community and its particular set of needs and requirements;
- Is supportive of local communities in their efforts to build social cohesion;
- Accepts primary care as the key component of the model of care and gives it priority over acute services as the place where health and social care options are accessed by the community.

To achieve this, action is required in three key areas if the basic model of care that is to underpin the health services is not to be undermined. There areas are: *Older People's Services*

> *Primary Care and Primary Care Teams*
> *Children and Family Services*
> *Disability and Mental Health*

and each is reviewed in turn below before we address related issues including medical cards and the health system reform process.

Older People's Services
If the health of older people is to be addressed appropriately then it is essential that there be support for older people to live at home by providing appropriate community-based services to meet their needs. This approach needs to be complemented by ensuring access to acute services is available in an appropriate manner when required. If this approach is to be followed then there is an urgent need to address the specific deficits in infrastructure that exist across the country. There should be an emphasis on replacement and/or refurbishment of facilities. If this is not done then we will see the inappropriate admission of older people to acute care facilities with the consequent negative impacts on acute services and unnecessary stress on older people.

Social Justice Ireland believes that what is required is a total investment of €500m over five years i.e. €100m each year is required.

Primary Care and Primary Care Teams

Primary Care has been recognised as one of the cornerstones of the health system. This was given recognition by the publication of a strategy *Primary Care – A New Direction* (2001). Between 90 and 95 per cent of the population are treated by the primary care system. The model of a primary care team presented in the document must be viewed in its most flexible form so that it can respond to the local needs assessment. The principle underlining this model should be a social model of health. This is in keeping with the World Health Organisation's definition on health. Universal access is needed to ensure that a social model of health as outlined in the document becomes a reality. For the development of *Primary Care – A New Direction* there is a clear need for the allocation of more resources. This would need an increase in the percentage of the healthcare budget being allocated for primary care.

The General Medical Service (GMS) system was first introduced in 1972 and it gave a commitment that 40 per cent of the population would be covered by this system. By 1977 some 39 per cent of the population were eligible for medical cards on income grounds. By 2007 this figure had decreased to approximately 29.5 per cent of the population. For families just over the eligibility level a visit to the GP and a prescription could cost some 25 per cent of their total weekly income. The implications of this for many individuals and families are that they cannot afford to access appropriate care at the time needed. We address the issue of medical cards later in this section.

The importance of paying attention to local people's own perspective on their health and to understand the impact of the conditions of their lives on their health is essential to community development and to community orientated approaches to primary care. There needs to be a community development approach to ensure that the community can define its own health needs, work out how these needs can best be met collectively and decide on a course of action to achieve the outcomes in partnership with service providers. This will ensure greater control over the social, political, economic and environmental factors that determine the health status of any community.

The Primary Care Strategy acknowledges the need for "community involvement" as a key factor in addressing health issues and recognises the need for partnership in both the planning and evaluation of all services. Community participation is an "essential component of a more responsive and appropriate care system which is truly people-centred" (Chief Medical Officers Report).

The decision by the new Government to appoint a Minister of State with specific responsibility for Primary Care is welcome. Government must now follow-up on this appointment with tangible progress in the development and delivery of Primary Care over the next few years.

Primary care teams
Ireland's healthcare system has struggled to provide an effective and efficient response to the health needs of its population. Despite a huge increase in investment in recent years great problems persist. One key initiative that would make a substantial positive impact on reducing these problems would be the development of primary care teams across the country.

Primary care teams draw the health professionals in an area together into a team that provides a one-stop shop where people can go locally rather than heading directly to the accident and emergency unit in the nearest hospital. A very large proportion of those who go to accident and emergency units should not be there.

At the moment the HSE is developing Primary Care Teams and Social Care Networks as the basic 'building blocks' of local public health care provision. We understand a Primary Care Team (or "PCT") to be a team of health professionals (catering for a population of 7-10,000) who work closely together and with the local community to meet the needs of people living in that community. These professionals include GPs and Practice Nurses, community nursing i.e. public health nurses and community RGNs, physiotherapists, occupational therapists and home-care staff. They provide the first point of contact when individuals need to access the health system. When fully developed, it is expected that 519 primary care teams could cover the whole country. PCTs are also expected to link in with other community-based disciplines to ensure that health and social needs are addressed. These include: speech & language therapists, dieticians, area medical officers, community welfare officers, addiction counsellors, community mental health nursing, consultant psychiatrists, etc. PCTs provide a single point of contact between the person and the health system. They facilitate navigation 'in', 'around' and 'out' of the health system.

The former Government had committed to putting 500 of these primary care teams in place by 2012. Progress has been made but more is required if this essential development is to be secured. *Social Justice Ireland* believes that what is required is €250m over a five-year period to support infrastructural development in putting in place the 519 primary care teams that are required to cover the whole country. We hope the new Minister of State makes the delivery of this proposal a priority.

Children and Family Services

In tandem with the development of Primary Care Team services there is a need to focus on health and social care provision to children and families. The obligation on the State to develop and provide services and facilities to support vulnerable and at risk children has been well highlighted recently. The standard of care as monitored by HIQA and the challenges posed to provide care to young people with complex needs have proven difficult to address both in public and private provision.

In many communities there are community & voluntary services being operated out of very poor facilities in need of refurbishment/rebuilding. Despite poor infrastructure, these services are the heart of local communities and provide vital services that are locally 'owned'. There is a need to support this activity and in particular meet the infrastructural requirements which will in the main be by way of minor development at local level.

Social Justice Ireland believes that what is required is a total of €250m over a five-year period to address the infrastructural deficit in Children and Family Services. This amounts to €27m per area for each of the nine Children Services Committee areas and a national investment of €7m in Residential and Special Care.

Social Justice Ireland welcomes the appointment of a Minister for Children by the new Government. This is an area with a substantial agenda that could, however, be addressed effectively in a relatively short period of time if the political will to do so were present. As well as the Children's Rights Referendum and the issue of Child Safeguarding that have been highlighted by the new Government, we believe the key issues for the new Department are the second National Children's Strategy, policy on early childhood care and education, child poverty, youth homelessness, disability among young people and the issue of young carers.

Disability and Mental Health

We welcome the 2011 *Programme for Government* commitment to complete a consultation to establish "a realistic implementation plan for the National Disability Strategy". There are many areas within the Disability Sector which are in need of further development and core funding and these areas need to be supported.[66]

---

[66] Other Disability related issues are addressed throughout this review.

Mental health

The National Health Strategy entitled *Quality and Fairness* (2001) identified mental health as an area to be developed. The Expert Group on Mental Health Policy invited written submissions and held consultation days with all relevant stakeholders and subsequently published a report entitled *A Vision for Change - Report of the Expert Group on Mental Health Policy* (2006). This report offered many worthwhile pathways to adequately address mental health issues in Irish society. Unfortunately, to date little has been implemented to achieve this vision.

There is an urgent need to address this whole area in the light of the World Health Report (2001) *Mental Health: New Understanding, New Hope* where it is estimated that, in 1990, mental and neurological disorders accounted for 10 per cent of the total Disability-Adjusted Life Years (DALYs) lost due to all diseases and injuries. This was 12 per cent in 2000. By 2020, it is projected that these disorders will have increased to 15 per cent. This has serious implications for services in all countries in the coming years.

Commitments in the 2011 *Programme for Government* offer hope that progress in this area will be made over the next few years. We welcome these commitments to better funding the sector and working to reduce the stigma of mental health and improve access to facilities and services for assisting those with mental health problems. *Social Justice Ireland* urges Government to continue to support progress in this area. We welcome the appointment of a Minister of State with responsibility in this area and trust it is an indication of the Government's serious commitment to addressing the needs that care clearly identifiable in this area of policy.

Areas of concern in mental health

There is a need for effective outreach and follow-up programmes for people who have been in in-patients institutions upon their discharge into the wider community. These should provide:

- Sheltered housing (high, medium and low supported housing)
- Monitoring of medication
- Retraining and rehabilitation
- Assistance with integration into community

A stronger emphasis on the development of community services for all levels of mental health is urgently required and *Social Justice Ireland* hopes the new Government will honour its *Programme for Government* commitment to deliver this.

While there has been some improvement in this area in recent years, people with an intellectual disability who require a mental health service frequently still find they do not have a psychiatric service available to them. Furthermore, while there has been some improvement in recent years, there is an issue with the lack of appropriate mental healthcare for all who need it, especially vulnerable groups including children, the homeless, prisoners, Travellers, asylum seekers, refugees and other minority or vulnerable groups. People in these and related categories have a right to a specialist service to provide for their often-complex needs. A great deal remains to be done before this right could be acknowledged as being recognised and honoured in the healthcare system.

When the social determinants of health (housing, income, childcare support, education etc.) are not met the connection between those who are disadvantage and ill health is well documented. This is also true where mental health issues are concerned.

Suicide – a mental health issue
A related problem to mental health is suicide. For many years the topic of suicide was one rarely discussed in Irish society and as a consequence the healthcare and policy implications of its existence were limited. Data show that the number of suicides in Ireland has climbed over the last decade and the current recession has accelerated this increase. In 1993 327 suicides were recorded and by 2009, the latest year for which data is available, the number of suicides had increased to 527. Over time Ireland's suicide rate has risen from 6.3 suicides per 100,000 people in 1980 to 11.7 suicides per 100,000 people in 2007 (OECD, 2005 and National Office of Suicide Prevention, 2010:25).

Table 3.6.3 provides details on the levels and sex distribution of suicides in Ireland since 2003. It shows that suicide is predominantly a male phenomenon with 80 per cent of suicide victims being male. When assessed by age group the data from the National Office of Suicide Prevention suggest that young people, and in particular young males, are the groups most at risk. In the period 2003-2007 young males aged between 20-24 years had a suicide rate of 34.7 per 100,000 in the population; three times the national average. Among this age-group in the population, suicide is one of the largest killers (2010:25-26).

The sustained high level of suicides in Ireland is a significant healthcare and societal problem. Of course the statistics in table 3.6.3 only tell one part of the story. Behind each of these victims are families and communities devastated by these tragedies.

Likewise, behind each of the figures is a personal story which leads to victims taking their own life. *Social Justice Ireland* believes that further attention and resources need to be given to addressing and researching Ireland's suicide problem. In that light, we welcomed the establishment of the national office of suicide prevention and the directions laid out in the N*ational Strategy for Action on Suicide Prevention* (2005-2014). Resources are also required for the support systems that must be provided for such vulnerable groups and we welcome the commitments in the 2011 *Programme for Government* to provide this. As a society we need to become more aware of this issue and more aware of methods to prevent it.

Table 3.6.3: Suicides in Ireland 2003-2009

Year**	Overall		Males		Females	
	No.	Rate	No.	Rate	No.	Rate
2003	497	12.5	386	19.5	111	5.5
2004	493	12.2	406	20.2	87	4.3
2005	481	11.6	382	18.5	99	4.8
2006	460	10.8	379	17.9	81	3.8
2007	458	10.6	362	16.7	96	4.4
2008★	424	9.6	332	15.0	82	3.8
2009★	527	11.7	422	19.0	105	4.7

Source: National Office of Suicide Prevention (2010:25-26)
Notes: ★ Provisional figures
★★Annual data is by year of occurrence (2003 to 2007) and by year of registration (2008 and 2009).
Rate is rate per 100,000 of the population.

Older people and Mental Health

Mental health issues affect all groups in society. A particularly vulnerable group are older people with dementia as they often fall between two stools i.e. mental health versus general medical care. Therefore there needs to be a co-ordinated service provided for this group. It is important that this service be needs-based and service-user-led and should be in keeping with international human rights standards and best practice in line with the principles in the World Health Organisation's 2001 annual report.

Research and development in all areas of mental health is needed to ensure a quality service is delivered. Providing good mental health services should not be viewed as a cost but rather as an investment for the future. Public awareness needs to be raised to ensure a clearer understanding of mental illness so that the rights of those with mental illness are recognised.

We acknowledge the significant investment made to develop services for older people. We welcomed the announcements of the introduction of '*A Fair Deal – The Nursing Home Care Support Scheme 2008*'. This initiative has been activated. It remains critical that sufficient capital investment is provided to ensure that the additional numbers of residential care beds are made available to meet the growing demand as identified. The focus on the development of community based services to support older people to remain in their own homes/communities for as long as this is possible is to be welcomed. Improved funding is also required for home help services, day care centres and home care packages - areas that have received serious and unwelcome cuts in recent Budgets and we continue to lobby for these cuts to be reversed and these services enhanced. There is a real danger that one outcome of these cuts is that the service would be nothing more than a 'Bed and Breakfast' facility that would be a travesty of what was intended and, more importantly, of what is required.

Medical Cards: Reform Needed
The introduction of 30,000 new medical cards and 200,000 'doctor visit only' cards in Budget 2005 was a small step in the right direction. However, a great deal more needs to be done before the necessary level of provision is in place. In 1996 1,252,384 people on low incomes were covered by full medical cards. After Budget 2005 1,069,934 people were similarly covered. Today there are approximately 1,400,000 people with medical cards and the recession is increasing this number.

The eligibility thresholds for full medical cards have not been raised but the numbers have grown because many newly unemployed people have seen their income slip below the threshold. The eligibility threshold for 'doctor-only' cards was raised in mid-2006 to a level 50 per cent above the standard medical card thresholds. As of December 2007 there were 75,542 doctor-only cards.[67]

What is required is full medical card coverage for all people in Ireland who are vulnerable. Currently, the income threshold for accessing a medical card is far below the poverty line. This in effect creates an employment trap as parents are often afraid

---

[67] Dail speech by Minister for Health and Children, December 19th 2007.

to take up a job and, consequently, lose their medical card even though their income remains low. The 'doctor visit only' cards are an improvement on the previous situation only if they are upgraded to full medical cards in due course. At present they create new problems as many people now find themselves in the most unenviable situation of knowing what is wrong with them but not having the resources to purchase the medicines they need to be treated.

The health budget

There are serious problems with the annual budget for health. In 2011 this is an especially difficult situation as the healthcare budget has been reduced dramatically. Government provides an inadequate budget each year to cover the expenditure that is required. Likewise, it provides too little investment in infrastructure now to enable the new model of health to emerge in the future. Government has had a 'pass the parcel' approach to the annual budget in this context with no clarity between the Department of Finance, the Department of Health and Children and the HSE on what exactly is to be delivered and how it is to be funded. A transparent and honest approach to the annual budget is required. It is important that there is clarity about the cost of each scheme and how this cost is being funded. Efficiencies are required and getting value for money is essential. However these should be targeted at areas where efficiencies can be delivered without compromising the quality of the service. *Social Justice Ireland* continues to argue that there is a need to be specific about the efficiencies that are needed and how these efficiencies are to be delivered. Within this framework it is then possible to insist, with credibility, on getting delivery in these areas.

Future healthcare costs

A number of the factors highlighted elsewhere in this review will have implications for the future of our healthcare system. The projected increases in population forecast by the CSO imply that there will be many more people living in Ireland in 10-15 years time. In this context, we recognise the development of the *National Intercultural Health Strategy 2007-2012*. One clear implication of this will be additional demand for more healthcare and more healthcare facilities. In the context of our past mistakes it is important that Ireland begin to plan for this additional demand and begin to train staff and construct facilities to cope.

As we indicated in section 3.2, on taxation, the ageing of the population over the next four decades will be an additional challenge to the provision of healthcare. Again, planning and investment is required.

Key Priorities on Healthcare

- Recognise the considerable health inequalities present within the Irish healthcare system and provide sufficient resources to tackle them.

- Give far greater priority to community care and restructure the healthcare budget accordingly. Overall, government should ensure that at least 35 per cent of the non-capital healthcare budget is allocated to community care. In the process care should be taken to ensure that the increased allocation does not go to the GMS or the drug subsidy scheme.

- Resource and implement the commitment to provide 500 primary care teams.

- Increase the percentage of the health budget allocated to health promotion and education in partnership with all relevant stakeholders.

- Address the serious problems with the annual budget for health. In particular ensure that government provides an adequate budget each year to cover the expenditure required and that the Department of Finance, the Department of Health, the Department of Children and the HSE co-ordinate on what exactly is to be delivered and how it is to be funded. A transparent and honest approach to the annual budget is required.

- Provide the childcare services with the additional resources necessary to effectively implement the Child Care Act.

- Provide additional respite care for elderly people and people with disabilities and ensure this is not compromised by the funding provided for the Fair Deal.

- Promote equality of access and outcomes to services within the Irish healthcare system.

- Ensure that structural and systematic reform of the health system reflects the key principles of the Health Strategy aimed at achieving high performance, person centred, quality of care and value for money in the health service.

- Develop and resource mental health services, and recognise that they will be a key factor in determining the health status of the population.

- Continue to facilitate and fund a campaign to give greater attention to the issue of suicide in Irish society. In particular, focus resources on educating young people in this context.

- Monitor and evaluate the National Health Reform Programme to ensure equity, people-centeredness, quality and accountability for all.

- Enhance the process of planning and investment so that the healthcare system can cope with the increase and diversity in population and the ageing of the population projected to happen over the next few decades.

3.7 Education and Educational Disadvantage

> **CORE POLICY OBJECTIVE:**
> **EDUCATION & EDUCATION DISADVANTAGE**
> To provide relevant education for all people throughout their lives, so that they can participate fully and meaningfully in developing themselves, their community and the wider society

Education can be an agent for social transformation. *Social Justice Ireland* believes that education can be a powerful force in counteracting inequality and poverty while recognising that, in many ways, the present education system has quite the opposite effect. Recent studies confirm the persistence of social class inequalities which are seemingly ingrained in the system. Even in the context of the increased participation and economic expansion of much of the last decade, the education system continues to mediate the vicious cycle of disadvantage and social exclusion between generations. While there are a number of programmes and initiatives to tackle educational disadvantage, many of these initiatives simply involve providing additional resources for disadvantaged schools. Our policy approach in this area is based on a belief that early school leaving is a particularly serious manifestation of wider inequality in education, which is embedded in and caused by structures in the system itself.

Education in Ireland – the numbers

There are almost 1 million full-time students in the formal Irish education system. Of these there are 498,914 at primary level, 341,312 at second level and 146,981 at third level. As such, the sector accounts for 22 per cent of the population and given recent increases in birth rates, the figures have continued to grow across the last decade. (CSO, 2010:46)

Ireland's expenditure on education equalled 4.9 per cent of GDP (5.66 per cent of GNI) in 2007, the latest year for which comparable EU-wide data is available (see table 3.7.1).[68] This compares to an EU-27 average of 4.96 per cent of GDP in that year. Over much of the last decade, as national income has increased the share allocated to education has slowly increased; a fact which we strongly welcome. In 1995 expenditure on education equalled 4.4 per cent of GDP and 5.4 per cent of GNP (OECD, 2005:30).

---

[68] GNI is similar to the concept of GNP and has a similar value.

Table 3.7.1: EU-27 expenditure on education as a percentage of GDP, 2007

Country	%	Country	%
Denmark	7.83	Poland	4.91
Cyprus	6.93	**IRELAND (GDP)**	**4.90**
Sweden	6.69	Estonia	4.85
Malta	6.31	Lithuania	4.67
Belgium	6.02	Germany	4.50
Finland	5.91	Spain	4.35
IRELAND (GNI)	**5.66**	Italy	4.29
France	5.59	Romania	4.25
Austria	5.40	Czech Republic	4.20
United Kingdom	5.39	Bulgaria	4.13
Netherlands	5.32	Greece*	4.00
Portugal	5.30	Slovakia	3.62
Hungary	5.20	Luxembourg**	3.40
Slovenia	5.19		
Latvia	5.00	**EU 27**	**4.96**

Source: Eurostat online database [accessed April 2011]
Notes: * Data for 2005; **Data for 2006

Using data from the Department of Education and Skills and the CSO we can analyse public non-capital education expenditure per student in Ireland over the 1999-2008 period – see Table 3.7.2. It shows that over the period there have been real increases at all three education levels; these increases have been 58 per cent in first level, 56 per cent for second level students and 2.4 per cent at third level. While a substantial proportion of these increases can be accounted for by increased pay for teachers, the increase is nevertheless noticeable. The trend is also partly explained by the aforementioned trend in student numbers. Between 1999/00 and 2008/09 the numbers of students in Ireland grew by 12.3 per cent at first level and declined by 3.5 per cent at second level. However, over the same period, the number of third level students increased by around 25 per cent (CSO: 2010:46). It should also be noted, however, that Ireland's young population as a proportion of total population is large by EU standards and, consequently, a higher than average spend on education might be expected.

A New and Fairer Ireland

Table 3.7.2: Ireland's non-capital public expenditure on education 1999-2008, expressed at 2008 prices

Year	€ per pupil			Total expenditure €m
	First level	Second level	Third level	
1999	4,136	6,069	11,288	5,473
2000	4,449	6,372	10,964	5,698
2001	4,613	6,985	11,412	6,020
2002	5,064	7,453	11,456	6,425
2003	5,532	8,000	11,257	6,847
2004	5,944	8,070	10,909	7,051
2005	6,060	8,397	11,316	7,274
2006	6,293	8,803	11,848	7,640
2007	6,442	9,268	11,673	7,967
2008	6,546	9,447	11,567	8,211

Source: CSO, 2010:46

When viewed in an international context, the most striking feature of investment in education in Ireland, relative to other OECD and EU countries, is our comparative under-investment in primary education relative to international norms (not to mention our very limited public funding for early childhood education)[69]. Irish investment in third-level education, which is widely regarded as inadequate, is approximately at the OECD average. However, our public investment at second level and, in particular, at primary level is substantially below the OECD average and is among the lowest of all OECD countries when the expenditure is standardised as a percentage of GDP.[70]

The importance of investment in education is widely acknowledged. For individuals, the rewards from education are clear. Those with higher qualifications earn, on average, far more over their lifetime than those with lower qualifications. However, for those who do not assign great value to improving education levels in themselves, a study published by Statistics Canada shows a clear and significant association between pro-active investment in education in any period and a country's subsequent growth and labour productivity (Coulombe et al, 2004). This study, which looked at adult literacy skills of people in 14 countries who entered

---

[69] Budget 2009#2 proposed some reforms in the area of early childhood education and we review these later in this section.
[70] See OECD (2004: 216; 2009:69-70).

the labour force in the period 1960 to 1995, identified a clear and significant association between investments in human capital in each period and a country's subsequent growth and labour productivity. Specifically, a rise of 1 per cent in literacy scores relative to the international average is associated with an eventual 2.5 per cent relative rise in labour productivity and a 1.5 per cent rise in GDP per head.

Planning for future education needs
Over the past number of years there has been minimal long-term strategic planning by the Department of Education and Skills as regards investment in education facilities at primary and secondary level. This factor was most strongly highlighted in Budget 2008 when the Government announced 'an immediate increase of €95m in funding for the Primary School Building programme'. However, it remains a worry that it is only at the end of 2007 that we began to plan for increases in child number at primary schools, starting September 2008. This is particularly the case given detailed data available from Census 2001 and 2006 which signalled these impending increases and their timing and spatial distribution.

In that context *Social Justice Ireland* believes it is important that Government, and in particular the Department of Education and Skills, pay attention to the population projections calculated by the CSO for the years to come. In its 2008 publication *Population and Labour Force Projections 2011-2041* the CSO signalled that the number of primary school children will increase from 433,900 in 2001 to almost 500,000 by 2011 and will climb further to almost 550,000 by 2016 (CSO, 2008:27, 33). They also specifically addressed the school population issue and stated that:

> "The projected changes will directly impact on the population of school-going age. Taking the "primary" school population as being broadly represented by those aged 5-12 years, the numbers in this category are projected to increase progressively under all combinations of assumptions in the period 2006-2021...Even in the absence of migration (M0) the "primary" school going population is projected to increase by between 30,000 and 68,000 over the period 2006-2021, depending on the fertility assumption chosen" (CSO, 2008: 28).

Addressing future needs at secondary school the CSO stated:

> "The numbers of children of "secondary" school age (i.e. persons aged 13-18 years) under all combinations of assumptions are projected to continue to decline until 2011 and to then experience a recovery by 2016 due to the higher number of births from 2003 onwards" (CSO, 2008: 28).

Table 3.7.3 summarises the CSO's projections.[71]

Table 3.7.3: School going population, CSO projections 2011-2041		
Year	Primary (ages 5-12)	Secondary (ages 13-18)
2001 (actual)	433,900	375,300
2006 (actual)	450,500	342,300
2011	497,200	337,900
2016	548,700	370,100
2021	599,500	401,500
2026	611,200	441,900
2031	583,000	463,500
2036	543,500	452,500
2041	528,500	420,500

Source: CSO (2004; 2008:27, 33) using M2F1 population projection assumption.

While it is likely that some of these projections will be reduced given the current recession and associated migration trends, *Social Justice Ireland* believes that these increases require long-term planning and more comprehensive programmes of school expansion; rapid reactions are neither prudent nor appropriate public policy.

Literacy and Adult Literacy
The issue of literacy has been contentious in recent times. Some years ago, in 1997, an OECD survey found that a quarter of Ireland's adult population performed at the very lowest level of literacy. More recently, results from the OECD's PISA study found that Ireland's fifteen-year olds rank at average reading levels among OECD countries. They also highlighted that average reading levels have been decreasing across all ability levels over time in Ireland and that 17 percent of students in Ireland are low-achieving in reading meaning that they are "below the basic level needed to participate effectively in society and in future learning" (OECD, 2010). Numeracy levels also displayed a similar pattern.

The OECD's findings suggest that while reading levels among the school-going population are better than the population generally, this difference is much smaller than should be expected. However, there is something fundamentally wrong with

---

[71] Recent economic events, including the return of emigration, are likely to have some impact on these figures, in particular those for primary school numbers. However, the scale of this impact is likely to be small.

an education system where 1 in 6 students are unable to read at the most basic level. Given these findings, it is clear that fundamental reforms are needed to Ireland's education system to address this problem. Left unresolved, it will store up continuous socio-economic problems for the decades to come. In that regard, *Social Justice Ireland* welcomes the November 2010 draft national plan to improve literacy and numeracy in schools, *Better Literacy and Numeracy for Children and Young People*, which sets out national targets and a range of significant measures to improve literacy and numeracy in early childhood education and in primary and post-primary schools. These measures include fundamental changes to teacher education, the curriculum in schools and radical improvements in the assessment and reporting of student progress at student, school and national level. Progress on this issue is overdue and necessary.

The Department of Education and Skills' policy for tackling literacy problems among adults is in the opinion of *Social Justice Ireland* simply unacceptable. As part of the 2007 *NAPinclusion* document a target for adult literacy policy was set stating that "the proportion of the population aged 16-64 with restricted literacy will be reduced to between 10%-15% by 2016, from the level of 25% found in 1997" where "restricted literacy" is defined as level 1 on the International Adult Literacy Scale. People at this level of literacy are considered to possess "very poor skills, where the individual may, for example, be unable to determine the correct amount of medicine to give a child from information printed on the package" (OECD).

As table 3.7.4 shows, in numerical terms this implies that the aim of government policy is to have "only" 301,960 adults of labour force age with serious literacy difficulties in Ireland by 2016.[72]

Table 3.7.4: Irish Government Adult Literacy Target for 2016	
Adult population (under 65 yrs) in 2016	3,019,600
10% "restricted literacy" target	301,960
15% "restricted literacy" target	452,940

Source: Calculated from CSO (2008:27) using the lowest CSO population projection for 2016 – the M0F2 population projection assumption.

---

[72] These calculations are based on the lowest CSO population projection for 2016. The CSO's calculation is based on their M0F2 demographic assumptions.

The question needs to be asked, how can policy aim to be so unambitious? How will these people with serious literacy problems function effectively in the economy and society that is emerging in Ireland? How can they get meaningful jobs? In reality achieving this target could only be interpreted as representing substantial and sustained failure.

Overall, *Social Justice Ireland* believes that the government's literacy target is illogical, unambitious and suggests a complete lack of interest in seriously addressing this problem. The lack of focus on this issue was further underscored by Budget 2011's decision to reduce funding for adult literacy programmes by 5 per cent. The current target on literacy should be revised downwards dramatically and the necessary resources committed to ensuring that the revised target is met. *Social Justice Ireland* believes that the government should adopt a new and more ambitious target of:

> reducing the proportion of the population aged 16-64 with restricted literacy to 5 per cent by 2016; and to 3 per cent by 2020.

This will still leave approximately 150,000 adults without basic literacy levels in 2016. However, this target is more ambitious and realistic in the context of the future social and economic development of Ireland.

Early school leaving and unemployment
Socio-economic background is closely linked to early school leaving as a high proportion of early school leavers come from semi-skilled and unskilled manual backgrounds. Employment opportunities and earning power are linked generally to level of education attained. People with no qualifications are more likely to be unemployed and if employed are less likely to gain promotion in their careers. As the analysis in section 3.1 of the review has shown, they are also more likely to be experiencing poverty. Even in the context of increased participation, the education system continues to mediate the transmission of disadvantage and social exclusion between generations.

The unemployment rate for persons in Ireland aged 18-24 was 25.2 per cent in 2009 while the rate for early school leavers was twice that. The significantly higher risk of unemployment attached to early school leaving underscores the need to give greater focus to this issue. High rates of early school leaving lead to the growth of a substantial group of people permanently excluded from the benefits of Irish society in the decades ahead.

Table 3.7.5: Early school leavers by labour force status and sex, 2009			
Labour force status	Persons	Males	Females
In employment	14,300	9,100	5,300
Unemployed	14,600	11,800	2,800
Unemployment rate of persons aged 18-24 (%)	25.2	32.2	18.0
Unemployment rate of early school leavers (%)	50.5	56.5	34.6

Source: CSO, 2010:51

In recent studies both the ESRI and the National Education Welfare Board (NEWB) have indicated that 800-1,000 children each year fail to make the transition from primary to secondary school. Retention from lower to upper second level completion is currently roughly 83 per cent through schooling (therefore 17 per cent are early school leavers). CSO figures suggest that further education and training opportunities are bringing a further 4-5 per cent of the cohort up to a level of or equivalent to 'at least upper second level' by the time they reach 20 to 24 years old, which is encouraging but serves to illustrate the scale of the problem that remains.

Government has invested heavily in trying to secure a school-based solution to this problem through, for example, the work of the NEWB. It may well be time to try alternative approaches aimed at ensuring that people in this cohort attain the skills required to progress in the future.

Key issues: Early childhood education

Budget 2009 #2 made a commitment that Government would introduce an early childhood education scheme. In the past the issue of early childhood education has not had a high profile within Ireland's policy development processes. However, this situation has changed in recent years with the growing realisation of the importance of early education for children. Nowadays the benefits of early education are acknowledged as studies show that it helps to determine how long children stay in school and how quickly they will find employment after leaving school. This requires a greater emphasis and additional resources within the Irish education system if the high non-completion rates outlined above are to be addressed successfully. We welcome the recent moves in this direction and encourage Government to promote and develop this scheme in a way which ensures it is accessible, appropriately resourced and monitored.

Key issues: Lifelong learning
One of the basic principles that should underpin lifelong learning is the democratic one of equality of status as people. Access in adult life to desirable employment and choices is closely linked to level of educational attainment. Equal political rights cannot exist where some are socially excluded and educationally disadvantaged. The lifelong opportunities of those who are educationally disadvantaged are in sharp contrast to the opportunities for meaningful participation of those who have completed a second or third level education. Therefore, lifelong education should be seen as a basic need. In this context, second chance education and continuing education are vitally important and require ongoing support.

Access to educational opportunity and meaningful participation in the system together with access to successful outcomes is central to the democratic delivery of education. This is not to suggest a one-menu approach for everyone; rather it posits a variety of channels leading to parity of esteem. Equally it does not suppose a similar timeframe for the completion of a particular phase of education for everyone. Such a vision mirrors the stated policy of the White Paper on Adult Education and Lifelong Learning (2000), which sought to develop a strategic and targeted response which is co-ordinated within itself and with other sectors. This strategy would also enable progressive movement between education/home/work as a prelude to the development of mass provision. However, certain priority groups would be targeted initially and in the future in the interests of social inclusion and economic efficiency.

Within this context it is important to emphasise that people should not be seen as failures if they choose not to progress to third level on successful completion of second level education. This is a fundamentally different issue to the failure to complete second level education. It should be acknowledged that it is perfectly acceptable for young people to take alternative pathways to adult self-reliance and participation in the labour market. However, this suggests that people who take this approach should have access (for education and training purposes) to the resources that would otherwise have been spent on them by the state if they had gone into full-time third level education directly from school. An initiative along these lines is required. The exchequer invests 2.5 times more money per capita in the education of those who complete three years of third-level education than it does for those who leave school before the completion of post-primary education. In the light of the barriers to educational participation of the more disadvantaged people, especially at post-school level, a basic educational allowance for full-time and part-time education should be available to each person between the ages of eighteen and forty who does not proceed to third level from school. Eligible parties seeking re-entry to second chance education at all levels could draw upon such monies on demand for educational courses. Such an initiative could serve to increase access over an extended period for people currently disadvantaged by financial constraints and third-level structures. In this way, a culture of access to continuing lifelong educational opportunity might become the norm. The right to equality of educational opportunity has long been accepted both by individuals and by the state. This concept of equality of educational opportunity implies equality of educational funding by the state for its citizens. Such funding is, in fact, an issue of rights, of equality, of social inclusion and of citizenship. It should be additional to funding for educationally disadvantaged, socially excluded and marginalised people. Also, it should be additional to funding provided to respond to educational disadvantage through the home and the community. Unfortunately, recent policy decisions have moved backwards rather than towards these objectives. Budget 2011 reduced funding for the School Completion Programme, Youthreach, Adult Literacy and Community Education by 5 per cent in each case. These programmes provide training and skills to those at risk. Again, poor and vulnerable people will not be provided with the skills to participate fully in Ireland's recovery and the cycle of disadvantage and social exclusion will continue.

Key issues: Contributing to higher education

There are strong arguments from an equity perspective that those who benefit from higher education, and who can afford to contribute to the costs of their higher education, should do so. This principle is well established internationally and is an important component of funding strategies for many of the better higher education systems across the world.

Social Justice Ireland believes that Government should introduce a system in which fees are paid by all participants in third level education with an income-contingent loan facility being put in place to ensure that all participants who need to do so can borrow to pay their fees and cover their living costs, and repay their borrowing when their income rises above a particular level. In this system:

- All students would be treated on the same basis insofar as both tuition and living cost loans would be available on a deferred re-payment basis;
- All students would be treated on the same basis as repayment is based on their own future income rather than on current parental income;
- Inclusion of all part-time students would reduce the present disparity between full-time and part-time students.

Were such a scheme introduced, Social Justice Ireland believes the gain to the Exchequer would be €445m on a full-year basis (2011 estimates) and €120m of this should go towards primary level and adult literacy programmes.

Resources required
The Irish public has consistently favoured a situation where government meets all the costs of first and second level education. There is also strong support for government supporting additional educational spending on children with learning difficulties. Likewise there is strong support for government providing the necessary support to ensure there are alternative pathways for those who fail to complete second level education. Government should act on this support and provide the required financing on condition that it can be shown that value is being got for the money invested.

There is also a need to secure funding for further developing early childhood education and for lifelong education. It is clear that substantial additional funding will be required to support these areas in the years ahead. This additional funding would be a good investment for the future and a good use of the resources being made available as a result of the economic growth of recent years.

Education is widely recognised as crucial to the achievement of our national objectives of economic competitiveness, social inclusion and active citizenship. However, the overall levels of public funding for education in Ireland are out-of-step with our social and economic aspirations. This under-funding is most severe in the early years of education and in the area of second-chance education - the very areas that are most vital in terms of the promotion of greater equity and fairness.

Key Priorities on Education and Educational Disadvantage

- Make access to ongoing educational opportunities the norm. To this end:
  - Ensure quality childcare and pre-school education, preferably in a community setting.
  - Ensure meaningful participation in education up to the end of second level.
  - Prioritise access to education for those outside the formal school system by the provision of user friendly structures and systems which enable equality of access for all.
  - Increase the resources available for adult and second chance education.

- Adopt a new and more ambitious adult literacy target.

- Significantly increase the funding provided to address literacy problems including the funding provided to the National Adult Literacy Agency (NALA).

- Introduce a Basic Educational Allowance for full-time and part-time education for each person between ages 18 and 40 who does not proceed to third level from school.

- Target resources and adjust the curriculum to address the problem of early school leaving and thereby minimise the future costs (for the individual and society) of this problem.

- Ensure the right to self-realisation and equal participation in society by
  - widening access to back-to-education initiatives
  - improved student support for the educationally disadvantaged
  - the provision of a basic educational investment allowance
  - work-linked and full-time literacy initiatives.

3.8 Intercultural & Migration Issues

> **CORE POLICY OBJECTIVE:**
> **INTERCULTURAL & MIGRATION ISSUES**
> To ensure that all people can contribute to developing the underpinning values and meaning of society and can have their own cultures respected in this process, and to ensure that Ireland is open to welcoming people from different cultures and traditions in a way that is consistent with our history, our obligations as world citizens and with our economic status

Respect for and recognition of their culture represents an important right of people within every society. Culture is defined by UNESCO as "the whole complex of distinctive spiritual, material, intellectual and emotional features that characterise a society or social group. It includes not only the arts and letters, but also modes of life, the fundamental rights of the human being, value systems, traditions and beliefs".

Many people in Ireland today – particularly Travellers, immigrants, refugees and asylum-seekers among others – do not experience a society where the majority population respects their cultures. In fact, as we became more racially diverse, it became evident that Irish society is capable of being as racist as any of our European neighbours who live in mixed racial societies. Government policy should continue to encourage the creation of a multi-racial, inclusive society and more progress is needed in this area.[73]

The Key Challenge of Integration
The rapid internationalisation of the Irish population in recent years presents this country with a key challenge - that of avoiding the mistakes made by many other countries through integrating rather than isolating these new migrant populations. While the scale of this internationalisation has declined with the onset of the recent recession, immigrants make up approximately ten per cent of the Irish labour force a figure that is unlikely to change significantly over the next few years, even when account is taken of emigration levels. The aforementioned CSO population

---

[73] Issues concerning migrant workers are dealt with in section 3.3.

projections (see section 2) also suggest that the immigrant population will continue to expand over forthcoming decades once the national and international economies have recovered. *Social Justice Ireland* believes that this is a major policy agenda and one that requires further attention.

It is worth noting the comments of President McAleese on this issue; delivered in a speech to the British Council in London in March 2007. There she stated that "drawing these newcomers deeply and happily into every facet of Irish society is one of the most important social issues we face over the next few decades…As one of the world's great exporters of people, as a culture steeped in the emigrant experience, we have both the challenge now, and the chance, to make the emigrant experience in Ireland something to be truly proud of".

Despite the fact that throughout this section we focus principally on the problems facing refugees, asylum-seekers and migrants, it is important to recognise that other groups, such as Travellers, also require their culture to be respected as of right.[74] Implementation of the recommendations of the Task Force on the Travelling People has progressed with the establishment of the structures recommended by the report. However, it is very important to ensure that the recommendations of the report are fully implemented.

Migrant Workers
Asylum-seekers are not the only foreigners who have come to Ireland in numbers over recent years. Many Irish companies recruited staff from abroad and various assessments of the performance of the Irish economy over the past decade have identified the input of these workers as of importance to the achievement of our economic growth over the period up to 2008. Others arrived here from new EU member states and many other countries.

A key requirement in this context is the need to integrate immigration policy with refugee and asylum-seeking policy. It also requires a recognition and acceptance of the importance of equality of respect and esteem in this area. We also note the need for more detailed information on the number of migrant workers living in Ireland. It is generally accepted that the Census 2006 figures were likely to be an underestimate of the true picture – for example the Census found that there were 63,276 Poles when the figure is generally accepted to be around 100,000 and it also

---

[74] We have addressed other issues concerning Travellers in a number of other sections of this review.

reported that there were 16,633 Chinese when the figure is likely to be between 60,000 and 100,000. While some members of these communities have left and are likely to leave over the next year or two, the provision of this information is important for the policy formation process and will be an important output from Census 2011.

Refugees and Asylum Seekers
For many years across the world the number of refugees forced to flee from their own countries in order to escape war, persecution and abuses of human rights was declining. In its most recent report the United Nations High Commission for Refugees (UNHCR) signalled a sizeable reversal of this trend. By the end of 2009, the latest period for which comprehensive statistics are available, the total population of concern to UNHCR was estimated at 36.5 million people, including 10.4 million refugees; 984,000 asylum-seekers; 251,000 refugees who had repatriated during 2009; 15.6 million internally displaced persons (IDPs) protected/assisted by UNHCR; 2.2 million IDPs who had returned to their place of origin in 2009; 6.6 million stateless persons; and 412,000 others of concern (UNHCR, 2010).

Irish people have a long tradition of solidarity with peoples facing oppression within their own countries, but that tradition is not reflected in our policies towards refugees and asylum-seekers. *Social Justice Ireland* believes that Ireland should use its position in international forums to highlight the causes of the displacement of peoples. In particular Ireland should use these forums to challenge the production, sale and free access to arms and the implements of torture.

Table 3.8.1 shows how the number of asylum-seekers in Ireland increased between 1992 and 2002. Since then the numbers declined and in 2010 they dropped below 2,000 for the first time since 1996. The main countries of origin of the 2010 applicants were Nigeria (21.4 per cent), Pakistan (11.2 per cent), China (9 per cent), Ghana (5.8 per cent) and Afghanistan (4.7 per cent).

The figures for asylum-seekers in 2002 represented the highest number of applications on record. In response the government amended the 1996 Refugee Act and created two independent statutory offices for the processing of asylum applications: the Refugee Applications Commissioner and the Refugee Appeals Tribunal. Additional staff and resources were been allocated to speed up the processing times for asylum applications; however the delay for some applicants is still considerable. The Refugee Legal Service was also been given more staff and resources.

Table 3.8.1: Applications for asylum in Ireland, 1992-2011			
Year	Number	Year	Number
1992	39	2002	11,634
1993	91	2003	7,900
1994	362	2004	4,766
1995	424	2005	4,323
1996	1,179	2006	4,314
1997	3,883	2007	3,985
1998	4,626	2008	3,866
1999	7,724	2009	2,689
2000	10,938	2010	1,939
2001	10,325	2011★	258

Source: Office of the Refugee Applications Commissioner Monthly Statistics (February, 2011).
Note: ★ 2011 figure for first 2 months of the year.

While asylum-seekers are assigned initial accommodation in Dublin, most are subsequently allocated accommodation at locations outside Dublin, pending completion of the asylum-seeking process. The Reception and Integration Agency (RIA) was established to perform this task. As of January 2011 the RIA had 46 accommodation centres including one reception centre and one centre to assist destitute nationals from EU and EU accession states, 42 accommodation centres and two self-catering centres spread across 18 counties in Ireland. A total of 6,042 people were resident in these centres (RIA, 2011).

The policy of "direct provision" employed in almost all of these centres results in these asylum-seekers receiving accommodation and board, together with €19.10 per week per adult and €9.60 per child. *Social Justice Ireland* believes that this is an inadequate amount of money. Furthermore, over time this sum has remained unchanged and its value has therefore been eroded by inflation. To assess the impact of inflation on the real value of these payments table 3.8.2 calculates the decreasing buying power of these sums since the introduction of the euro currency on January 1st 2002. Prior to the arrival of the euro payments equalled £15 per week per adult and £7.50 per week per child.

Table 3.8.2: The Real Value of Direct Provision Payments, 2002-2010

Year	Inflation rate	Real Adult Value	Real Child Value	% devaluation versus 2002
Start 2002		€19.10	€9.60	-
2002	4.6%	€18.22	€9.16	-4.60%
2003	3.5%	€17.58	€8.84	-7.94%
2004	2.2%	€17.20	€8.64	-9.96%
2005	2.5%	€16.77	€8.43	-12.22%
2006	4.0%	€16.10	€8.09	-15.73%
2007	4.9%	€15.31	€7.69	-19.86%
2008	4.1%	€14.68	€7.38	-23.14%
2009	-4.5%	€15.34	€7.71	-19.68%
2010	-1.0%	€15.49	€7.79	-18.88%

Source: Calculated from CSO (2011:2)

Over these years inflation has decreased the buying power of these payments by almost 19 per cent. Even if there is some justification for such a small income support payment for these asylum-seekers receiving accommodation and board it is incomprehensible that it should be allowed to constantly decrease in real terms year after year. *Social Justice Ireland* believes that these direct provision payments should be increased immediately to at least €65 a week for an adult and €38 for a child. Based on the 2010 data, *Social Justice Ireland* estimates that this change would cost €12.5m per annum and provide notable improvements in the subsistence life being lead by these asylum-seekers.

Ireland has both a moral and legal responsibility towards refugees and asylum-seekers. As a nation whose own people have themselves experienced the pain of emigration in the past, we should be to the forefront in implementing our obligations under the 1951 UN Geneva Convention relating to the Status of Refugees. The non-governmental organisations (NGOs), already playing a major role in addressing the many issues that arise in this context, should be resourced to continue and develop their work.

Asylum-seekers are among the most excluded and marginalised in Ireland, yet they are treated in a very unjust way by Irish society. The single most important issue in this context is the fact that they are denied access to employment. Consequently we propose that asylum-seekers who currently are not entitled to take up employment should be allowed to do so with immediate effect. Removing this restriction would have a major impact on reducing their poverty and exclusion.

Key Priorities on Intercultural & Migration Issues

- Develop and resource a cultural policy which involves a dynamic conserving of traditions and beliefs, while also developing a vision for the future which incorporates hope, confidence and involvement.

- Establish a new framework to address the broader issue of integration policy. In doing so recognise that this is a key policy objective necessary for the long term wellbeing and stability of Irish society.

- Recognise the right to work of all asylum-seekers whose application for asylum is at least six-months old (and who are not entitled to take up employment).

- Provide fully resourced language training as well as free full-time education, certified courses and public health education for migrants and asylum-seekers.

- Ensure proper protection and care of minors, while safeguarding their rights and the integrity of the migration and asylum processes.

- Give to asylum-seekers on 'direct provision' who are more than six months awaiting the processing of their application, equal rights to accommodation and other social welfare provision, in line with the rights enjoyed by other Irish residents.

- Immediately increase the weekly allowance allocated to asylum-seekers on 'direct provision' to at least €65 a week for an adult and €38 for a child.

- Ensure that appropriate measures are taken to address the trafficking of women and children for sexual exploitation and recognise that prostitution is violence in its own right.

- Government should argue that the production and sale of arms and instruments of torture be curtailed and should lobby for the elimination of child soldiers.

3.9 Participation

> **CORE POLICY OBJECTIVE: PARTICIPATION**
> To ensure that all people have a genuine voice in shaping the decisions that affect them and to ensure that all people can contribute to the development of society

The changing nature of democracy has raised many questions for policy-makers and others concerned about the issue of participation. Decisions often appear to be made without any real involvement of the many affected by the decisions' outcomes. The context of the 2011 general election dissipated some of the voter apathy that had been widespread over previous years. Indeed the election also reminded voters of the importance of governance and decision making in democratic societies. As chart 3.9.1 shows voter turnout has been falling over time reaching a low point of 62.6 per cent in 2002. The 2011 turnout, at 70.1 per cent, was an improvement on previous elections and brought Ireland's turnout above the European average for the first time since the 1980s; the EU-27 average turnout is 69.7 per cent (CSO, 2010:44).[75]

The most recent in-depth analysis of voter participation was done in 2003 by the CSO. In a quarterly national household survey module on voter participation and abstention issued in April 2003 the CSO provided an insight into how people regarded the electoral process. It examined participation in the May 2002 general election and found high levels of non-participation among young people.[76] Just over 40 per cent of those aged 18-19 and only 53 per cent of those aged 20-24 years voted in the 2002 election. This contrasts with participation figures of well above 80 per cent for older voters aged over 65.

---

[75] The 2006 review of the accuracy of the electoral register may suggest that the official figures for 2002 and 2007 are somewhat understated.

[76] A similar study was not carried out following the 2007 General Election.

Chart 3.9.1: Percentage turnout in Irish General Elections, 1973-2011.

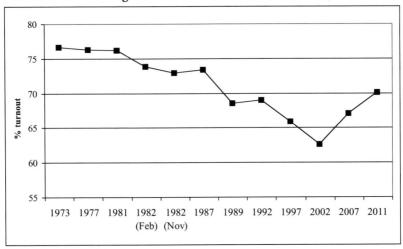

Source: CSO (2010:44) and Department of Environment, Heritage and Local Government (2011).

The survey also examined why people did not participate in the election and found that 20.4 per cent of non-voters said they had "no interest"; 10.6 per cent were "disillusioned" with politics; 3.7 per cent felt that their "vote would make no difference"; and 2.9 per cent were "lacking understanding/information" and so did not vote. Other reasons for not voting were: *not registered* (21.8 per cent); *away* (15.6 per cent); *too busy* (8.5 per cent); *illness/disability* (6 per cent); *no polling card* (3.8 per cent); and *lack of transport* (1.3 per cent). Across the age groups young people were more likely to be *not registered* and *not interested* (CSO, 2003:5). Finally the survey also found that it is those people who participate least in other areas of society (employment, voluntary groups, organisations) that do not participate in elections.

The implications of these findings suggest that many people, especially young people, have little confidence in the political process. They have been disillusioned because the political process fails to involve them in any real way, while also failing to address many of their core concerns. Transparency and accountability are demanded but rarely delivered. Many of the developments of recent years will simply have added to the disillusionment of many people. A new approach is clearly needed to address this issue.

An agreed forum and structure for argument on issues on which people disagree is a need that is becoming more obvious as political and mass communication systems develop. Most people are not involved in the processes that produce plans and decisions which affect their lives. They know that they are being presented with a *fait accompli*. More critically, they realise that they and their families will be forced to live with the consequences of the decisions taken. A lack of structures and systems to involve people in the decision-making process results in the exclusion and alienation of large sections of society. It causes and maintains inequality.

Any exclusion of people from debate on the issues that affect them is suspect. Such exclusion leaves those responsible for it open to charges concerning the arbitrary use of power. Some of the decision-making structures of our society and of our world allow people to be represented in the decision-making process. However, almost all of these structures fail to provide genuine participation for most people affected by their decisions. Our society and the world in which we live need decision-making structures that enable participation. To enable real participation to occur a process of deliberative democracy is required. Deliberative democratic structures enable discussion and debate to take place without any imposition of power differentials. Issues and positions are argued and discussed on the basis of the available evidence rather than on the basis of assertions by those who are powerful and unwilling to consider the evidence. Deliberative democracy produces evidence-based policy.

Deliberative participation by all is essential if society is to develop and, in practice, to maintain principles guaranteeing satisfaction of basic needs, respect for others as equals, economic equality, and religious, social, sexual and ethnic equality. Modern means of communication and information make it relatively easy to involve people in dialogue and decision-making. It is a question of political will - will the groups who have the power share it with others?

Some progress was made over the past decade. At local government level the development of Community Forums, Strategic Policy Committees and County/City Development Boards were moves in the right direction. So also were some of the developments in social dialogue at national level, most importantly the creation of the Community and Voluntary Pillar and the Environmental Pillar. However, these initiatives failed to develop real deliberative processes. In practice power differentials were used to undermine the validity of evidence-based policy proposals. While evidence-based proposals can be undermined in this way the issue of real participation has quite some distance to go before the rhetoric of participation is matched by reality.

Task Force on Active Citizenship
The Task Force on Active Citizenship was established in 2006. It was asked to recommend measures which could become part of public policy to facilitate and encourage a greater degree of engagement by citizens in all aspects of life and the growth and development of voluntary organisations as part of a strong civic culture. Its final report, published in March 2007, provided a total of 25 broad ranging recommendations for enhancing citizen's participation in all aspects of Irish life. *Social Justice Ireland* considers this an important report. Arising from the work of this Task Force, consideration should be given to the development of appropriate measures and indicators of social capital, and to future approaches in relation to citizenship education and voter participation.

A forum for dialogue on civil society issues

An issue that is contributing to disillusionment with the political process concerns the range of civil society issues that are of major concern to large numbers of people but are never really discussed. There are many issues that people feel are not being addressed adequately; insofar as a discussion or debate does take place, they feel that they are not allowed to participate in any real way.

The development of a new forum within which a civil society debate could be conducted on an ongoing basis would be a welcome addition to the political landscape in Ireland. Such a forum could make a major contribution to improving participation by a wide range of groups in Irish society.

Social Justice Ireland proposes that government authorise and resource an initiative to identify how a civil society debate could be developed and maintained in an ongoing way in Ireland, and to examine how it might connect to the growing debate at European level around civil society issues.

There are many issues such a forum could address. One such issue that comes to mind, given recent developments in Ireland, is the issue of citizenship, its rights, responsibilities, possibilities and limitations in the twenty-first century. Another topical issue is the shape of the social model Ireland wishes to develop in the decades ahead. Do we follow a European model or an American one? Or do we want to create an alternative - and, if so, what shape would it have and how could it be delivered? The issues a civil society forum could address are many and varied. Ireland would benefit immensely from having such a forum.[77]

---

[77] For a further discussion of this issue see Healy and Reynolds (2003:191-197).

Impact on the democratic process

Would a civil society forum and a new social contract against exclusion take from the democratic process? Democracy means "rule by the people". This implies that people participate in shaping the decisions that affect them most closely. What we have, in practice, is a highly centralised government in which we are "represented" by professional politicians. The more powerful a political party becomes, the more distant it seems to become from the electorate. Party policies on a range of major issues are often difficult to discern. Backbenchers have little control over, or influence on, government ministers, opposition spokespersons or shadow cabinets. Even within the cabinet some ministers seem to be able to ignore their cabinet colleagues.

The democratic process has certainly benefited from the participation of various sectors in different arenas. It would also benefit from taking up the proposals to develop a new social contract against exclusion and a new forum for dialogue on civil society issues.

The decline in participation is exacerbated by the primacy given to the market by so many analysts, commentators, policy-makers and politicians. Many people feel that their views or comments are ignored or patronised, while the views of those who see the market as solving most if not all of society's problems are treated with the greatest respect. This situation seems to be persisting despite the total failure of market mechanisms in recent years during which these very mechanisms combined to produce Ireland's range of current crises – and the linked EU-level crises that are not currently being recognised by most decision-makers.

Markets have a major role to play. But it needs to be honestly acknowledged that markets produce very mixed results when left to their own devices. Recent experience has shown clearly that in terms of many policy goals, markets are extremely limited. Consequently other mechanisms are required to ensure that some re-balancing, at least, is achieved. The mechanisms proposed here simply aim to be positive in improving participation in a twenty-first century society.

Supporting the Community and Voluntary Sector

The issue of governance is of major importance for Government and for society at large. Within this wider reality it is an especially crucial issue for the Community and Voluntary sector. There is a substantial role for civil society in addressing both the causes and the consequences of the multi-faceted crises Ireland currently faces (economic, banking, fiscal, social and reputational).

The Community and Voluntary sector is playing a major role in responding to both the causes and the consequences of these crises. Support for this work is crucial and it should not be left to the charity (welcome but very limited) of philanthropists. Funding is required by the sector and has been provided over many years by Government. In recent years much of that funding has been reduced with obvious consequences for those depending on the Community and Voluntary sector. It is crucial that the new Government appropriately resource this sector into the future and that it remains committed to the principle of providing multi-annual statutory funding.

Social dialogue is a critically important component of any effective decision-making in a modern democracy. The Community and Voluntary Pillar provides a mechanism for social dialogue that should be engaged with by the new Government. All aspects of governance must be characterised by transparency and accountability. Social dialogue contributes to both transparency and accountability. We believe governance along these lines can and should be developed in Ireland.

Key Priorities on Participation

- **Establish and resource a forum for dialogue on civil society issues. This initiative should identify how a civil society debate could be developed and maintained in an ongoing way in Ireland and should examine how it might connect to the growing debate at European level around civil society issues.**

- **Significantly increase the funding to C&V sector organisations providing services, facilitating participation at national and local level and addressing both the causes and the consequences of Ireland's current series of crises.**

- **Ensure that there is real and effective monitoring of policy implementation. Involve a wide range of perspectives in this process, thus ensuring inclusion of the experience of those currently excluded.**

- **Resource voter education programmes for young people and socially excluded people.**

- **Strengthen the mechanisms of engagement between the state and the C&V sector.**

3.10 Sustainability

> **CORE POLICY OBJECTIVE: SUSTAINABILITY**
> To ensure that all development is socially, economically and environmentally sustainable

Sustainability is a crucial issue for people and the environment in the 21st century. Too often, however, sustainability is defined in terms that are too narrow. Sustainability is about a range of issues including environmental, economic and social. To complement the economic and social analysis elsewhere in this publication, this section focuses first on promoting sustainable development before then turning to assess environmental issues.

(a) Promoting Sustainable Development

The search for a humane, sustainable model of development has gained momentum in recent times. After years of people believing that markets and market forces would produce a better life for everyone, major problems and unintended side-effects have raised questions and doubts. There is a growing awareness that sustainability must be a constant factor in all development, whether social, economic or environmental.

This fact was reiterated by Kofi Annan, the then Secretary-General of the United Nations, at the opening of the World Summit on Sustainable Development in Johannesburg, South Africa (September 2002). There he stated that the aim of the conference was

> to bring home the uncomfortable truth that the model of development that has prevailed for so long has been fruitful for the few, but flawed for the many.

And he further added that

> The world today, facing the twin challenges of poverty and pollution, needs to usher in a season of transformation and stewardship – a season in which we make a long overdue investment in a secure future.

Sustainable development has been defined in many different ways. Perhaps the best-known definition is that contained in *Our Common Future* (World Commission on Environment and Development, 1987:43):

development that meets the needs of the present without compromising the ability of future generations to meet their own needs.

It is crucial that the issues of environmental, economic and social sustainability be firmly at the core of the decision making process.

The need for shadow national accounts

Conventional economic models of development or progress fail to meet the needs of millions and millions of people on this planet today. This failure is evident even within better-off countries such as Ireland. These conventional economic models also compromise the ability of future generations to meet their needs. As this becomes more evident, there is a growing demand worldwide to find new models that will conserve the planet and its resources and empower people to meet their own needs and the needs of others.

Central to any model of development which has sustainability at its core must be a realisation of the need to move away from money-measured growth, as the principal economic target and measure of success, towards sustainability in terms of real-life social, environmental and economic variables. Already within mainstream decision-making, this realisation has begun to have some impact. This can be seen, for example, in the growing awareness that environmental taxation should be recognised as a key policy instrument in dealing with environmental concerns. Public concern in the area of genetically modified (GM) food stands as another example. In the context of income and social welfare policy, the increasing recognition of the benefits of a basic income are a further example of the same search for policies that will be sustainable into the future (see section 3.1(d)). The growing demand for the recognition of unpaid work being done in society stands as yet another example. As can be seen from these examples, however, there is a long way to go before Ireland or the EU can claim to have placed sustainability at the centre of their development models.

A central initiative in this context should be the development of "satellite" or "shadow" national accounts. Our present national accounts miss fundamentals such as environmental sustainability. Their emphasis is on GNP/GDP as scorecards of wealth and progress. These measures, which came into widespread use during World War II, more or less ignore the environment, and completely ignore unpaid work. Only money transactions are tracked. Ironically, while environmental depletion is ignored, the environmental costs of dealing with the effects of economic growth, such as cleaning up pollution or coping with the felling of rain forests, are added to, rather than subtracted from, GNP/GDP. New scorecards are needed.

Already a number of alternative scorecards exist, such as the United Nations' Human Development Index (HDI), former World Bank economist Herman Daly's Index of Sustainable Economic Welfare (ISEW) and Hazel Henderson's Country Futures Index (CFI). A 2002 study by Wackernagel et al presented the first systematic attempt to calculate how human demands on the environment are matched by its capacity to cope. It found that we currently use 120 per cent of what the earth can provide sustainably each year.

In the environmental context it is crucial that dominant economic models are challenged on (among other things) their assumptions that nature's capital (clean air, water and environment) are essentially free and inexhaustible; that scarce resources can always be substituted; and that the planet can continue absorbing human and industrial wastes which most economists tend to downplay as externalities.

Some governments and international agencies have picked up on these issues, especially in the environmental area. They have begun to develop "satellite" or "shadow" national accounts, which include items not traditionally measured. Our 2009 publication *Beyond GDP: What is prosperity and how should it be measured?* explored many of these new developments (from the OECD and the New Economics Foundation among others). It also proposed a series of policy developments which would assist in achieving similar progress in Ireland. Here, there has been limited progress in this area, including commitments to better data collection and broader assessment of well-being and progress by the CSO, ESRI and EPA. However, much remains to be achieved and *Social Justice Ireland* strongly urges government to adopt this broader perspective and commit to producing these accounts alongside more comprehensive indicators of progress.

Principles to underpin sustainable development
Principles to underpin sustainable development were proposed in a report for the European Commission prepared by James Robertson in May 1997. Entitled *The New Economics of Sustainable Development*, the report argued that these principles would include the following:

- systematic empowerment of people (as opposed to making and keeping them dependent) as the basis for people-centred development

- systematic conservation of resources and environment as the basis for environmentally sustainable development
- evolution from a "wealth of nations" model of economic life to a "one-world" economic system
- evolution from today's international economy to an ecologically sustainable, decentralising, multi-level one-world economic system
- restoration of political and ethical factors to a central place in economic life and thought
- respect for qualitative values, not just quantitative values
- respect for feminine values, not just masculine ones.

At first glance, these might not appear to be the concrete guidelines that policy-makers so often seek. Yet they are principles that are relevant to every area of economic life. They also apply to every level of life, ranging from personal and household to global issues. They impact on lifestyle choices and organisational goals. If these principles were applied to every area, level and feature of economic life they would provide a comprehensive checklist for a systematic policy review.

It is also important that any programme for sustainable development should take a realistic view of human nature, recognising that people are altruistic and selfish, co-operative and competitive. Consequently it is important to develop the economic system to reward activities that are socially and environmentally benign (and not the reverse, as at present). This in turn would make it easier for people and organisations to make choices that are socially and environmentally responsible. A simple example is the tax on plastic bags. It shows how quickly people can and will change. In just one week some retail outlets were reporting a 90 per cent reduction in the use of plastic bags. Overall the Department of Environment and Local Government estimated that usage had declined by 95 per cent (approximately one billion bags) in 2002. Since then there has been some increase in usage despite an increase in the levy. This highlights the need to sustain the effort required in relevant areas to ensure the need for sustainable development is recognised and pursued.

Any programme for sustainable development has implications for public spending. In addressing this issue it needs to be understood that public expenditure programmes and taxes provide a framework which helps to shape market prices, rewards some kinds of activities and penalises others. Within this framework there are other areas which are not supported by public expenditure or are not taxed. This framework should be developed to encourage economic efficiency and enterprise, social equity and environmental sustainability. Systematic reviews should be carried out and published on the sustainability effects of all public subsidies and other relevant public expenditure and tax differentials. Such reviews could then lead to the elimination of subsidies that favour unsustainable development. Systematic reviews should also be carried out and published on the possibilities for re-orientating public spending programmes, with the aim of preventing and reducing social and environmental problems.

Monitoring sustainable development: some problems
Many studies have highlighted the lack of socio-economic and environmental data in Ireland required to assess trends in sustainable development. A chapter by Carrie in the Feasta review (2005) focused on the lack of long-run socio-economic data on issues such as education participation, crime and healthcare. Another paper by Scott (ESRI, 2005) outlined the empirical and methodological gaps which continue to impede the incorporation of sustainable development issues into public policy making and assessment. It is only through a sustained commitment to data collection in all of these areas that these deficiencies will be addressed. We welcome recent developments in this area, particularly at the CSO, and look forward to all of these data impediments being removed in the years to come.

(b) Environmental Issues
Our environment is a priceless asset. Its protection is of major importance not just to current times but also to the generations that will follow us. However, the environment is regularly taken for granted; it is often mistreated and excessively exploited. We start this section with a brief overview of some key environmental facts about Ireland. Then, we examine a number of environmental issues that are of concern at this time.

Ireland: some key environmental facts
Recent publications from the CSO and the EPA (Environmental Protection Agency) offer some very interesting figures on environmental issues and policies in Ireland. While it is only possible to assess a fraction of the issues covered by these documents, the following are among the key figures reported:

- Air pollution in Dublin, Cork and Limerick has decreased significantly since the introduction of legal restrictions on the sale of non-smokeless coals. Dublin, Cork and 21 other Irish towns now record pollution levels comfortably below the EU limits. Dublin last exceeded that limit in the period of 1998-1999 and it has not been broken anywhere in Ireland since then.

- 'Acid rain precursor emissions' decreased by 34 per cent between 1990 and 2008. However, they are still five per cent above the agreed targets for 2010 set out in the Gothenburg protocol.
- 30 per cent of Ireland's river water is classified by the EPA as polluted. Progress on reducing this percentage has been limited over the past twenty years.
- Between 1999 and 2008, Ireland's greenhouse gas emissions increased 20 per cent despite commitments in the Kyoto protocol. Since then these have significantly reduced due to the economic recession.
- The number of private cars in Ireland per 1,000 population has increased from 227 in 1990 to 435 in 2008 (137 per cent). Over the same period related CO_2 emissions increased by 179 per cent.
- In 1997 93.1 per cent of all inland freight was transported by road. This increased to 99.4 per cent in 2008, 23.4 percentage points higher than the EU-27 average.
- There were 730,494 hectares of afforested land in Ireland in 2008. This represents a gain of almost 6,248 hectares on 2007 and an increase of 51.8 per cent since 1990.
- In 2008 trees removed 2,167 kilotonnes of CO_2 from the Irish atmosphere while road transport created 14,062 kilotonnes.
- Oil and gas accounted for 80.7 per cent of Ireland's energy supply in 2009.
- In 2009 renewable energy provided only 4.5 per cent of Ireland's electricity generation needs.
- In 2009, 41.5 per cent of Ireland's energy demands derived from transport, 25.3 per cent from residential households, 17.5 per cent from industry, 13.4 per cent from services and 2.3 per cent from agriculture.
- In 2008 Ireland produced 3.22 million tonnes of waste – a 7 per cent increase since 2003. Of this waste, 60.1 per cent was landfilled and 36.1 per cent was recycled.

(Data from *Measuring Ireland's Progress 2009* (CSO 2010: 67-73), *The Statistical Yearbook of Ireland 2010* (CSO 2010: 307-317); and *Ireland's Environment 2008* (EPA, 2009).)

(i) Waste disposal and recycling

In 1995 the total household and commercial waste collected in Ireland equalled 1.385 million tonnes. Since then, the volume of waste has increased significantly to reach 3.104 million tonnes in 2008; a 124 per cent increase (CSO, 2010:316). While the recession and construction industry collapse has decreased these levels from a peak in 2007, the scale of this increase over such a short period of time highlights the importance of this issue. At this rate of growth it is no surprise that our landfill capacity will soon be reached. In that context continued efforts to encourage reductions in waste generation and additional recycling are necessary.

The management of this growing volume of waste remains a challenge. In 2008, 36.1 per cent of our waste was recovered/recycled and 60.1 per cent went to landfill. This represents an improvement on 2003, when 24.2 per cent of waste was recovered (CSO, 2009:72). Using data from 2007, when 34.1 per cent of waste was recycled and 59.3 per cent landfilled, table 3.10.1 shows there are still some problematic areas where levels of landfill remain very high. Targeted policies in the areas of plastics, textiles and organic waste are clearly needed if we are to further increase this recycling figure. However, it should be noted that the increase to 36.1 per cent of waste recycled in 2008 represented the first year in which Ireland reached the EU target of 35 per cent. This target was to be met by 2013 and its early achievement proves that through good policies, real changes and improvements in environmental policies can be achieved.

Table 3.10.1: Total waste collected and landfilled in Ireland in 2007		
Material	Tonnes (000s)	% Landfilled
Paper and cardboard	914.1	42.0
Glass	182.6	26.3
Plastic	288.8	77.5
Metals (Aluminium etc)	133.5	37.5
Textiles	244.9	95.6
Organic Waste	918.4	92.4
Wood	240.7	7.1
Others	251.7	86.6
Total	**3,174.6**	**63.5**

Source: CSO (2009:70)

Social Justice Ireland welcomes this development and we echo the call by the EPA that "a revised target to present new challenges and build on this success is required". While Ireland has achieved the EU recycling target we have some distance to go to match some European countries and the US city of San Francisco which have set targets to eliminate all landfill by 2020. In Germany, Netherlands, Sweden, Austria, Denmark and Belgium less than 5 per cent of municipal waste is landfilled; Germany is the lowest at 0.5 per cent (CSO, 2010:72).

Sustainability

A welcome innovation has been the production of performance league tables of local authority waste management. This comparison has been produced by the Local Government Management Services Board (LGMSB) and its most recent edition was published in February 2011 and related to the year 2009. Their report examined how local authorities have been dealing with the waste produced in their area and in particular it identified the proportion of waste being landfilled. Table 3.10.2 sets out the results for the 4 best and 4 worst local authorities as reported by the LGMSB.

Table 3.10.2: League table of local authority waste management – best and worst

	% Recycling	% Landfill
4 Best		
Longford County Council	45.32	36.3
Fingal County Council	42.19	49.3
Galway City Council	40.64	44.8
Waterford City Council	39.84	49.1
4 Worst		
Meath County Council	16.19	71.7
Carlow County Council	11.16	71.1
South Dublin County Council	23.14	70.6
Limerick City Council	20.87	70.1

Source: LGMSB, 2011: 32-34
Note: Data sorted by percentage recycled (best) and percentage landfilled (worst)

Longford county council topped the league table by recycling 45.32 per cent of their waste. Meath remains the worst performer, having landfilled 71.7 per cent of their waste, though this represents an improvement on 91.7 per cent in 2007. *Social Justice Ireland* welcomes the publication of this league table. Its continued production will ensure that local authorities are incentivised to improve their performance. We also note that it is important to monitor local authority policies which aim to reduce and reuse commodities rather than purely dispose of them.

Both industry and households need to change their attitude towards recycling. Industry in all sectors will have to use fewer material inputs and emit fewer wastes. To facilitate this, government needs to move towards making material inputs and waste disposal far more expensive, and towards making increasing demands for the durability, repairability and recyclability of goods. The highly successful Waste Electrical & Electronic Equipment (WEE) directive marks considerable progress in the right direction. Further EU directives which will force car companies to take back their products at the end of their useful lives are also a necessary step in this direction. The 2008 Finance Bill also allowed companies to claim the full cost of investments in energy efficient equipment against their taxable income. However, more needs to be done. Households will also have to change their behaviour. Sustained campaigns to further encourage and facilitate recycling are necessary, while incentives to recycle rather than landfill need to be put in place.

(ii) Greenhouse gases, air pollution and carbon credits

Over time, Ireland's air has become more and more polluted. Between 1990 and 2008 the EPA reported that Ireland's greenhouse gas emissions grew by 21.3 per cent (see Table 3.10.3). Total combined Irish emissions of the three main greenhouse gases regarded as having global warming potential amounted to 65.9m tonnes of CO_2 equivalent in 2008, up from 55m tonnes in 1990 (CSO, 2010:314).

The most recent figures indicate that current levels of emissions now exceed the limits agreed under the Kyoto protocol. The Irish government and the European Commission agreed a target of an 8 per cent reduction in European CO_2 emissions on their 1990 level by 2012. Within this agreement, Ireland agreed to limit its increase of CO_2 emissions to 13 per cent between 1990 and 2012. Table 3.10.3 reports the level of greenhouse gas emissions versus the 1990 level (set at 100 on the emissions index). *Social Justice Ireland* welcomes Ireland's ongoing commitment to this protocol, despite the refusal of some countries, including the USA, to ratify its implementation. However, these emissions are a major cause of climate change, and it is in all our interests to ensure that the limits agreed in the Kyoto protocol are met.

The recent decline in economic activity is expected to reduce emissions levels although the state will still have to purchase carbon credits to offset our excessive pollution in 2012. However despite recent decreases, it would seem inappropriate to abandon the plans and policy developments of recent years. Clearly, there are additional changes that Ireland can continue to make which will further reduce our emissions levels. In particular, the transport sector has a central role to play. While launching the 2007 figures, the EPA noted that the transport sector recorded the greatest increase between 2006 and 2007 (of 4.7 per cent) and that that sector's pollution contribution has grown by 178 per cent since 1990. If simple policy options are available to address this sustained growth in transport related emissions, they should be adopted.

Table 3.10.3: Ireland's Greenhouse Gas Emissions and the Kyoto Target

Year	Emissions Index	+ / - Kyoto Target	% from target
1990	100	-13.00	-11.5
1998	117.73	+4.73	+4.2
1999	119.0	+5.98	+5.3
2000	121.9	+8.86	+7.8
2001	125.2	+12.18	+10.8
2002	121.8	+8.83	+7.8
2003	121.4	+8.42	+7.5
2004	121.0	+8.04	+7.1
2005	123.8	+10.77	+9.5
2006	122.8	+9.84	+8.7
2007	121.7	+8.66	+7.7
2008	121.3	+8.28	+7.3

Source: CSO (2010:67)

Further issues relating to air quality have also been highlighted by the EPA (2008a: 43). Its report indicates that while the quality of Irish air is generally good and meets the standards set out in EU directives, there are some outstanding issues.

Firstly, the EPA underlines as a key issue the reduction of Ireland's emissions of trans-boundary air pollutants in line with international commitments (EPA, 2008a: 43).

Secondly, traffic emissions in Cork and Dublin have caused levels of nitrogen dioxide and particulate matter to approach EU limits. In Ireland, the growth in traffic on our roads has been one of the more visible elements of our recent economic growth. This enormous growth in car usage (see earlier data at the start of this subsection) is attributed to the lack of an extensive public transport system. The EPA (2008a) concludes that "government departments, national agencies and local authorities must make air quality protection an integral part of their planning and traffic management processes, and there needs to be a modal shift from the private car to high-quality public transport." An integrated, efficient public transport system is urgently required. Infrastructure to divert heavy vehicles away from city and town centres is also essential" (2002: viii). A welcome step in this direction was Budget 2008's reform of VRT and motor taxes. The general thrust of these reforms meant that both VRT and motor taxes have been increased on the most heavily polluting cars and reduced on those with the lowest engine sizes and the smallest carbon dioxide emissions levels. In particular, there would be significant increases in the taxes levied on the highest polluting and largest engine cars. While car sales have slowed due to the economic recession, this is a welcome long-term policy reform.

(iii) Climate change: international and Irish implications

Over the past number of years many questions have been raised with regard to the appropriateness and reliability of the scientific evidence on climate change. In particular, there have been a number of politicians and academics who have dismissed the available evidence and suggested that the identified effects of global warming are part of the Earth's natural cycle. In response to this uncertainty the British Government commissioned an independent report to critically examine the available evidence. Nicholas Stern, a former chief economist of the World Bank and the current head of the British Government Economic Service, researched and wrote the report. Among the key findings of the report are the following:[78]

- Carbon emissions have already pushed up global temperatures by half a degree Celsius
- If no action is taken on emissions, there is more than a 75 per cent chance of global temperatures rising between two and three degrees Celsius over the next 50 years
- Rising sea levels could leave 200 million people permanently displaced
- Up to 40 per cent of species could face extinction
- There will be more examples of extreme weather patterns
- Extreme weather could reduce global gross domestic product (GDP) by up to 1 per cent
- A two to three degrees Celsius rise in temperatures could reduce global GDP by 3 per cent
- In the worst case scenario global consumption per head would fall 20 per cent
- To stabilise at manageable levels, emissions would need to stabilise in the next 20 years and fall between 1 per cent and 3 per cent after that. This would cost 1 per cent of GDP

---

[78] A full version of the report can be downloaded from the website: www.sternreview.org.uk

International reports such as those issued by the Intergovernmental Panel on Climate Change (IPCC, 2001 and 2007) have provided further details on the international implications of climate change. To complement these, two reports focusing on Ireland have been prepared for the EPA by the Department of Geography at the NUI, Maynooth (Sweeney et al, 2003; McElwain and Sweeney, 2007). These presented an assessment of the magnitude and likely impacts of climate change in Ireland over the course of the current century.

The 2003 report entitled *Climate Change: scenarios & impacts for Ireland* predicted the following:

- Current mean January temperatures in Ireland are predicted to increase by 1.5°C by mid-century with a further increase of 0.5–1.0°C by 2075.
- By 2055, the extreme south and south-west coasts will have a mean January temperature of 7.5–8.0°C. By then, winter conditions in Northern Ireland and in the north Midlands will be similar to those currently experienced along the south coast.
- Since temperature is a primary meteorological parameter, secondary parameters such as frost frequency and growing season length and thermal efficiency can be expected to undergo considerable changes over this time interval.
- July mean temperatures will increase by 2.5°C by 2055 and a further increase of 1.0°C by 2075 can be expected. Mean maximum July temperatures in the order of 22.5°C will prevail generally with areas in the central Midlands experiencing mean maxima of up to 24.5°C.
- Overall increases of 11 per cent in precipitation are predicted for the winter months of December–February. The greatest increases are suggested for the north-west, where increases of approximately 20 per cent are suggested by mid-century. Little change is indicated for the east coast and in the eastern part of the Central Plain.
- Marked decreases in rainfall during the summer and early autumn months across eastern and central Ireland are predicted. Nationally, these are of the order of 25 per cent with decreases of over 40 per cent in some parts of the east.

(Sweeney at al, 2003)

Both reports also examine the specific implications of these findings for agriculture, water resources, forestry, sea-levels and eco-systems in Ireland.

A more recent report by the Community Climate Change Consortium for Ireland (2008) published the following key findings:

- Warming of the climate is to continue, particularly in autumn and winter, and in the South and East. Possible increases of 3 to 4°C are expected towards 2100.
- Towards the end of the century, autumns and winters will become 15-25 per cent wetter, while summer will become 10-18 per cent drier. As a result stream flows will be reduced in summer and increase in winter, increasing the risk of flooding.
- An increase in the frequency of very intense cyclones is probable.
- The seas around Ireland will continue warming at trend – 0.3-0.4°C per decade, except for over the Irish Sea, which will continue to warm by 0.6-0.7°C.
- Sea levels are rising 3.5cm per decade.
- Changes in climate may impede the recovery of the ozone layer, bringing the negative health consequences of UV radiation.
- Demand for heating energy is likely to decline significantly with further warming.

Overall these reports suggest that there are considerable implications of climate change for Ireland and they underscore the necessity to adequately address this issue in the immediate future.

(iv) River water quality

Slowly the quality of Ireland's surface waters is improving. In total Ireland has a network of 13,200km of river channels. Table 3.10.4 outlines the findings of the EPA *Water Quality in Ireland 2007-2008* report (2009). The table presents the figures from the earliest data, for the years 1987-1990, and the data for the 2001-2003 and the two most recent assessments. The figures for 2006-2008 recorded a marginal decline in water quality since 2004-06 but an overall improvement across the period. However, it is of concern that 30 per cent of river channels are still classified as polluted to some extent.

Table 3.10.4: Irish River Quality, 1987-2008 (%)				
	1987-90	2001-03	2004-06	2006-08
Unpolluted	77.3	69.3	71.4	70.0
Slightly Polluted	12.0	17.9	18.1	19.0
Moderately Polluted	9.7	12.3	10.0	10.6
Seriously Polluted	0.9	0.6	0.5	0.5
Total	**100.0**	**100.0**	**100.0**	**100.0**

Source: CSO (2010:316)

The EPA (2008) cites a number of sources of this problem. Cases of slight pollution are in the majority caused by agriculture, with municipal sources and forestry also featuring prominently. Moderate pollution is largely caused by municipal and agricultural sources. The bulk of cases of serious pollution are attributed to municipal sources. In all cases, municipal sources most frequently refers to sewage discharge. All of the abovementioned sources pollute waters with phosphorous and nitrates. The EPA's *Environment in Focus* (2006) report suggests that there is a need to promote better farmyard management, to reduce the over-application of fertilisers and to expand the system of nutrient management planning. At river basin district level, improvements were noted in the South Western and South Eastern regions, with more significant deteriorations taking place in the North Western and Shannon regions.

Groundwater quality is also of concern. In the period 1995 to 2006, there have been elevated nitrate concentrations in groundwater in the south-east and east, and elevated phosphate concentrations in the west (EPA, 2008: 5-26). Intensive agricultural practices are likely the source of the former, while the latter is probably caused by the vulnerable nature of Karst aquifers. Protection of groundwater will have to be improved if these problems are to be adequately addressed and if the EU water framework directive is to be fully implemented.

(v) Genetic engineering (GE)
Genetic engineering refers to a set of technologies that artificially move genes across species boundaries to produce new organisms. The techniques involve the manipulation of genetic material and other biologically important chemicals. The resultant organisms have new combinations of genes, and therefore new combinations of traits that are not found in nature and, indeed, are not possible through normal breeding techniques. Proponents of the technology, mainly multinational agribusiness corporations, argue that genetically engineered crops are necessary to feed a growing world population.

By contrast, opponents of agricultural biotechnology claim that genetic engineering will not feed the hungry people in our world. Only sustainable agriculture and equitable social and economic policies at local and global level can effectively tackle malnutrition, hunger and poverty.

Critics of genetic engineering maintain that it is hazardous to human health and the environment, and that it will undermine biodiversity. Given the risks to human health and the environment, and the complex ethical, economic and social issues involved, we believe that a moratorium should be placed on the deliberate release of genetically engineered organisms.

(vi) Environmental taxation and poor households

The extent of Ireland's pollution problem is clear from the studies outlined above. Furthermore, it is also clear that if we are to seriously address this problem then new environmental taxes are necessary. In particular, *Social Justice Ireland* welcomed the announcement of carbon taxation in Budget 2010 and its (slow) implementation across 2010.

One of the objections presented to the increase of excise duties on fuels is that they would substantially damage the economic position of poor households. Indeed research by the ESRI has confirmed this. However, a series of research papers by the ESRI has shown that it is possible to insulate poorer households from the effects of these new taxes (see Bergin et al 2002:25; Scott and Eakins, 2002). Scott and Eakins have suggested that a proportion of the revenue generated by new carbon taxes should be transferred to the Department of Social and Family Affairs and used by them to increase payments (in particular fuel allowances) given to poor households. Such an increase in these payments would therefore compensate poorer households for the effect of the new tax and consequently ensure that Ireland's poorest households do not suffer.

Social Justice Ireland believes that the compensation mechanism proposed for poorer households should have accompanied the introduction of these environmental taxes. They are even more relevant now given recent significant income declines and the commitments in the *National Recovery Plan 2011-2014* and *Memorandum of Understanding* (i.e. the Bailout Agreement) to increase the current carbon tax from €15 to €30 per tonne of CO_2.[79]

---

[79] Taxation issues, including environmental taxes are discussed further in section 3.2.

Sustainability

Key Priorities on Sustainability

- Sustainability-proof all public policy initiatives and provision.

- Restructure the tax system in favour of environmentally benign development and high levels of employment and useful work.

- Terminate subsidies and other public-expenditure programmes that encourage unsustainable development.

- Introduce public purchasing policies that encourage contractors to adopt sustainable practices.

- Develop more self-reliant local economies.

- Develop and implement a programme of accounting, auditing and reporting procedures to establish the sustainability performance of businesses and other organisations.

- Introduce demand-reduction policies in areas such as energy and transport, and tackle the implications of such reduction.

- Fully introduce the *National Climate Change Strategy.*

- Publish the renewed *National Sustainable Development Strategy*.

- **Engage pro-actively and positively in the Rio+20 process.** [This UN Conference on Sustainable Development (UNCSD) marks the 20th anniversary of the 1992 United Nations Conference on Environment and Development (UNCED), in Rio de Janeiro, and the 10th anniversary of the 2002 World Summit on Sustainable Development (WSSD) in Johannesburg.]

3.11 Rural Development

> **CORE POLICY OBJECTIVE:**
> **RURAL DEVELOPMENT**
> To secure the existence of substantial numbers of viable communities in all parts of rural Ireland where every person would have meaningful work, adequate income and access to social services, and where infrastructures needed for sustainable development would be in place

Rural Ireland continues to change dramatically. The 1996 census recorded that 46 per cent of Ireland's population lived in small villages and in the open countryside. This figure declined to 40.4 per cent according to the results of census 2002 and to 39.3 per cent (1,665,535 people) in Census 2006 (CSO, 2003:53; 2007:19). A factor in that reduction is the sustained decline in farm numbers. Agriculture, forestry and fishing now account for only 4.8 per cent (89,500 people) of all those classified as employed in Ireland (CSO, 2011:9). At present those in farming comprise one-quarter of the rural labour force, and are a minority of the rural population. Furthermore, fewer farm children seek a future in farming.

This section addresses a variety of issues relevant to rural Ireland and to its long-term development. A central and persistent theme is that rural Ireland is currently in transition from an agricultural to a rural development agenda.

Farm incomes
We have already reviewed rural income data from the SILC reports (see section 3.1). Those data reflect the fact that among its many characteristics rural Ireland has high dependency levels, increasing out-migration and many small farmers living on very low incomes. Only a minority of farmers are at present generating an adequate income from farming and, even on these farms, income lags considerably behind the national average. An important insight into the income of Irish farmers is provided by Teagasc in their National Farm Survey (2010).

The latest survey, reporting income for 2009 and published in 2010, collected data from a representative sample of 1,029 farm households nationwide. Its results indicate that the average family farm income (FFI) (excluding off-farm income) was €11,968 in 2009, a decrease of 30 per cent from the figure of €16,993 recorded in 2008 and the lowest figure since 1999. The report notes that this income decrease was derived from a reduction in agricultural prices rather than from any reductions in EU and Government transfer payments. Overall, average FFI has fallen by 40 per cent since 2007. Amongst more commercial full-time farmers the average income was €24,214 in 2009, down from €37,590 in 2008 (-36 per cent), while among part-time farmers FFI equalled an average of €6,611 a decline of 13 per cent since 2008 (Teagasc, 2010).

The survey also noted great variations in income depending on the size of the farm and the type of farming pursued. Farmers involved in cattle rearing had an average income of €6,563 while those in dairying had an average from-farm income of €23,684. Farmers mainly in tillage and sheep farming had average incomes of €15,547 and €9,688 respectively. An examination of the distribution of farm income reveals that 6.3 per cent of farmers had an income exceeding €40,000 while 48 per cent of farmers had a 'from-farm' income of less than €6,500. Teagasc found that 143 per cent of average family farm incomes in 2009 were comprised of direct payments or subsidies; the figure in excess of 100 per cent is explained by costs incurred in farming which reduce the amount of the payment available to be used as family income (2010:16). This also suggests that the income derived from market-based output is insufficient to cover total costs of production (i.e. the farm is making a loss).

Off-farm income is extremely important among farm families, especially in the western region. The National Farm Survey indicates that on 52.6 per cent of farms the farmer and/or spouse had an off-farm job and that overall on over 79 per cent of farms the farmer and/or spouse had some source of off farm income be it from employment, pension or social assistance. The results of the Household Budget Survey (CSO, 2007:15) further indicate that less than 47 per cent of farm-household income came from farming in 2004-2005. While the current recession is having a considerable impact on the availability of off-farm jobs, in the long-run the dependence on off-farm incomes is likely to continue thus increasing the importance of additional off-farm income being available if rural poverty and social exclusion are to be addressed.

Table 3.11.1 presents an interesting analysis from the National Farm Survey which assesses the real value of FFI over the period 1995-2009. It reveals a marked decline in farm income in real terms. Measuring in real terms removes the effect of inflation (price increases) and essentially represents the buying power of agricultural earnings. The same method is used to assess national income figures such as GDP/GNP whose growth rates are also recorded in real terms. Therefore the table shows that the buying power of family farm incomes in 2009 is equivalent to €8,181 in 1995 terms. More simply, FFI is 42.5 per cent lower in real terms in 2009 than it was in 1995.

Table 3.11.1: Family Farm Income in cash and buying power terms, 1995-2009			
	Cash value	Buying power (1995 terms)	% change in buying power since 1995
1995	€14,236	€14,236	0.0
1996	€13,866	€13,634	-4.2
1997	€14,042	€13,607	-4.4
1998	€13,442	€12,717	-10.7
1999	€11,088	€10,324	-27.5
2000	€13,499	€11,903	-16.4
2001	€15,840	€13,322	-6.4
2002	€14,917	€11,991	-15.8
2003	€14,765	€11,467	-19.5
2004	€15,557	€11,822	-17.0
2005	€22,459	€16,651	+17.0
2006	€16,680	€11,789	-17.2
2007	€19,687	€13,379	-6.0
2008	€16,993	€11,093	-22.1
2009	€11,968	€8,181	-42.5

Source: Calculated from Teagasc (2011:5)

The decline of agriculture

A key element in the evolution of any developed world society/economy has been a noticeable shift away from dependence on agriculture. That natural phase of economic development has been slowly occurring in Ireland over the past few decades. As Ireland develops, the size of its agricultural sector and the numbers employed in that sector continue to decline. The focus of that sector has also shifted from being producer driven to being consumer driven.

Two insights into the future shape of Irish agriculture have been provided over recent years. The first, published in November 2004, is that of the Government-appointed Agri-vision 2015 committee. In their report the committee concluded that:

The number of Irish farms is expected to decline by 23%, from 136,000 in 2002 to 105,000 in 2015. By 2015, one third of the farm population will be classed as economically viable, another third of farms will be economically unviable with the operators working primarily off the farm and the remaining third will be transitional farms characterised by adverse demographic features, such as having an elderly farm operator and/or lacking an identified heir.

Of the third of farms that will remain economically viable by 2015, 75% will be farmed on a part-time basis, with the on-farm enterprise providing a return sufficient to remunerate the labour and capital used. Of those farms that are operated on a full time basis, and which are economically viable, the vast majority are expected to be dairy enterprises (2004:37).

During 2005 a second major report set out the expected future direction of rural Ireland up to 2025. Funded by the Department of Agriculture and Food and a number of other Government bodies it was compiled by some of the leading experts on rural Ireland at Teagasc, NUI Maynooth and University College Dublin. The report is entitled *Rural Ireland 2025: Foresight Perspectives* (2005) and it indicates a further sizeable change in the shape of rural Ireland over the next two decades.

Looking to the future of agriculture the expert group concluded that "it is unlikely that by 2025 Ireland will have appreciably more than 10,000 full-time commercial farmers, comprising predominantly dairy farmers, a thousand or so commercial dry stock farmers, with roughly a similar number of sheep producers and a few hundred pig enterprises" (2005:10). This conclusion was reached on the basis of there being no unexpected major policy changes (nationally and at EU level) between now and 2025. The report also projected that the remainder of farmers (a further 30,000 full time equivalent jobs implying approximately 60,000 part-time workers) will be working part-time (2005: 10-11). Overall the report projected that many of these part-time farmers as well as a number of the projected 10,000 full-time commercial farmers will be involved in producing green energy fuels, such as wood biomass, as an important component of their farming enterprises.

A more recent Teagasc (2008b) report describes the medium-term outlook for beef, tillage and dairy farms. Cattle farms are very reliant on subsidies – only 32 per cent of beef sector output is generated at a market profit, but this figure increases to 81 per cent when the new Suckler Cow Welfare Payment and costs of compliance with the Single Farm Payment Scheme are taken into consideration.

The proportion of economically viable tillage farms is estimated at just over three quarters, expected to decline to two thirds by 2018. Finally, the proportion of dairy farms considered economically viable declined from 68 to 53 per cent in 2008. It is projected that dairy farm numbers will decline from 20,000 in 2008 to approximately 12,000 in 2014, with two thirds of these being economically viable.

Rural development

As agriculture declines there is need for a more comprehensive set of rural development policies. Long-term strategies to address the failures of current policies on critical issues such as infrastructure development, the national spatial imbalance, local access to public services, public transport and local involvement in core decision-making are urgently required. Recognition that current development policies are largely city-led is also necessary and this approach needs to be re-balanced.

The 1999 White Paper on rural development was welcome in that it provided an outline of a vision to guide rural development policy as we had advocated for over a decade previously. In so doing, it accepted that the statement of a vision is a necessary first step in moving forward. *Social Justice Ireland* also welcomed the identification by the White Paper of much that was already being done under a variety of headings in all areas of rural development. However, there was little in terms of new and imaginative policies proposed for the implementation of the vision, and no commitment of new and measurable resources to attain the objectives set out.

The context of current rural development policy more than a decade later, however, is one where

- EU policies in particular ensure that production is concentrated among larger producers, and where regulations, policies and financing all militate against small local producers,
- direct payments favour large volume, higher income farmers,
- there is a dominance of the agri-model of rural development,
- there is very limited progress in achieving balanced regional development. Areas such as the western region have been losing ground to the rest of the country in recent years.

It is clear that the scale of the infrastructure and investment deficit in rural Ireland is unacceptably high. In recent years there have been major spatial changes and there are major spatial disparities as well. The failure of current policies in so many crucial areas requires that long-term strategies be developed to address these failures.

The *Rural Ireland 2025* report succinctly summarises the objectives for rural development contained within government policies. It states that "government policy for rural areas aims to build a rural economy where enterprises will be commercially competitive without damaging the environment. It seeks to have vibrant sustainable communities, with a quality of life that will make them attractive places in which to work and live. It aspires for equity of opportunity between rural and urban areas, and for balanced development between the regions. These initiatives are underpinned by EU policy for rural areas, which subscribes to the attainment of 'living countrysides' within the context of balanced regional development across the Union" (2005: *v*).

To successfully move rural Ireland closer to these policy goals the *Rural Ireland 2025* report suggested a series of rural development strategies which should be immediately pursued (2005:*v-vi*). These include taking action on:

- The National Spatial Strategy, implemented in conjunction with successive regionally focused national plans, would result in a more balanced distribution of population and economic activity throughout the country.
- Rapid communications and supporting infrastructure would provide greater accessibility throughout all parts of the country.
- The rural economy could sustain more competitive enterprises through the development of additional entrepreneurial and management skills, as well as further innovation in products, business organisation and marketing.
- The agri-food industry could have more developed business, technological and innovative capacities, with a widely differentiated product portfolio selling in international markets.
- Forestry and the ocean economy could be sizeable suppliers to the energy sector and provide valued public goods.
- Maintenance of an attractive rural environment could be secured by compliance with EU Directives and payment for public goods, as well as better management systems nationally.
- A knowledge-based bio-economy could emerge built on the comparative advantage of Ireland's natural resources.
- 'Old economy' enterprises could be upgraded, and manufacturing small and medium sized enterprises (SMEs) could increase their contribution to the rural economy.

- Tourism could be a vibrant sector of the rural economy, providing knowledge-based environmental goods and services, focused on Ireland's unique landscapes and culture.
- Clusters of internationally oriented companies could exploit the full potential of natural resources in food, the marine, forestry and tourism.

Other rural development issues
As the rural development agenda moves forward, there are a series of other issues that deserve consideration. To complete this section of our review, we highlight a number of these issues.

Rural transport
The availability of transport as a means of access to both public and private services is a major issue for people living in rural areas and one that we have addressed earlier (see section 3.4). Progress towards this goal is not helped by the continued centralisation of public services. When rural schools closed there was no account taken of the transport costs of bringing children to the larger schools. Despite the recent transport initiatives, many communities in rural areas are not well served. Some of the difficulties faced by these initiatives have stemmed from the lack of regulation and the constant debate on who should have the profitable routes. There are also considerable problems associated with providing a service in areas where the population is scattered over a large area. *Social Justice Ireland* believes that we are now reaching a crucial juncture that requires key decisions in ensuring that rural communities receive adequate public transport infrastructure services. It is also worth mentioning that it is vital that a quality public transport infrastructure is put in place if the government is to meet its commitment to sustainable balanced regional development. In that regard we support the call from Irish Rural Link to establish a National Rural Transport Office (NRTO), perhaps within the Department of Transport, Tourism and Sport, which links and supports the development of rural transport within the overall auspices of developing public transport in general.

Accessibility of transport for older people is vital in terms of accessing health and other services, social networks and remaining active. The Rural Transport Initiative (RTI) is making a very important contribution to supporting community-based living.

Rural Development

Rural public services

Section 3.4 of this review has already addressed issues associated with current and future regulation of public services. One key element of policy in this area which is relevant to rural Ireland is the current and sustained existence of so-called 'public service obligations'. These require services to be made available on a nationwide basis and as a policy they play an important role in ensuring the possibility and sustainability of rural communities. For service providers, be they public or private, there are additional costs associated with adhering to these obligations and therefore there is a clear incentive for them to seek their removal. Government policy should ensure that these obligations remain and that permanent residents of rural areas are not disadvantaged through their removal.

Social Exclusion

Many rural areas continue to lose population as highlighted in the Audit of Innovation report (2005) prepared by the BMW regional assembly. Such a loss means that there is an increasing dependant population, including a higher cohort of older people and others requiring care. Because of such dependency social exclusion, including the incidence and risk of poverty, becomes more associated with remoteness and rurality. Indeed the CLAR initiative based on areas with most population decline had demonstrated this danger – the programme received a 94 per cent cut in Budget 2011. This pattern will worsen unless population growth is significantly redistributed throughout the regions.

Settlement Patterns

Housing has become a controversial topic because of the once off house debate. However this masks many issues in terms of settlement that need attention. Many rural villages are victims of poor planning and design in terms of long life tenure. Social housing provision according to the Local Authority Assessment of Social Housing Needs is particularly low in towns and villages around the country (Department of Environment, Heritage and Local Government, 2005). While many experts continue to argue against the practice of one off housing in terms of the social and economic benefits to the community, the lack of any serious alternative is detrimental to the needs of many people who cannot afford basic housing within their own community.

There is a huge need to ensure that local authorities, organisations involved in housing provision, and local communities are resourced to ensure that rural villages can be the focus of long life housing design.

Retrieving energy from agricultural sources
Two issues raised over this and the last section of this review are worth reflecting on. The decline in the number of people employed in farming (outlined above) and the increasing challenges posed by environmental targets that Ireland must meet (as considered in section 3.10b). *Social Justice Ireland* believes that both of these issues could be simultaneously addressed by the development of energy focused on bio-fuels, biomass, bio-gas and wind energy.

To date, Ireland is far from fully utilising its ability to take advantage of the direction that EU policy is taking on the production of renewable energy. EU policy has set an objective that consumption of energy from renewable sources will be over 20 per cent by 2020 - in 2007 Ireland consumed only 2.9 per cent (CSO, 2009b: 329). The intention of the EU is to add one million jobs in the Union by adopting a range of renewable energy targets.

Social Justice Ireland believes that Ireland has the advantage of an agriculture sector undergoing radical transition, and therefore it is a sector that is extremely receptive to new ideas that build on existing skills. Within a short period of time this potential might well have disappeared. Through the development of these energy sources Ireland can align itself with EU policy while simultaneously establishing social and economic stability in rural areas.

Key Priorities on Rural Development

- **Recognise that rural Ireland is currently in transition from an agricultural to a rural development agenda and adopt policies to further support this transition. In doing so, recognise and support the multi-dimensional nature of rural development.**

- **Ensure the provision of basic infrastructure and services, (and their attendant public service obligations), based more on principles of equity and social justice, than on cost effectiveness, and take particular account of rural disadvantage.**

- **Ensure the provision of a reliable and appropriate transport system, by providing resources for the development of local-transport strategies and initiatives tailored to meet the needs of the local community (e.g. the Rural Transport Initiative).**

- Structure housing lists to reflect rural needs. In particular, in rural areas, develop a framework to guide planning policy, which is focused on supporting and sustaining viable rural communities and protecting and enhancing the rural environment.

- Reappraise programmes to create employment for part-time farmers with a view o targeting effectively the needs of smaller farmers.

- Investigate the use of farm land as a means of meeting Ireland's renewable energy requirements by maximising the retrieval of energy from agricultural sources.

3.12 The Developing World

> **CORE POLICY OBJECTIVE:**
> **THE DEVELOPING WORLD**
> To ensure that Ireland plays an active and effective part in promoting genuine development in the developing world and to ensure that all Ireland's policies are consistent with such development

Globally, the scale and extent of underdevelopment and inequality remains large. An indication of the size of this problem is outlined bi-annually in the United Nations Human Development Report. Table 3.12.1 presents an insight into the scale and extent of these problems using UN data from the *2010 Human Development Report*.

Table 3.12.1: United Nations development indicators by region and worldwide

Region	GDP per capita (US$ PPP)*	Life Expectancy at Birth (yrs)	Adult Literacy %**
Least Developed Countries	1,393	57.7	59.9
Arab States	7,861	69.1	72.1
East Asia + Pacific	6,403	72.6	n/a
Europe + Central Asia	11,462	69.5	97.5
L. America + Caribbean	10,643	74.0	91.1
South Asia	3,417	65.1	62.4
Sub-Saharan Africa	2,050	52.7	62.4
OECD	37,077	80.3	n/a
Worldwide total	**10,631**	**69.3**	**n/a**

Source: UNDP (2010: 146, 196)
Notes: * Data adjusted for differences in purchasing power.
** Adult defined as those aged 15yrs and above

Tables 3.12.1 and 3.12.2 show the sustained differences in the experiences of different regions in the world. There are sizeable differences in income levels (GDP per person) between the most developed countries of the world, those in the OECD, and the rest (i.e. the vast majority) of the world. These differences go beyond just income and are reflected in each of the indicators reported in both tables. Today, life expectancies are almost 30 years higher in the richest countries than in Sub-Saharan Africa. Similarly, the UN reports that more than 1 in 3 Southern Asians and Sub-Saharan Africans are unable to read.

These phenomena are equally reflected in high levels of absolute poverty (there are over 1,300m people worldwide living below the international poverty line of $1.25 a day) and in the various mortality figures in table 3.12.2. The 2010 *Human Development Report* shows that almost 9 per cent of all children born in Sub-Saharan Africa died before their first birthday. These mortality rates reach almost 15 per cent by the fifth birthday. Figures are not as high elsewhere; however the mortality rates reported by the UN for developing regions contrast with the very low rates in the OECD countries including Ireland.

Table 3.12.2: United Nations development indicators by region and worldwide

Region	% Net Primary Enrolment Rate	Infant mortality rate*	Under-5yrs mortality rate*
Least Developed Countries	75.5	82	126
Arab States	80.9	38	50
East Asia + Pacific	93.3	23	28
Europe + Central Asia	92.3	20	22
L. America + Caribbean	94.4	19	23
South Asia	86.9	56	73
Sub-Saharan Africa	73.6	86	144
OECD	95.6	5	6
Worldwide total	**86.1**	**44**	**63**

Source: UNDP (2010: 196, 201)
Notes: * number of deaths per 1,000 live births (infant = less than 1 year old)

UN millennium development goals

In response to these problems the UN Millennium Declaration was adopted in 2000 at the largest-ever gathering of heads of state. It committed countries - both rich and poor - to doing all they can to eradicate poverty, promote human dignity and equality and achieve peace, democracy and environmental sustainability. World leaders promised to work together to meet concrete targets for advancing development and reducing poverty by 2015 or earlier. Emanating from the Millennium Declaration, a set of Millennium Development Goals was agreed.

These bind countries to do more in the attack on inadequate incomes, widespread hunger, gender inequality, environmental deterioration and lack of education, healthcare and clean water. They also include actions to reduce debt and increase aid, trade and technology transfers to poor countries. These goals and their related targets are:

Goal 1: Eradicate extreme poverty and hunger
- *Target 1:* Halve, between 1990 and 2015, the proportion of people whose income is less than $1 a day.
- *Target 2:* Halve, between 1990 and 2015, the proportion of people who suffer from hunger.

Goal 2: Achieve universal primary education
- *Target 3:* Ensure that, by 2015, children everywhere, boys and girls alike, will be able to complete a full course of primary schooling.

Goal 3: Promote gender equality and empower women
- *Target 4:* Eliminate gender disparity in primary and secondary education, preferably by 2005 and in all levels of education no later than 2015.

Goal 4: Reduce child mortality
- *Target 5:* Reduce by two-thirds, between 1990 and 2015, the under-five mortality rate.

Goal 5: Improve maternal health
- *Target 6:* Reduce by three-quarters, between 1990 and 2015, the maternal mortality ratio.

Goal 6: Combat HIV/AIDS, malaria and other diseases
- *Target 7:* Have halted by 2015 and begun to reverse the spread of HIV/AIDS.
- *Target 8:* Have halted by 2015 and begun to reverse the incidence of malaria and other major diseases.

Goal 7: Ensure environmental sustainability
- *Target 9:* Integrate the principles of sustainable development into country policies and programmes and reverse the loss of environmental resources.

Target 10: Halve by 2015 the proportion of people without sustainable access to safe drinking water.

Target 11: Have achieved by 2020 a significant improvement in the lives of at least 100 million slum dwellers.

Goal 8: Develop a global partnership for development

Target 12: Develop further an open, rule based, predictable, nondiscriminatory trading and financial system (includes a commitment to good governance, development, and poverty reduction – both nationally and internationally).

Target 13: Address the special needs of the least developed countries (includes tariff and quota free access for exports, enhanced programme of debt relief for and cancellation of official bilateral debt, and more generous official development assistance for countries committed to poverty reduction).

Target 14: Address the special needs of landlocked countries and small island developing states (through the Programme of Action for the Sustainable Development of Small Island Developing States and 22nd General Assembly provisions).

Target 15: Deal comprehensively with the debt problems of developing countries through national and international measures in order to make debt sustainable in the long term

Target 16: In cooperation with developing countries, develop and implement strategies for decent and productive work for youth.

Target 17: In cooperation with pharmaceutical companies, provide access to affordable essential drugs in developing countries.

Target 18: In cooperation with the private sector, make available the benefits of new technologies, especially information and communications technologies.

(UNDP, 2003: 1-3)

While we are 10 years into the MDG process, progress on these goals and targets has been mixed with some regions doing better than others. In particular the UN suggests that East Asia and the Pacific are progressing satisfactorily but that overall human development is proceeding too slowly. Writing in the 2010 MDG Progress Report the UN Secretary General Ban Ki-Moon stated that "*it is clear that improvements in the lives of the poor have been unacceptably slow, and some hard-won gains are being eroded by the climate, food and economic crises*" (2010:3). Social Justice Ireland believes that the international community needs to play a more active role in assisting less developed countries achieve these goals. Central to this will be the provision of additional financial support and cutbacks in this support (see below) are likely to undermine progress.

Poverty and its associated implications remains the root cause of regional conflicts and civil wars in many of these poor countries. States and societies that are poor are prone to conflict. It is very difficult for governments to govern adequately when their people cannot afford to pay taxes, and industry and trade are almost non-existent. Poverty is also a major cause of environmental degradation. Large-scale food shortages, migration and conflicts lead to environmental pressures.

Clearly poverty in the southern world threatens the very survival of all peoples. It is the major injustice in a world that is not, as a unit, poor. Now more than ever the Irish government must exercise its voice within the European Union and in world institutions to ensure that the elimination of poverty becomes the focus of all policy development.

Trade and debt
A further implication of the earlier tables is to underscore the totally unacceptable division that currently exists between rich and poor regions of the world. The fact that this phenomenon persists is largely attributable to unfair trade practices and to the backlog of unpayable debt owed by the countries of the South to other governments, to the World Bank, the International Monetary Fund (IMF) and to commercial banks.

The effect of trade barriers cannot be overstated; by limiting or eliminating access to potential markets the Western world is denying poor countries substantial income. At the 2002 UN Conference on Financing and Development Michael Moore, the President of the World Trade Organisation, stated that the complete abolition of trade barriers could "boost global income by $2.8 trillion and lift 320 million people out of poverty by 2015". Research by Oxfam (2002) further shows that goods from poor countries are taxed at four times the rate of goods from rich countries and that 120 million people could be lifted out of poverty if Africa, Latin America and Asia increased their share of world markets by just 1 per cent. It is clear that all countries would gain from trade reform. Such reform is now long overdue.

The high levels of debt experienced by Third World countries have disastrous consequences for the populations of indebted countries. Governments that are obliged to dedicate large percentages of their country's GDP to debt repayments cannot afford to pay for health and educational programmes for their people. In 1997, Third World debt totalled over $2.2 trillion. In the same year nearly $250 billion was repaid in interest and loan principal. Africa alone spends four times more on interest on its loans than on healthcare. For every €1 given in aid by rich countries, poor countries pay back nearly €4 in debt repayments. It is not possible for these countries to develop the kind of healthy economies that would facilitate debt repayment when millions of their people are being denied basic healthcare and education and are either unemployed or earn wages so low that they can barely survive.

A process of debt cancellation has been argued for over a number of years and should be further developed beyond the basic schemes introduced in recent years. *Social Justice Ireland* welcomes moves in this direction and in particular we welcome the ongoing commitment of the Irish government to support such a move. This was a major policy shift, following entrenched opposition to the move by the Department of Finance. It is now important that Ireland campaign on the international stage to see this process implemented. Given Ireland's current economic circumstances, the Irish population now has a greater appreciation of the implications of these debts and the merit in having them reduced.

Social Justice Ireland believes that Ireland's representatives at the World Bank and the IMF should be more critical of the policies adopted by these bodies. The Department of Finance's annual reports on Ireland's involvement in these organisations reveal an alarming degree of unconditional support. According to these reports Ireland has unconditionally supported the World Bank's positions in all of the following areas: poverty reduction, gender issues, private-sector development, governance issues and corruption, military spending, post-conflict initiatives and environmentally sustainable projects. This level of support does not match Irish public opinion. NGOs, such as the Debt and Development Coalition, which have done much work on these issues, are very critical of the World Bank in its policies on issues such as poverty reduction, gender and the environment. We believe that this criticism of government is well founded.

Ireland's commitment to ODA

The international challenge to significantly increase levels of Overseas Development Assistance (ODA) was set out by the former UN Secretary General Kofi Annan shortly after the adoption of the MDGs. He stated that:

> *We will have time to reach the Millennium Development Goals – worldwide and in most, or even all, individual countries – but only if we break with business as usual. We cannot win overnight. Success will require sustained action across the entire decade between now and the deadline. It takes time to train the teachers, nurses and engineers; to build the roads, schools and hospitals; to grow the small and large businesses able to create the jobs and income needed. So we must start now. And we must more than double global development assistance over the next few years. Nothing less will help to achieve the Goals.*

These comments lay down a clear challenge to the international community and *Social Justice Ireland* believes that Ireland can lead the way in responding to that challenge; even in the context of out current economic circumstances. We welcomed the announcement at the United National General Assembly by the former Taoiseach Bertie Ahern that Ireland would reach the UN target of 0.7 per cent of GNP on overseas aid by 2012. In particular we welcomed the accompanying funding timetable announced by the Department of Foreign Affairs. We regret that Government rapidly abandoned these commitments once the economy experienced recession. We very much welcome the new Government's commitment to meet this target by 2015.

As table 3.12.3 shows, over time Ireland has achieved sizeable increases in our ODA allocation. In 2006 a total of €814m (0.53 per cent of GNP) was allocated to ODA – reaching the interim target set by the Government. Budget 2008 further increased the ODA budget to reach €920.7m (0.6 per cent of GNP). However, since then the ODA budget has been a focus of government cuts and has fallen by €285m – more than 31 per cent. In 2009 and 2010 these have been cuts focused on the poorest countries and people in the world and we regret this policy choice. Budget 2011 adopted a better approach and focused that Budget's cut, of €35m, on Ireland ODA contributions to international institutions such as the World Bank and the IMF.

Rebuilding our commitment to ODA and honouring the UN target should be important policy paths for Ireland to pursue in the years to come. Not only would its achievement be a major success for government, and an important element in the delivery of promises made in the national agreement, but it would also be of significance internationally. Ireland's success would not only provide additional assistance to needy countries but would also provide leadership to those other European countries who do not meet the target. To date the Irish Aid programme has received deserved praise from the OECD's Development Assistance Committee who reviewed the performance of Ireland's aid budget in 2007 and described it being in international terms at the 'cutting edge' (OECD, 2009). Despite the challenges, we believe that this commitment should be honoured. We strongly urge the new Government to honour their very welcome commitment on ODA.

Table 3.12.3: Ireland's net overseas development assistance, 1993-2011

Year	€m's	% of GNP
1993	69.4	0.18
1994	95.5	0.23
1995	122	0.26
1996	142.3	0.27
1997	157.6	0.26
1998	177.3	0.26
1999	230.3	0.30
2000	254.9	0.28
2001	319.9	0.33
2002	422.1	0.40
2003	445.7	0.38
2004	488.9	0.39
2005	578.5	0.42
2006	814.0	0.53
2007	870.9	0.53
2008	920.7	0.60
2009	696	0.55
2010	671	0.53
2011	636	0.50

Source: CSO (2010:45), Irish Aid (2010:67-69) and various Budget Documents.

HIV/AIDS

In March 2011 the UN AIDS Report showed that there are 33.3 million people living with HIV. This is a 27% increase since 1999. Globally nearly 23% of all people living with HIV are under 24 years and people aged 15-24 years account for 35% of all people becoming newly infected. The poorer African countries are the most severely affected, accounting for 68% of all people living with HIV. They also have 72% of AIDS deaths.

In launching the report the UN Secretary General Ban Ki-Moon noted, "Every day 7,000 people are newly infected, including 1,000 children. Weak national infrastructures, financing shortfalls and discrimination against vulnerable populations are among the factors that continue to impede access to HIV prevention, treatment, care and support services". The current uncertain economic climate is very challenging to those combating the HIV/AIDS epidemic. The UN notes that in 2009 the funding was lower than in 2008. Despite our difficulties *Social Justice Ireland* urges Government to meet its commitments in this area.

Key Priorities on the Developing World

- **Ensure that Ireland delivers on its promise to meet the United Nations target of contributing 0.7 per cent of GNP to Overseas Development Assistance by the EU deadline of 2015.**

- **Take a far more proactive stance at government level on ensuring that Irish and EU policies towards countries in the South are just.**

- **Adopt a more critical perspective towards the policies of the World Bank and the IMF.**

- **Continue to support the international campaign for the liberation of the poorest nations from the burden of the backlog of unpayable debt and take steps to ensure that further progress is made on this issue.**

- **Continue to support the implementation of the Millennium Development Goals.**

- **Engage pro-actively and positively in the Rio+20 process already referred to in section 3.10 on sustainability.**

- **Work for changes in the existing international trading regimes, to encourage fairer and sustainable forms of trade. In particular, resource the development of Ireland's policies in the WTO to ensure that this goal is pursued.**

- **Ensure that the government takes up a leadership position within the European and international arenas to encourage other states to fund programmes and research aimed at resolving the AIDS/HIV crisis.**

4. VALUES

"Few can doubt that we have been in a period of economic transition. The financial collapse has shown that many aspects of the 'new economy', so widely praised just a few years ago, are unstable and unsustainable. For years we were told that we had entered a brand new world of unlimited financial possibilities, brought about by sophisticated techniques and technologies, starting with the internet and the information technology revolution, spread through the world by "globalisation" and managed by 'financial engineers' who, armed with the tools of financial derivatives, could eliminate risk and uncertainty. Now we can see that the new financial structure was a house of cards built on sand, where speculation replaced enterprise, and the self-interest of many financial speculators came at the expense of the common good.

While there were many factors that contributed to the financial meltdown of 2008, they start with the exclusion of ethics from economic and business decision making. The designers of the new financial order had complete faith that the 'invisible hand' of market competition would ensure that the self-interested decisions of market participants would promote the common good." (Clark and Alford, 2010).

In Ireland we regularly hear the questions; "Where did the wealth go?" "When we had the resources what did we as a society fix?" We are conscious of much fear, anxiety and anger in our communities. Today, more and more of society are questioning how the policies and decisions of the past decade could have failed Irish society so badly.

These reflections brings to the fore the issue of values. Our fears are easier to admit than our values. Do we as a people accept a two-tier society in fact, while deriding it in principle? The earlier chapters of this review document many aspects of this two tiered society. This reality is made possible by the support of our value system. This dualism in our values allows us to continue with the status quo, which, in reality, means that it is okay to exclude almost one sixth of the population from the mainstream of life of the society, while substantial resources and opportunities are channelled towards other groups in society. This dualism operates at the levels of individual people, communities and sectors.

Christian Values

Social Justice Ireland's concerns in this area are deeply rooted in Christian values. Christianity subscribes to the values of both human dignity and the centrality of the community. The person is seen as growing and developing in a context that includes other people and the environment. Justice is understood in terms of relationships. The Christian scriptures understand justice as a harmony that comes from fidelity to right relationships with God, people and the environment. A just society is one that is structured in such a way as to promote these right relationships so that human rights are respected, human dignity is protected, human development is facilitated and the environment is respected and protected (Healy and Reynolds, 2003:188).

As our societies have grown in sophistication, the need for appropriate structures has become more urgent. While the aspiration that everyone should enjoy the good life, and the goodwill to make it available to all, are essential ingredients in a just society, the good life will not happen without the deliberate establishment of structures to facilitate its development. In the past charity, in the sense of alms-giving by some individuals on an arbitrary and ad hoc basis, was seen as sufficient to ensure that everyone could cross the threshold of human dignity. Calling on the work of social historians it could be argued that charity in this sense was never an appropriate method for dealing with poverty. Certainly it is not a suitable methodology for dealing with the problems of today. As recent world disasters have graphically shown, charity and the heroic efforts of voluntary agencies cannot solve these problems on a long-term basis. Appropriate structures should be established to ensure that every person has access to the resources needed to live life with dignity.

Few people would disagree that the resources of the planet are for the use of the people - not just the present generation, but also the generations still to come. In Old Testament times these resources were closely tied to land and water. A complex system of laws about the Sabbatical and Jubilee years (Lev 25: 1-22, Deut 15: 1-18) was devised to ensure, on the one hand, that no person could be disinherited, and, on the other, that land and debts could not be accumulated. This system also ensured that the land was protected and allowed to renew itself

These reflections raise questions about ownership. Obviously there was an acceptance of private property, but it was not an exclusive ownership. It carried social responsibilities. We find similar thinking among the leaders of the early Christian community. St John Chrysostom, speaking to those who could manipulate the law so as to accumulate wealth to the detriment of others, taught that *"the rich are in the possession of the goods of the poor even if they have acquired them honestly or inherited them legally"* (Homily on Lazarus). These early leaders also established that a person in extreme necessity has the right to take from the riches of others what s/he needs, since private property has a social quality deriving from the law of the communal purpose of earthly goods (*Gaudium et Spes* 69-71).

In more recent times, Pope Paul VI said *"private property does not constitute for anyone an absolute and unconditional right. No one is justified in keeping for his/her exclusive use what is not needed when others lack necessities.... The right to property must never be exercised to the detriment of the common good"* (*Populorum Progressio* No. 23). Pope John Paul II has developed the understanding of ownership, especially in regard to the ownership of the means of production. One of the major contributors to the generation of wealth is technology. The technology we have today is the product of the work of many people through many generations. Through the laws of patenting and exploration a very small group of people has claimed legal rights to a large portion of the world's wealth. Pope John Paul II questions the morality of these structures. He says *"if it is true that capital as the whole of the means of production is at the same time the product of the work of generations, it is equally true that capital is being unceasingly created through the work done with the help of all these means of production"*. Therefore, no one can claim exclusive rights over the means of production. Rather that right *"is subordinated to the right to common use, to the fact that goods are meant for everyone"*. (*Laborem Exercens* No. 14). Since everyone has a right to a proportion of the goods of the country, society is faced with two responsibilities regarding economic resources: firstly each person should have sufficient to access the good life; and secondly, since the earth's resources are finite, and since "more" is not necessarily "better", it is time that society faced the question of putting a limit on the wealth that any person or corporation can accumulate. Espousing the value of environmental sustainability requires a commitment to establish systems that ensure the protection of our planet.

Interdependence, mutuality, solidarity and connectedness are words that are used loosely today to express a consciousness which is very Christian. All of creation is seen as a unit that is dynamic - each part is related to every other part, depends on it in some way, and can also affect it. When we focus on the human family, this means that each person depends on others initially for life itself, and subsequently for the resources and relationships needed to grow and develop. To ensure that the connectedness of the web of life is maintained, each person is meant to reach out to support others in ways that are appropriate for their growth and in harmony with the rest of creation. This thinking respects the integrity of the person, while recognising that the person can achieve his or her potential only in right relationships with others and the environment.

Most people in Irish society would subscribe to the values articulated here. However these values will only be operative in our society when appropriate structures and infrastructures are put in place. These are the values that *Social Justice Ireland* wishes to promote. We wish to work with others to develop and support appropriate systems, structures and infrastructures which will give practical expression to these values in Irish society.

5. CONCLUSION

The events of the past few years underscore the need for us to build a new and fairer Ireland. In this socio-economic review *Social Justice Ireland* has presented its analysis of the present socio-economic situation in Ireland and how it came to be in this situation. We also presented a vision of a New Ireland and sketched out the nature and structure of a pathway towards this vision. We proposed an agenda to ensure economic development, social equity and sustainability in the medium to long term. Within this, we outlined and proposed a wide range of policy initiatives that should form the basis of any movement towards building for the future. All our proposals are made within responsible fiscal parameters.

Given the parameters of this review we have not been able to go into the level of detail that some people would like to see. However, we refer people to our constantly updated website, *www.socialjustice.ie*, where we will continue to develop this analysis and approach.

We do not claim to have all the answers. However, we make our proposals as a contribution to the public debate on what the key priorities in the socio-economic arena should be now and in the years ahead. All responses are most welcome.

REFERENCES

Allied Irish Banks (2011), *Macroeconomic Forecasts*, Dublin, AIB Bank.

Bacon and Associates (1998), *An Economic Assessment of Recent House Price Developments*, Dublin, Stationery Office.

Begg, D. (2003), "The Just Society – Can we afford it?" in Reynolds B. and S. Healy (eds.) *Ireland and the Future of Europe: leading the way towards inclusion?*, Dublin, CORI.

Bennett M., D. Fadden,. D. Harney, P. O'Malley, C. Regan and. L. Sloyan (2003) *Population Ageing in Ireland and its Impact on Pension and Healthcare Costs*. Report of Society of Actuaries Working Party on Population Studies. Society of Actuaries in Ireland.

Bergin A., Fitz Gerald J. and Kearney I. (2002), *The Macro-economic Effects of Using Taxes or Emissions Trading Permits to Reduce Greenhouse Gas Emissions*, paper presented to ESRI conference entitled "The sky's the limit: efficient and fair policies on global warming", December, Dublin.

Bristow, J. (2004). *Taxation in Ireland: an economist's perspective*, Dublin, Institute of Public Administration.

Brooke, S. (2004), *Housing Problems and Irish Children,* Children's Research Centre, Trinity College Dublin.

Brueggermann, W. (2009), *From Anxiety and Greed to Milk and Honey*, http://www.sojo.net/

Carrie, A. (2005) "Lack of long-run data prevents us tracking Ireland's social health" in *Feasta Review No 2 Growth: The Celtic Cancer*. Dublin, Feasta.

Central Bank of Ireland (various), *Quarterly Bulletins*, Dublin, Central Bank.

Central Statistics Office (2003), *Census 2002: Various Volumes*, Dublin, Stationery Office.

References

Central Statistics Office (2003), *Quarterly National Household Survey: Voter participation and abstention*, Dublin, Stationery Office.

Central Statistics Office (2005), *EU Survey on Income and Living Conditions 2004 Results*, Dublin, Stationery Office.

Central Statistics Office (2006), *EU Survey on Income and Living Conditions 2005 Results*, Dublin, Stationery Office.

Central Statistics Office (2006), *Industrial Earnings and Hours Worked*, Dublin, Stationery Office.

Central Statistics Office (2007), *Census 2006: Principal Demographic Results*, Dublin, Stationery Office.

Central Statistics Office (2007), *Census 2006: Various Volumes*, Dublin, Stationery Office.

Central Statistics Office (2007), *EU Survey on Income and Living Conditions 2006 Results*, Dublin, Stationery Office.

Central Statistics Office (2007), *Household Budget Survey*, Dublin, Stationery Office.

Central Statistics Office (2008), *EU Survey on Income and Living Conditions 2007 Results*, Dublin, Stationery Office.

Central Statistics Office (2008), *Measuring Ireland's Progress 2007*, Dublin, Stationery Office.

Central Statistics Office (2008), *Population and Labour Force Projections 2011-2041*, Dublin, Stationery Office.

Central Statistics Office (2009), *Measuring Ireland's Progress 2008*, Dublin, Stationery Office.

Central Statistics Office (2009), *Survey on Income and Living Conditions 2008 Results*, Dublin, Stationery Office.

Central Statistics Office (2010), *Earnings and Labour Costs*, Dublin, Stationery Office.

Central Statistics Office (2010), *Measuring Ireland's Progress 2009*, Dublin, Stationery Office.

Central Statistics Office (2010), *Statistical Yearbook of Ireland*, Dublin, Stationery Office.

Central Statistics Office (2010), *Survey on Income and Living Conditions 2009 Results*, Dublin, Stationery Office.

Central Statistics Office (2011), *Quarterly National Accounts*, Dublin, Stationery Office.

Central Statistics Office (various), *Live Register*, Dublin, Stationery Office.

Central Statistics Office (various), *Quarterly National Household Survey*, Dublin, Stationery Office.

Central Statistics Office (various). *National Income and Expenditure Accounts*, Dublin, Stationery Office.

Chambers of Commerce of Ireland (2004), *Local Authority Funding – Government in Denial*, Dublin.

Clark C. M. A. and H. Alford (2010), *Rich & Poor: Rebalancing the economy*, London, CTS.

Clark C.M.A. (2002), *The Basic Income Guarantee: ensuring progress and prosperity in the 21st century*, Dublin, Liffey Press and CORI Justice Commission.

Collins, M.L. (2004), "Taxation in Ireland: an overview" in B. Reynolds, and S. Healy (eds.) *A Fairer Tax System for a Fairer Ireland*, Dublin, CORI Justice Commission.

Collins, M.L. (2006), "Poverty: Measurement, Trends and Future Directions", in Healy, S., B. Reynolds and M.L. Collins, *Social Policy in Ireland: Principles, Practice and Problems*, Dublin, Liffey Press.

Collins, M.L. (2011), *Establishing a Benchmark for Ireland's Social Welfare Payments*. Paper for Social Justice Ireland. Dublin, Social Justice Ireland.

References

Collins, M.L. and C. Kavanagh (1998), "For Richer, For Poorer: The Changing Distribution of Household Income in Ireland, 1973-94", in Healy, S. and B. Reynolds, *Social Policy in Ireland: Principles, Practice and Problems*, Dublin, Oak Tree Press.

Collins, M.L. and C. Kavanagh (2006), "The Changing Patterns of Income Distribution and Inequality in Ireland, 1973-2004", in Healy, S., B. Reynolds and M.L. Collins, *Social Policy in Ireland: Principles, Practice and Problems*, Dublin, Liffey Press.

Collins, M.L. and M. Walsh (2010), *Ireland's Tax Expenditure System: International Comparisons and a Reform Agenda – Studies in Public Policy No. 24*, Dublin, Policy Institute, Trinity College Dublin.

Comhar (2008), *A Study in Carbon Allocation: Cap and Share*, Dublin, Comhar Sustainable Development Council.

Commission on Taxation (1982), *Commission on Taxation First Report*. Dublin, Stationery Office.

Commission on Taxation (2009), *Commission on Taxation Report 2009*. Dublin, Stationery Office.

Coulombe, S. J. Tremblay and S. Marchand (2004) *Literacy scores, human capital and growth across 14 OECD countries* Statistics Canada, Canada.

Delaney, L. and T. Fahey (2005), *Social and Economic Value of Sport in Ireland*. Dublin, ESRI.

Department of Agriculture and Food (1999), *White Paper on Rural Development*, Dublin, Stationery Office.

Department of Agriculture and Food (2004), *Agri Vision 2015 Committee Report*, Dublin, Stationery Office.

Department of Education and Science (2000), *Learning for Life: White Paper on Adult Education*, Dublin, Stationery Office.

Department of Finance (2003), *Budget 2004*, Dublin, Stationery Office.

Department of Finance (2006), *Budget 2006 – Review of Tax Schemes Volumes I, II and III.* Dublin, Stationery Office.

Department of Finance (2007), *Budget 2008*, Dublin, Stationery Office.

Department of Finance (2008), *Budget 2009*, Dublin, Stationery Office.

Department of Finance (2009), *Budget 2009 #2 – Supplementary Budget*, Dublin, Stationery Office.

Department of Finance (2009), *Budget 2010*, Dublin, Stationery Office.

Department of Finance (2010), *Budget 2011*, Dublin, Stationery Office.

Department of Foreign Affairs (2006), *White Paper on Irish Aid*, Dublin, Stationery Office.

Department of Health (2005), *National Strategy for Action on Suicide Prevention 2005-2014,* Dublin: Stationery Office.

Department of Health (2006), *A Vision for Change – Report of the Expert Group on Mental Health Policy,* Dublin: Stationery Office.

Department of Health (2008), *A Fair Deal – The Nursing Home care Support Scheme,* Dublin: Stationery Office.

Department of Health and Children (2001), *Primary Care A New Direction Health Strategy,* Dublin: Stationery Office.

Department of Health and Children (2001), *Quality and Fairness: A Health System for You,* Dublin: Stationery Office.

Department of Health and Children (2008) *National Intercultural Health Strategy 2007-2012,* Dublin: Stationery Office.

Department of Social, Community and Family Affairs (2000), *Supporting Voluntary Activity*, Dublin, Stationery Office.

Department of the Environment and Local Government (2000), *Planning and Development Act 2000*, Dublin, Stationery Office.

Department of the Environment and Local Government (2002), *National Spatial Strategy*, Dublin, Stationery Office.

Department of the Environment, Heritage and Local Government (various), *Housing Statistics Bulletin*, Dublin, Stationery Office.

Department of the Taoiseach (2001), *Final Report of the Social Welfare Benchmarking and Indexation Group*, Dublin, Stationery Office.

Department of the Taoiseach (2002), *Basic Income, A Green Paper*, Dublin, Stationery Office.

Department of the Taoiseach (2006) *Towards 2016 - Ten-Year Framework Social Partnership Agreement 2006-2015*, Dublin, Stationery Office.

Disability Federation of Ireland (2007), *Pre-Budget Submission for Budget 2008*, Dublin, DFI.

Disability Federation of Ireland (2008), *Pre-Budget Submission for Budget 2009*, Dublin, DFI.

Dowthwaite, R. (2004), "Tradable Quotas: the fairer alternative to eco-taxation" in B. Reynolds, and S. Healy (eds.) *A Fairer Tax System for a Fairer Ireland*, Dublin, CORI Justice Commission.

Drudy, P.J (2005) "Housing: the case for a new philosophy" in B. Reynolds and S. Healy (eds.) *Securing Fairness and Wellbeing in a Land of Plenty*, Dublin, CORI Justice Commission.

Drudy, P.J. (2006), "Housing in Ireland: Philosophy, Problems and Policies", in Healy, S., B. Reynolds and M.L. Collins, *Social Policy in Ireland: Principles, Practice and Problems*, Dublin, Liffey Press.

Drudy, PJ and M. Punch (2005) *Out of Reach: Inequalities in the Irish Housing System*, Dublin, Tasc at New Island.

Dunne, T. (2004), "Land Values as a Source of Local Government Finance" in B. Reynolds, and S. Healy (eds.) *A Fairer Tax System for a Fairer Ireland*, Dublin, CORI Justice Commission.

Economic and Social Research Institute (2003), *National Development Plan Mid-Term Review*, Dublin, ESRI.

Economic and Social Research Institute (various), *Quarterly Economic Commentary (QEC)*, Dublin, ESRI.

Eivers, E., Shiel, G., and Shortt, F. (2005), *Literacy in disadvantaged primary schools: Problems and solutions*. Dublin: Educational Research Centre, 2005.

Environmental Protection Agency (2006), *Environment in Focus*, Dublin, EPA.

Environmental Protection Agency (2008), *Ireland's Environment – 2008*, Dublin, EPA.

Environmental Protection Agency (2009), *Water Quality in Ireland 2007-2008*, Dublin, EPA.

European Union (1997), *Stability and Growth Pact*, EU Commission, Brussels.

Eurostat (2004), *Taxation Trends in the European Union*, Luxembourg, Eurostat.

Eurostat (2008), *Taxation Trends in the European Union*, Luxembourg, Eurostat.

Eurostat (2009), *Taxation Trends in the European Union*, Luxembourg, Eurostat.

Eurostat (2010), *Taxation Trends in the European Union*, Luxembourg, Eurostat.

Feasta and New Economics Foundation (NEF) (2006), *The Great Emissions Rights Give-Away*. Feasta and NEF.

Fine Gael and the Labour Party (2011). Programme for Government. Dublin.

Flannery, Austin (1982), *Gaudium et Spes*: Pastoral Constitution on the Church in the Modern World (Second Vatican Council, December 7, 1964.

Goldberg, F.T., L.L. Batchelder and P.R. Orszag (2006), *Reforming Tax Incentives into Uniform Refundable Tax Credits*, Washington, Brookings.

Government of Ireland (2010), *National Recovery Plan*. Dublin, Stationery Office.

References

H.M. Treasury (2004). *Financial Statement and Budget Report, 2004.* London, H.M. Treasury.

Healy, S. and B. Reynolds (2003), "Christian Critique of Economic Policy and Practice" in J.P. Mackey and E. McDonagh (eds.) *Religion and Politics in Ireland at the turn of the millennium*, Dublin, Columba Press.

Healy, S. and B. Reynolds (2003), "Ireland and the Future of Europe – a social perspective" in Reynolds B. and S. Healy (eds.) *Ireland and the Future of Europe: leading the way towards inclusion?*, Dublin, CORI.

Healy, S. and B. Reynolds (2004), "Towards a Fairer Tax System for the 21st Century" in B. Reynolds, and S. Healy (eds.) *A Fairer Tax System for a Fairer Ireland*, Dublin, CORI Justice Commission.

Homeless Agency (2008), *Counted in 2008,* Dublin, Homeless Agency.

IMD (2007), *IMD World Competitiveness Yearbook*, Lausanne, Switzerland.

Indecon (2005), *Indecon Review of Local Government Funding – Report commissioned by the Minister for Environment, Heritage and Local Government.* Dublin, Stationery Office.

Institute for Public Health (2007), "*Fuel Poverty and Health*", Dublin, IPH.

Intergovernmental Panel on Climate Change (IPCC, 2007), *Climate Change 2007: The Physical Science Basis*, Geneva, IPCC.

International Monetary Fund (2004), *World Economic Outlook*, Washington DC, IMF.

International Monetary Fund (2008), *World Economic Outlook*, Washington DC, IMF.

IPCC (2001), *Climate Change 2001: The Scientific Basis: Contribution of Working Group 1 to the Third Assessment Report of the Intergovernmental Panel on Climate Change.* Cambridge University Press, UK.

Irish Aid (2010), *Annual Report 2009*, Dublin, Stationery Office.

John Paul II (1981), *Laborem Exercens*, Encyclical Letter of the Supreme Pontiff John Paul II on Human Work, Catholic Truth Society, London.

Lawless, M. and C. Corr (2005), *Drug Use Among the Homeless Population in Ireland*. Dublin, National Advisory Committee on Drugs.

Library Council (2004), *A Public Space for All*, Dublin, Library Council.

Local Government Management Services Board (2011), *Service Indicators in Local Authorities in 2009*, Dublin, LGMSB.

McAleese, M (2007), 'The Changing Faces of Ireland - Migration & Multiculturalism'. Speech by the President of Ireland to the British Council Wednesday 14th March 2007. www.president.ie

McCashin A (2000), *The Private Rented Sector in the 21st Century – Policy Choices*. Dublin, Threshold and St Pancras Housing Association.

McGinnity, F. and H. Russell (2008), *Gender Inequalities in Time*, Dublin, ESRI.

McGrath, R, P. Lynch, S. Dunne, J. Hanafin, E. Nishimura, P. Nolan, J. Venkata Ratnam, T. Semmler, C. Sweeney and S. Wang. *Ireland in a Warmer World. Scientific Predictions of the Irish Climate in the Twenty-First Century. Final report of C4I*, Dublin, 2008.

National Action Plan for Social Inclusion 2007-2016 (2007), Dublin, Stationery Office.

National Anti-Poverty Strategy (1997), *Sharing in Progress*, Dublin, Stationery Office.

National Anti-Poverty Strategy Review (2002), *Building an Inclusive Society* Dublin, Stationery Office.

National Asset Management Agency (2011), *Third Quarter Report and Accounts*, Dublin, NAMA.

National Economic and Social Council (1995), *New Approaches to Rural Development,* Dublin, NESC.

National Economic and Social Council (2003), *An Investment in Quality: Services, Inclusion and Enterprise*, Dublin, NESC.

References

National Economic and Social Council (2004), *Housing in Ireland: performance and policy*, Dublin, NESC.

National Economic and Social Council (2005), *The Developmental Welfare State*, Dublin, NESC.

National Economic and Social Council (2009), *Ireland's Five Part Crisis*, Dublin, NESC.

National Economic and Social Forum (2006), *Improving the Delivery of Quality Public Services*. Dublin, Stationery Office.

National Education Welfare Board (various), *Annual Report*, Dublin, Stationery Office.

National Office for Suicide Prevention (2010), *Annual Report 2010*, Dublin, Stationery Office.

Nolan, B. (2006), "The EU's Social Inclusion Indicators and Their Implications for Ireland", in Healy, S., B. Reynolds and M.L. Collins, *Social Policy in Ireland: Principles, Practice and Problems*, Dublin, Liffey Press.

NUI Maynooth, University College Dublin and Teagasc (2005). *Rural Ireland 2025 - Foresight Perspectives*. NIRSA NUI Maynooth, RERC Teagasc, UCD Dublin.

O'Reilly and Thompson (2006), 'Paper on the Accessibility of Healthcare' delivered to the Irish College of General Practitioners Conference, Galway 2006.

O'Siochru, E. (2004), "Land Value Tax: unfinished business" in B. Reynolds, and S. Healy (eds.) *A Fairer Tax System for a Fairer Ireland*, Dublin, CORI Justice Commission.

O'Toole, F. and N. Cahill (2006), "Taxation Policy and Reform", in Healy, S., B. Reynolds and M.L. Collins, *Social Policy in Ireland: Principles, Practice and Problems*, Dublin, Liffey Press.

OECD (2004), *Education at a Glance*, Paris, OECD.

OECD (2005), *Society at a Glance*, Paris, OECD

OECD (2008), *Economic Survey of Ireland,* Paris, OECD.

OECD (2008), *OECD Factbook,* Paris, OECD.

OECD (2009), *Economic Survey of Ireland 2009,* Paris, OECD.

OECD (2010), *Labour Force Statistics, 1989-2009,* Paris, OECD.

OECD (2010), *PISA Study Report,* Paris, OECD.

OECD (2010), *Revenue Statistics,* Paris, OECD.

OECD Development Assistance Committee (2009), *Ireland –Peer Review,* Paris, OECD.

Office of the Refugee Applications Commissioner (2011) *Monthly Statistics - February,* Dublin, ORAC.

Oxfam (2002). *Make Trade Fair Campaign.* www.maketradefair.com.

Pope Paul VI, (1967) *Populorum Progressio* No. 23, Vatican City, Rome.

Private Residential Tenancies Board (2010), *Annual Report and Accounts 2009,* Dublin, PRTB.

Public Health Alliance Ireland (2004), *Health in Ireland – An Unequal State,* Dublin, PHAI.

Public Health Alliance Ireland (2007), *Health Inequalities on the Island of Ireland – the facts, the causes, the remidies,* Dublin, PHAI.

Punch, A. (2006), "Projecting Ireland's Population at a Time of Major Demographic Change", in Healy, S., B. Reynolds and M.L. Collins, *Social Policy in Ireland: Principles, Practice and Problems,* Dublin, Liffey Press.

Rapple, C. (2004), "Refundable Tax Credits" in B. Reynolds, and S. Healy (eds.) *A Fairer Tax System for a Fairer Ireland,* Dublin, CORI Justice Commission.

References

Reception and Integration Agency (2011), *Monthly Statistical Report - January*, Dublin.

Revenue Commissioners (2009), *Analysis of High Income Individual's Restriction 2007*, Dublin, Stationery Office.

Revenue Commissioners (various), *Effective Tax Rates for High Earning Individuals*, Dublin, Stationery Office.

Revenue Commissioners (various), *Statistical Report various years,* Dublin, Stationery Office.

Reynolds, B. and S. Healy (1989) *Poverty and Taxation Policy,* Dublin, CORI Justice Commission.

Reynolds, B. and S. Healy (2004) *A Fairer Tax System for a Fairer Ireland,* Dublin, CORI Justice Commission.

Reynolds, B. and S. Healy (2005) *Securing Fairness and Wellbeing in a Land of Plenty,* Dublin, CORI Justice Commission.

Reynolds, B. and S. Healy (2009), *Beyond GDP: What is progress and how should it be measured?* Dublin, Social Justice Ireland

Robertson, J. (1997), *The New Economics of Sustainable Development*, report to the European Commission, Brussels.

Russell, H., B. Maitre and N. Donnelly (2011), *Financial Exclusion and Over-indebtedness in Irish Households*, Dublin, ESRI.

Scott S. and Eakins J. (2002), *Distributive effects of carbon taxes*, paper presented to ESRI conference entitled "The sky's the limit: efficient and fair policies on global warming", December, Dublin.

Social Justice Ireland (2010), *Analysis and Critique of Budget 2011.* Dublin, Social Justice Ireland.

Social Justice Ireland (2010), *Building a Fairer Taxation System: The Working Poor and the Cost of Refundable Tax Credits.* Dublin, Social Justice Ireland.

Social Justice Ireland (2010), *Policy Briefing: Budget Choices*. Dublin, Social Justice Ireland.

Social Justice Ireland (2011), *Policy Briefing: Poverty and Income Distribution*. Dublin, Social Justice Ireland.

Society of St.Vincent de Paul, Combat Poverty Agency and Crosscare (2004), *Food Poverty and Policy*. Dublin, Combat Poverty Agency.

Stern, N (2006) *Stern Review: The Economics of Climate Change*. London, HM Treasury.

Sweeney, J., T. Brereton, C. Byrne, R. Charlton, C. Emblow, R. Fealy, N. Holden, M. Jones, A. Donnelly, S. Moore, P. Purser, K. Byrne, E. Farrell, E. Mayes, D. Minchin, J. Wilson and Jh. Wilson (2003). *Climate change: scenarios & impacts for Ireland*. Dublin, Environmental Protection Agency.

Sweeney, P. (2004), "Corporation Tax: leading the race to the bottom" in B. Reynolds, and S. Healy (eds.) *A Fairer Tax System for a Fairer Ireland*, Dublin, CORI Justice Commission.

Teagasc (2008), *Medium Term Outlook for the Beef, Tillage and Dairy Farm Sectors 2008*, Athenry, Teagasc.

Teagasc (2010), *National Farm Survey 2009*, Athenry, Teagasc.

UNAIDS (2005), *Annual Update,* UNAIDS/WHO, Switzerland.

UNAIDS (2008), *AIDS epidemic update,* UNAIDS/WHO, Switzerland.

United Nations Development Program (2003), *Human Development Report,* New York: United Nations Publications.

United Nations Development Program (2010), *Human Development Report,* New York: United Nations Publications.

United Nations Development Program (2010), *Millennium Development Goals Report 2010,* New York: United Nations Publications.

United Nations High Commission for Refugees (2009), *Statistical Yearbook 2008*, Geneva: United Nations Publications.

Vincentian Partnership for Social Justice (2006), *Minimum Essential Budgets for Six Households*, Dublin, VPSJ.

Vincentian Partnership for Social Justice (2010), *Minimum Essential Budgets for Households in Rural Areas*, Dublin, VPSJ.

Wackernagel, M., Schulz N.B., Deumling D., Linares A.C., Jenkins M., Kapos V., Monfreda C., Loh J., Myers N., Norgaard R. and Randers J. (2002), Tracking the ecological overshoot of the human economy in *Proc. National. Academy of Science*, Vol. 99, Issue 14, 9266-9271.

Whelan, C.T., R. Layte, B. Maitre, B. Gannon, B. Nolan, W. Watson, J. Williams (2003) *Monitoring Poverty Trends in Ireland: Results from the 2001 Living in Ireland Survey*. ESRI Dublin, Policy Research Series No. 51, December.

World Commission on Environment and Development (1987), *Our Common Future*, Oxford University Press.

World Economic Forum (2003). *Global Competitiveness Report 2003-04*. www.weforum.org.

World Economic Forum (2010), *Global Competitiveness Report 2010-11*. www.weforum.org.

World Health Organisation (2001), *Mental Health: New Understanding, New Hope* Geneva, Switzerland.

ONLINE DATABASES [all accessed April 2011]

CSO online database, web address: http://www.cso.ie/px

Eurostat online database, web address: http://epp.eurostat.ec.europa.eu

OECD online database, web address: http://www.oecd.org

APPENDIX

As chapter two, section 2.1, notes there are figures available for total government expenditure as a percentage of national income for 2009 – more recent than the 2007 figures used in the comparisons on table 2.5. However, these figures are problematic given that they report a notable increase in spending as a proportion of national income for almost all EU countries as GDP declined while government spending was, in many cases, boosted to stimulate the economy and pay for increased unemployment related expenditure. This was particularly so in the countries worst hit by the recession and in the case of Ireland they also include one-off expenditure associated with capital injections into the banking sector. The abnormal nature of fiscal policies in 2009 (as was the case in 2008 and most likely 2010-11) across all EU countries suggests that it would be inappropriate to make structural comparisons using this data. For this reason the analysis presented in table 2.5 uses the 2007 data. However, for completeness, we present the data for 2009 and historic data from Ireland and the EU-27 in table A2.

Table A1: Total Government Expenditure as a % of GDP, for the EU-27 in 2009

Country	% of GDP	Country	% of GDP
IRELAND GNP	**59.5**	Portugal	48.2
Denmark	58.2	Germany	47.5
Finland	56.2	Czech Republic	45.9
France	56.0	Spain	45.8
Sweden	54.9	Cyprus	45.8
Belgium	54.2	Poland	44.4
Greece	53.2	Latvia	44.2
Austria	52.3	Malta	43.9
Italy	51.9	Lithuania	43.6
United Kingdom	51.7	Luxembourg	42.2
Netherlands	51.4	Slovakia	41.5
Hungary	50.5	Romania	41.0
Slovenia	49.0	Bulgaria	40.6
IRELAND GDP	**48.9**	Estonia★	33.6

Source: Eurostat online database (2011) and CSO (2011:4)
Notes: EU-27 average of 50.8% of GDP.
        ★ 2006 data

Table A2: Ireland and EU-27 Total Government Expenditure as a % of GDP, 1995-2008

Year	Ireland	EU-27	Year	Ireland	EU-27
1995	41.1	n/a	2002	33.4	46.6
1996	39.1	n/a	2003	33.2	47.2
1997	36.6	n/a	2004	33.6	46.7
1998	34.5	47.3	2005	34.0	46.8
1999	34.1	46.7	2006	34.4	46.2
2000	31.3	45.1	2007	36.8	45.6
2001	33.1	46.1	2008	42.7	46.9

Source: Eurostat online database (2011), CSO (2011:4) and CSO online database (2011)